INDUSTRY MATTERS

Englisch für Industriekaufleute

von
Michael Benford
Caroline Okerika
Ken Thomson

in Zusammenarbeit mit
der Verlagsredaktion

Cornelsen

Verfasser:	Michael Benford, Bochum Caroline Okerika, Loxstedt Ken Thomson, Berlin
Berater:	Joanne Glen, Bad Nauheim Ina Herrmann, Tübingen Christian Schmidt, Nördlingen Hartmut Terkhorn, Köln
Projektleitung:	Jim Austin
Verlagsredaktion:	Merlene Griffin
Redaktionelle Mitarbeit:	Oliver Busch (Wortlisten), Felix Bellermann, Stefanie Heimann
Layout und technische Umsetzung:	Arnold & Domnick, Leipzig
Bildredaktion:	Gertha Maly
Umschlaggestaltung:	Sergio Vitale, VitaleDesign, Berlin
Titelfoto:	Getty Images RM / David Leahy

Erhältlich sind auch:	**Handreichungen für den Unterricht mit CD-ROM und Audio-CD ISBN 978-3-06-450569-8**
Online-Ergänzungen unter:	**www.cornelsen.de/matters**

www.cornelsen.de

1. Auflage, 3. Druck 2016

Alle Drucke dieser Auflage sind inhaltlich unverändert
und können im Unterricht nebeneinander verwendet werden.

Druck: Grafisches Centrum Cuno GmbH & Co.KG, Calbe

ISBN 978-3-06-450488-2

PEFC
PEFC/04-31-1370

PEFC zertifiziert
Dieses Produkt stammt aus nachhaltig bewirtschafteten Wäldern und kontrollierten Quellen.

www.pefc.de

Stella Ebert

VORWORT

Industry Matters – 2nd Edition ist die komplett aktualisierte Neubearbeitung des bewährten Lehrwerks für Industriekaufleute und wurde für die Ausbildung in Berufsschulen sowie die innerbetriebliche Aus- und Weiterbildung konzipiert. Das Lehrwerk basiert auf den Lehrplänen der Bundesländer für Berufsschulen.

Es ist auf Lernende zugeschnitten, deren Englischkenntnisse den Anforderungen eines mittleren Bildungsabschlusses bzw. eines durchschnittlichen gymnasialen Grundkursabschlusses entsprechen und setzt Englischkenntnisse, die der Stufe B1 des Europäischen Referenzrahmens *(Common European Framework of Reference)* entsprechen, voraus. Darüber hinaus gibt es in den Rubriken *Extra material* auch anspruchsvolleren Lernstoff für fortgeschrittene Schüler/innen (B2). Neu an der *2nd Edition* ist auch die durchgängige Vorbereitung auf die KMK-Zertifikatsprüfung in Englisch (Stufe II). Dies geschieht anhand prüfungsbezogener und mit einem KMK-Symbol gekennzeichneter Aufgaben im Schülerbuch, einer KMK-Seite pro Unit sowie einem KMK *mock exam* im Anhang.

Industry Matters – 2nd Edition besteht aus zehn Units, in denen handlungsorientiert aktuelle Themen aus unterschiedlichen Bereichen des industriellen Alltags aufgegriffen werden und von denen jede eine in sich abgeschlossene Handlung enthält. Es ist möglich, einzelne Units auszulassen, jedoch wird empfohlen, wann immer Zeit und Lehrpläne es ermöglichen, die gegebene Reihenfolge einzuhalten, um einen kontinuierlichen Aufbau des Fachvokabulars zu gewährleisten. Landeskundliche Informationen über englischsprachige Länder werden ebenfalls vermittelt.

Industry Matters – 2nd Edition ist für einen handlungsorientierten und praxisbezogenen Unterricht konzipiert. In den Units werden die Lernenden aufgefordert, an den dargestellten Handlungen aktiv mitzuwirken, indem sie Aufgaben übernehmen, die im kaufmännischen Betrieb anfallen, z. B. Telefonate entgegennehmen, Buchungen tätigen, Besucher empfangen, Preise und Lieferbedingungen vereinbaren, u. v. m. Die Sprachkompetenz der Schülerinnen und Schüler wird anhand zahlreicher Leseverständnis-, Hörverständnis- und Sprechübungen, die von gelenkten Dialogen bis zu freien Diskussionen reichen, geschult. Das nötige Fachvokabular und wichtige Redewendungen, die in *Language boxes* sowie in erweiterter Form im Anhang aufgeführt sind, werden in Rollenspielen und Partnerübungen gefestigt. Anhand motivierender Aufgaben werden Hemmungen, sich in der Fremdsprache auszudrücken, abgebaut. Neben der Aufarbeitung des Fachvokabulars und der spezifischen Redemittel werden auch Grundlagen der Grammatik zur Wiederholung angeboten. Sie werden in deutscher Sprache mit Hilfe von Beispielen erklärt und im handlungsbezogenen Kontext geübt.

Webcodes, die auf der *Matters*-Webseite (www.cornelsen.de/matters) eingegeben werden können, motivieren zu eigenverantwortlichem Arbeiten.

Im Anhang wird eine komplette KMK-Zertifikatsprüfung angeboten. Weiterhin werden *Partner files*, zwei Wörterlisten – alphabetisch sowie nach Units gegliedert – ein Deutsch-Englisches Glossar, eine Aufstellung von nützlichen technischen Redewendungen und die Incoterms® 2010 aufgeführt.

Der Verlag, die Autoren und die Berater/innen wünschen Ihnen viel Erfolg und Freude bei der Arbeit mit **Industry Matters – 2nd Edition**.

2	Dialog bzw. Hörtext auf der Audio-CD
KMK	Übungen zur Vorbereitung auf die KMK-Zertifikatsprüfung
PAGE 135	Verweis auf nützliche Materialien im Anhang
WEBCODE INDMU0101	Die Webcodes weisen auf Zusatzmaterial zur selbstständigen Weiterarbeit hin und können unter www.cornelsen.de/matters abgerufen werden.

UNIT 1

A presentation about Cantec GmbH

- Presenting company statistics
- Welcoming visitors to a company
- Introducing yourself and others

1 Warm-up

A Complete the sentences (1–6) with the words from the box. Then match them to the pictures (a–f).

a

b

c

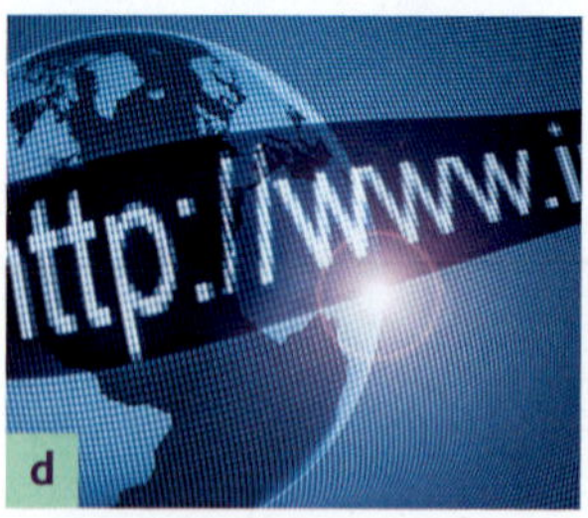
d

e

f

brochures • guided tour • presentation • booth at a trade fair or an exhibition • video • website

1. Companies often offer visitors a … of the company.
2. A … gives visitors a good overview of the company's goods and services.
3. It's a good idea to get some … about the company to read later.
4. A promotional … is a good way to show customers how a product actually works.
5. To get more detailed information on a company, just click on its … .
6. A … is a good place to meet customers and do deals.

B Describe which methods your company uses to present itself to the outside world. Think about the following:

- when there are visitors to your company
- when your company's sales representatives visit a customer
- when your company has a booth at a trade fair or an exhibition
- the internet

2 Presenting Cantec GmbH, Essen

WEBCODE **INDMU0101**

02

Dirk Sauerwald is the Head of Sales for Africa and Asia at Cantec GmbH in Essen. Today he is giving a presentation to some representatives from a Chinese company.

A Listen to Dirk's presentation and put the slides (a–f) in the correct order.

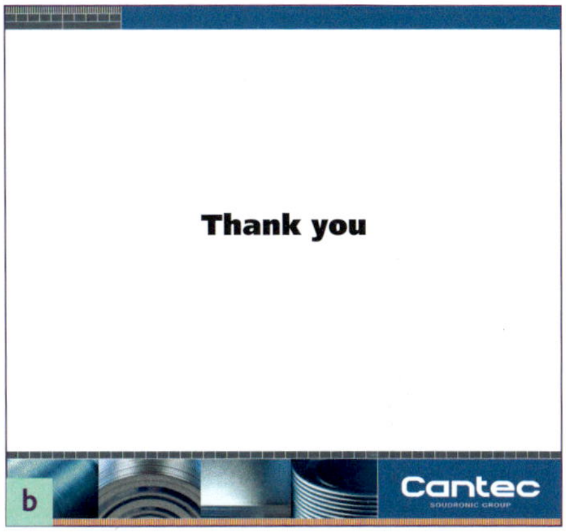

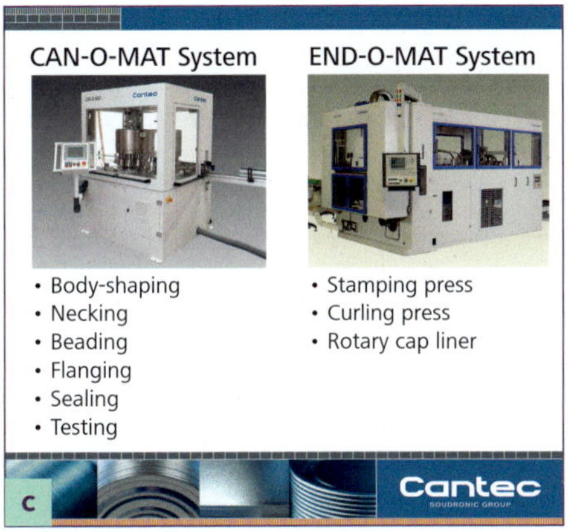

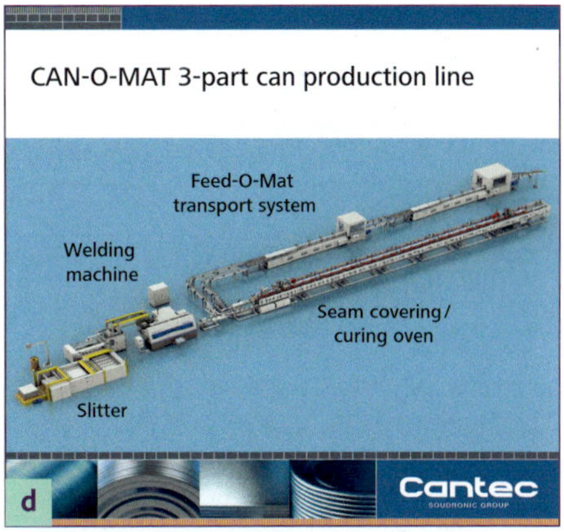

B Listen again or read the slides on page 7 and answer the following questions.

1. How many people work for Cantec in Germany?
2. What percentage of Cantec's products are exported?
3. Where is the Soudronic Group based and where are its subsidiaries?
4. What are the two machines shown in the presentation called?

C Now read the slides and find words to match the following definitions.

1. someone who works at a company
2. the total amount of goods and services sold by a company
3. about, not exactly
4. head office
5. the top of a can or bottle
6. whole, complete
7. production
8. the part of the production line where the cans are baked at a high temperature

3 Language of presentations

02

A Use the words from the box to complete Dirk's presentation. Then listen to the CD to check your answers.

assemble • customer • design • located • manufacturing • parent • production • providing • range • share • state-of-the-art • subsidiaries • turnover • workforce

[Slide 1]
Good morning, ladies and gentlemen and welcome to Cantec, Germany. My name is Dirk Sauerwald and I'm the Head of Sales for Africa and Asia. The agenda for today's meeting is in the folder in front of you. Right, I'd like to begin by giving you a presentation about the company. I'll start with some background information and company statistics, and will then move on to our products and services. Then at the end, I'll be happy to answer any questions you may have.
Cantec in Germany is a high-tech company …[1] high-end can-making machines. We have a …[2] of 158, ranging from engineers to technicians and trainees, and our annual …[3] last year was 35 million euros. We export 98% of our products all over the world and have a global market …[4] of approximately 40%.

[Slide 2]
As you can see from this slide, we belong to a group of companies. The …[5] company is Soudronic which is …[6] in Switzerland. The Soudronic Group has …[7] in Germany, France and Italy.

[Slide 3]
Now, let's move on to our next point: the products and services that Cantec has to offer. Our speciality at Cantec is …[8] the customer with a high-quality turnkey system with high-speed machines. We have the know-how to make a wide …[9] of 3-part cans and lids, and guarantee optimal …[10] service.

[Slide 4]
These illustrations show our two main machines in more detail. The machine on the left – the Can-O-Mat – turns out up to 1,300 can bodies per minute. The End-O-Mat on the right produces up to 4,000 can ends per minute. Our machines are …[11].

[Slide 5]
Now let's take a look at production in more detail. This is a slide of one of our …[12] lines which shows our Can-O-Mat machine for can bodies. This line consists of a metal cutter, a conveyor belt, the Can-O-Mat body-making machine and an oven. We transport all the components to our customer in containers and …[13] them on site. Customers can …[14] their cans themselves or choose one of our standard models.

[Slide 6]
That was a brief overview of Cantec, Germany. Many thanks for listening. Now if you'd like to ask any questions, I'd be delighted to answer them.

B Copy the table below and complete it using the appropriate highlighted phrases in Dirk's presentation.

Welcoming the audience	Introducing your topic	Structuring your presentation	Moving to the next point	Describing visuals	Dealing with questions	Conclusion
…	…	…	…	…	…	…

4 Over to you

PAGE 131

In groups of two or three, give a presentation on your own company. Use the highlighted expressions in Dirk's presentation and the tip box below to help you structure your presentation.

TIP

Giving a presentation

- Prepare an agenda, including when there will be a question-and-answer session.
- Use visual aids (e. g. transparencies, posters, photos, objects) or PowerPoint.
- Decide if it is best to give out handouts before, during or after the presentation.
- Do not fill your transparencies or slides with text.
- Speak slowly and freely with the help of key words on hand-held prompt cards only.
- Face your audience! Do not turn your back to them to point to the screen.
- Make sure you make eye contact with your audience.
- Remember to take cultural differences into account (e. g. gestures and body language).
- If working in pairs, practise with your partner before giving the presentation in public.
- Introduce yourself and then let your partner introduce him/herself.
- Make sure you do not speak for too long before handing over to your partner.
- Sit down or stand to one side when you are not speaking.

5 Forms of enterprise

KMK

Ihr Vorgesetzter erwartet Besuch von einem neuen Geschäftspartner aus Großbritannien und bittet Sie, ihm Informationen über seine Firma zu besorgen. Auf der Homepage des britischen Unternehmens finden Sie folgendes Porträt.

Fassen Sie auf Deutsch die wichtigsten Inhalte für Ihren Vorgesetzten zusammen. Die Illustration (unten) kann Ihnen helfen.

http://freshfare.com

Google

Freshfare Ltd, Portmead, Wales

Company profile

15 years ago we started out as a small food-packing business located in a 6,000-sq-ft unit on an industrial estate near Swansea in South Wales. The company was called Freshfare Foods and was owned and run by Roger Jenkins. Our main customers were schools, factories and hospitals in the local area, and Roger was helped by his son, William, and two other employees.

Demand for high-quality food products grew rapidly, and after only five years, our turnover had doubled to £100,000. When Roger retired three years later, William diversified the company's product portfolio to include organic varieties, and started to sell them all over the UK.

William rented three more units on the industrial estate and two years later incorporated the company as Freshfare Ltd. William became the managing director of the new company, and the new members of the board were Lynn Evans, an accountant, and Alec Jones, a solicitor.

Since being incorporated five years ago, we have seen great demand for healthy, organic and conventional food products, and our reputation has spread to Europe, where we have an increasing number of overseas buyers. For this reason we have rented a further unit on the industrial estate in South Wales, so we can keep up with the volume of demand from Europe.

Our turnover reached £5 million last year, and we plan to open a new factory in Christchurch in the south of England next year.

Common forms of enterprise in the UK, US, Australia and South Africa

Sole trader
(Einzelunternehmer)

- The company belongs to the sole trader.
- The sole trader takes decisions alone.
- He gets all the profit.
- He could lose everything.

UK: Private limited company (Ltd)
US: Limited liability company (LLC)
AU: Proprietory Limited company (Pty Ltd)
SA: Proprietory Limited company (Pty Ltd)
(GmbH)

- The company belongs to a closed circle of members.
- The members decide what is best for the company.
- The members share the profits.
- The members can only lose the money they have invested.

UK: Public limited company (plc)
US: Corporation (Corp./Inc.)
SA: Limited company
(AG)

- The company belongs to the shareholders (members of the public).
- The directors decide what is best for the company and the shareholders.
- The shareholders share the profit.
- The shareholders can only lose the money they paid for the shares.

6 Welcoming visitors to your company

03

A group of Chinese technicians has come to Cantec GmbH to learn how to operate the canning machinery their company has purchased.

A Listen to the dialogue and answer the following questions.

1 In which department does Mareike Steinwender work?
2 Who is John Wang?
3 Where does Mareike take the visitors first?
4 What is Mr Lohmann going to do?
5 What does Mr Nierfeld give the visitors?
6 In which country did the group stop on the way to Germany?

B Listen again and complete the following sentences with words from the dialogue.

1 Good morning, gentlemen and … Cantec!
2 … to meet you.
3 Please take a … and make yourselves … .
4 Would you like something to …?
5 Mr Nierfeld, Mr Lohmann let me … you to John Wang.
6 Did you have a good … over from China, Mr Wang?
7 Is your … comfortable?
8 Here is a … of the programme for the week.

LANGUAGE

Introducing yourself and others

Introducing yourself

Formal

You:	Hello, my name is Jürgen Meier. I'm from Decker Design.
Business partner:	Pleased to meet you. I'm Debbie Diamond from Web Solutions.
You:	Pleased to meet you.

Informal

You:	Hi, I don't think we've met. I'm Jürgen from Decker Design.
Business partner:	Nice to meet you. I'm Debbie from Web Solutions.
You:	Nice to meet you.

Introducing someone else

Formal

You:	Let me introduce you to Mareike Schneider, our Marketing Manager.
Business partner:	Pleased to meet you.
Mareike:	Pleased to meet you (too).

Informal

You:	Have you met Mareike?
Business partner:	No, I haven't actually.
You:	Debbie. This is Mareike.
Debbie:	Hi, Mareike.
Mareike:	Hi. (Nice to meet you.)
Debbie:	(You too.)

7 Introductions

PAGE 131

In groups of three, use your own name and the business cards below to (a) introduce yourself and (b) introduce another person both formally and informally.

Soyang Europe GmbH
www.soyang-europe-gmbh.de

Dr. *(your name)* Koch
Managing Director

Tel.: +49 (2131) 51 62
Mobile: +49 (160) 96 4539 81
Fax: +49 (2131) 51 60
EMail: koch@soyang.eu

Soyang Europe GmbH
Hammer Landstraße 1a
41460 Neuss
Germany

GLOBAL SOLUTIONS plc
www.global-solutions.com

Jonathan Sykes
Marketing Director

20 New Street
YORK
YO1 8RA
United Kingdom

Tel: + 44 1904 67467227
Mobile: + 44 7084 652855
Fax: + 44 1904 67467200
Email: j.sykes@global.com

IMPEX GROSSHANDEL / TRADING

Maike Erdmenger
Verkaufsleiterin / Sales Manager

Impex Großhandel GmbH
Eiserne Hand 88
45127 Essen (GERMANY)

Tel.: + 49 201 1732243
Mobile: + 49 151 123456712
Email: maike.erdmenger@impex.de

8 Role-play: welcoming a visitor

KMK

Erstellen Sie in Partnerarbeit einen Dialog aus folgender Zick-Zack Übersicht. Für die nötigen Satz-Konstruktionen können Sie die *Language Box* auf Seite 11 verwenden.

Mitarbeiter/in Ihrer Firma	Fiona/Fred Miles von TopTech Ltd, UK
Sie heißen Frau/Herrn Miles willkommen und stellen sich vor.	
	Sie stellen sich vor.
Sie geben die entsprechende Antwort und bitten Frau/Herrn Miles, Ihnen zum Besprechungsraum zu folgen.	
	Sie reagieren entsprechend.
Sie bieten Frau/Herrn Miles etwas zu trinken an.	
	Sie bestellen ein Getränk.
Sie fragen, ob sie/er eine gute Reise hatte und ob ihr/ihm das Hotel gefällt.	
	Sie antworten entsprechend.
Sie geben Frau/Herrn Miles ein Exemplar vom Programm für die nächsten zwei Tage und fragen, ob sie/er dazu Fragen hat.	
	Sie bedanken sich für das Programm und fragen, ob Sie heute den Geschäftsführer kennen lernen werden.
Sie improvisieren weitere Fragen und Antworten.	
	Sie improvisieren weitere Fragen und Antworten.
Sie bitten Frau/Herrn Miles für die Führung durch den Betrieb mitzukommen.	
	Sie reagieren entsprechend.

GRAMMAR

Simple present and present progressive

1 He or she **gets** a contract. He **passes** it **on** to us in Essen.
2 **Do** you usually **give** them written instructions? – No, we **don't**.
3 She **understands**.
4 **I'm writing** a report on project management at the moment.
5 **Are** the men downstairs **working on** the project?
6 She**'s not expecting** any visitors.

- Das **simple present** wird für wiederholte, oft regelmäßige Handlungen und Zustände verwendet (1–3). Es steht oft in Verbindung mit Signalwörtern wie *regularly, usually, always* usw. (2).
- Manche Verben, die keine Handlung sondern einen Zustand darstellen (z. B. *contain, know, like, mean, need, understand, want*), stehen immer im *simple present* (3).
- In der 3. Person *(he, she, it)* wird ein *-(e)s* an die Grundform angefügt (1, 3). Frage und Verneinung werden mit einer Form von *do (do/does, don't/doesn't)* + Grundform gebildet (2).

- Das **present progressive** wird für eine nur vorübergehend andauernde Handlung verwendet, die im Augenblick des Sprechens geschieht (4–6). Es steht oft in Verbindung mit Signalwörtern wie *at the moment, now* usw. (4).

9 Practice

A Use the simple present or the present progressive to complete Sally's conversation with a sales rep below.

Sally: How … (you / normally / get)¹ in touch with a customer?
Sales rep: I … (often visit)² them at their own company.
Sally: … (you / work)³ on a big order at the moment?
Sales rep: Yes, but this order … (take)⁴ a long time.
Sally: … (the customer / want)⁵ a lower price?
Sales rep: Yes, he … (try to)⁶ reduce the price significantly.
Sally: What … (you / normally / do)⁷ if a customer wants to reduce the price?
Sales rep: We … (change)⁸ the terms of our offer.
Sally: … (the customer / now / wait for)⁹ you to contact him with a new offer?
Sales rep: Yes, but he … (also look for)¹⁰ another supplier.

10 Interaktion

Erstellen Sie in Partnerarbeit einen Dialog aus folgenden Rollenkarten.

Situation
James/Jenny Carter von Bell Inc. aus Delaware in den USA ist auf der Hannover Messe und sucht englische Verkaufsliteratur von verschiedenen deutschen Firmen. Die Person, die gerade Standdienst macht, nutzt diese Gelegenheit, ihre Firma kurz zu präsentieren.

Eigener Name und Position in Ihrem Betrieb

Sie beschreiben:
- die Produkte Ihres Unternehmens (kurze Beschreibungen)
- die Dienstleistungen (z. B. Installation, Wartung, Reparatur)
- die Lieferzeiten
- den/die Standort/e

Sie geben dem Besucher / der Besucherin:
- Verkaufsliteratur
- Ihre Karte

James/Jenny Carter

Sie stellen Fragen über:
- die Qualität der Produkte
- Lieferung bzw. Installation bzw. Wartung
- Problemlösung / Troubleshooting (z. B. Wartezeit bei Pannen)
- Gewährleistung

Sie geben dem/der Mitarbeiter/in Ihre Visitenkarte.
Sie bitten um ein Angebot für … (Produkt).

11 Produktion

Ihr Unternehmen erhält zunehmend Aufträge von englischsprachigen Kunden und braucht deshalb eine Website auf Englisch. Ihr Vorgesetzter bittet Sie, englische Texte für den Webdesigner Ihrer Firmenhomepage zu folgenden Überschriften zu verfassen.

Wählen Sie vier der fünf Überschriften und schreiben Sie zu jedem Thema einen kurzen Text von 60 – 70 Wörtern.

- company profile
- products
- services
- careers
- locations

Extra material

(http://websitesetupguide.com/) Google

The Basics

I'm a professional web designer. In this beginner's guide I show you exactly how to set up a normal website with a *dot com* (or other) domain name, from start to finish. Creating a website and running it this way will cost you about $4–5 per month in total. The information I give you on this site is all free.

To set up a website, you only need to do two things:
- Sign up for website hosting, and choose a domain name (e.g. *something*.com).
- Create your website.

What is web hosting?

Web hosting is where your website actually sits, on a computer in a building somewhere, when you put it on the internet. It can be anywhere in the world.

What is a domain name?

A domain name is the internet address of a website. It will cost around US$10–20 per year.

Some domain name advice
- It should be simple, short and memorable.
- Don't stuff your whole business name into your domain name.

Web hosting and a domain name are the only things you have to pay for to set up a website. This will probably cost you up to US$10 per month. Everything else can be done for free.

My recommendation for web hosting

On this site, I only promote one web host – the one I think is the best. After investigating all the major hosts and doing my own research, I recommend HostGator. Their prices are good, their tech support isn't outsourced, and they just seem to be a high-quality and ethical company.

Website design

I recommend you use WordPress to design and manage your site. It's a very popular, free online system that lets you build a professional looking website without any previous knowledge of web design or technical know-how.

Extra information

How to create a profitable business site:
- Include important keywords on your site.
- Advertise your site on Google.
- Sell things on your website (via PayPal).
- Get links to your site from other sites.
- Charge for advertising on your site.

Source: http://websitesetupguide.com/

12 Looking at the text

Read the text and do the following tasks.

1. The writer claims that a website will cost about $ 4–5 per month. Look at the other expenses he names and work out if they come to the same price.
2. Explain why web hosting can be anywhere in the world.
3. Name the reasons the writer gives for recommending HostGator.
4. Give reasons for not putting a whole company name into a domain name.
5. Explain what it means if a company outsources its technical support.
6. Which things under *Extra information* might the website operator need to pay for?

13 Discussion

In groups of three or four, discuss one or more of the following questions. Then share your ideas with the whole class.

1. When is it best to set up a website (a) yourself or (b) using a web designer?
2. Do you agree or disagree with the writer's recommendations in *Extra information* about how to set up a business site?
3. Do you think your own company's website presents the company successfully? Give reasons for your opinion and make constructive recommendations if appropriate.

UNIT 2

Roles and responsibilities at Cantec GmbH

- Showing visitors around
- Getting to know the departments
- Talking about your job

1 Warm-up: what job would you like to do?

A Use the words from the box to talk about the pictures (a–f).

company car • independence • office job • outdoor work • promotion prospects • responsibility • salary • self-employed • small / medium-sized / large company • travel • working with people

B Find out what sort of job your partner would like to do after finishing his or her traineeship and why. The language box below will help you.

LANGUAGE

Career choices

I'd like to …
I'd prefer … + *infinitive*
I like … + *ing*
I've always wanted to …
Working for a … would mean … + *ing*
In the long/short term, …
For the time being, …

What would you like to do when you've finished your traineeship?

I've always wanted to be independent and set up my own business. What about you?

2 In-house exhibition week at Cantec GmbH

04

Cantec GmbH, a canning machinery manufacturer in Essen, is having an in-house exhibition week for its customers from all over the world.

A Listen as Mareike Steinwender at the reception desk greets some English-speaking visitors and say where the visitors are from.

B Listen again and follow the directions that Mareike gives the visitors on the plan below. Then write down the following:

1 each visitor's name and company
2 who each visitor wishes to see
3 the name of the department in which the person works

3rd floor

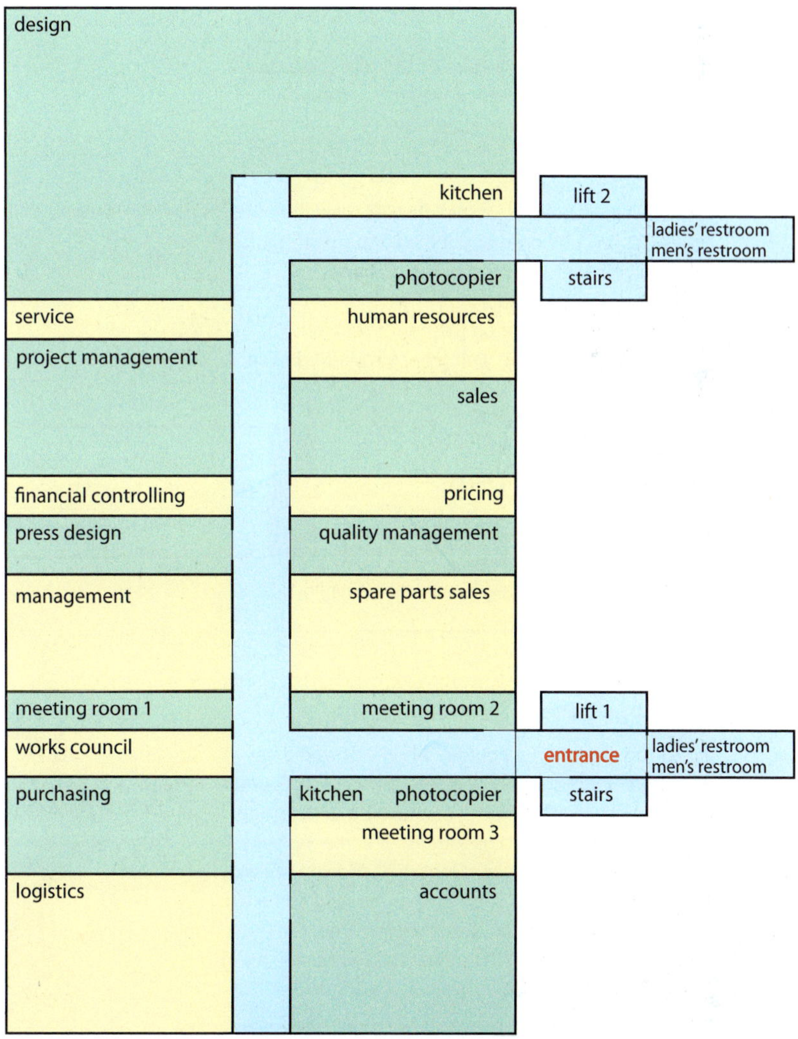

3 How do I get to ...?

A **Use the partner files at the back of the book to give each other directions to different people and offices. Use the floor plan on page 17 and the language box below for help.**

Student A: turn to partner file 1 on page 113.
Student B: turn to partner file 9 on page 116.

B **In pairs, use a floor plan of your own company to practise giving visitors directions to people and departments.**

LANGUAGE

Asking for and giving directions

Asking for directions
Excuse me, I'm trying to find ...
I'm looking for ...
Can you tell me where I can find ..., please?
Could you tell me the way to ..., please?
Do you happen to know ...?

Giving directions
Please take one of the lifts (BE)/elevators (AE) to the first (second/third/fourth, etc.) floor.
When you come out of the lift, turn left/right.
Continue to the end of the corridor.
Go straight ahead/on.
It's the first door on the right, just after ...
Thanks. – You're welcome, Mr/Ms/Mrs/Miss ... /My pleasure.

Useful expressions
to the left/right of ...
between (the) ... and (the) ...
next to (the) ...
opposite (the) ...
upstairs/downstairs
to take the lift/elevator/escalator/stairs

!
DE: *Erdgeschoss, 1. OG, 2. OG, 3.OG*
BE: ground floor, 1st floor, 2nd floor, 3rd floor
AE: 1st floor, 2nd floor, 3rd floor, 4th floor

TIP

Of course

Do not say "Of course" when you would say *Natürlich / Sicher / Selbstverständlich* in German because "Of course" can also be understood to mean "Stupid question!". If someone asks you: "Do you speak English?" and you answer, "Yes, of course", this can sound as if you are saying: "Do I look like someone who can't speak English?". The best answer here is a short answer (three words): "Yes, I do."

4 A departmental meeting

05

Sally Bowles, a student from London University, has come to Cantec for a week's training. Today she is sitting in on a departmental meeting.

A List the ten departments mentioned in the correct order. The organization chart on page 20 will help you.

Sauerwald OK, let's get started, shall we? I'm pleased to announce that we in the sales department have an enquiry from Sweet Corn South Africa Pty Ltd. They're interested in an entire production line and I think we can give them exactly what they want.

Bauerdiek Well that's good news, Mr Sauerwald!

Sauerwald Yes, it certainly is, but just so that Miss Bowles is aware how an order is processed, I'll explain a few things as I go along. Before we here can make the South Africans an offer, we'll have to get the pricing department to work out how much it will cost. They'll have to talk to Dr Lentz in the design department. Has he got the capacity at the moment?

Bauerdiek I'll ask him after the meeting, but I'm sure there'll be no problems. The next step after that is to send the details to project management. Can you follow all this, Miss Bowles?

Sally Well, I'm doing my best! I think we've got as far as project management.

Bauerdiek Exactly. Will the purchasing department need to buy anything from outside companies for this, Mr Sauerwald?

Sauerwald Well, I've had a quick look at the customer's requirements and I think we'll need to buy some components from Siemens for this one.

Bauerdiek OK. So after project management, it's the purchasing department. What's next?

Sauerwald Well, once we know the exact price, we'll make the customer a firm offer. For this South African project our terms are a down payment of 30% with order and the rest on completion, so the next step is for the accounts department to send the customer an invoice for the down payment. As soon as the customer has paid the 30%, we can buy the parts we need and send the order to the logistics department. Logistics then co-ordinates the materials and manpower needed for the job, draws up a schedule and sends it to production. After the components have been made by production, they go to assembly where the production line is put together. Are you with us, Miss Bowles?

Sally I think so.

Sauerwald Good. Finally, I'll arrange for the South African technicians to come to Germany for a week's training by our service department. Then we ship the production line to South Africa …

KMK

B Entscheiden Sie, ob folgende Aussagen (1–3) richtig oder falsch sind. Begründen Sie Ihre Antwort. Danach beantworten Sie die Verständnisfragen (4–6) in kurzen Stichworten auf Deutsch.

1. Herr Sauerwald hat eine wichtige Anfrage einer südafrikanischen Firma erhalten.
2. Cantec wird Produkte an Siemens verkaufen.
3. Bei Fertigstellung der Anlage wird der südafrikanische Kunde eine Zahlung von 70% des Rechnungsbetrages leisten.
4. Welche Abteilungen haben Entscheidungsgewalt bei der Angebotsunterbreitung von Cantec an den südafrikanischen Kunden?
5. Wann kann Cantec erst mit der Produktion der Ware beginnen?
6. Warum kommen die südafrikanischen Techniker nach Deutschland?

5 Cantec's organization chart

WEBCODE **INDMU0201**

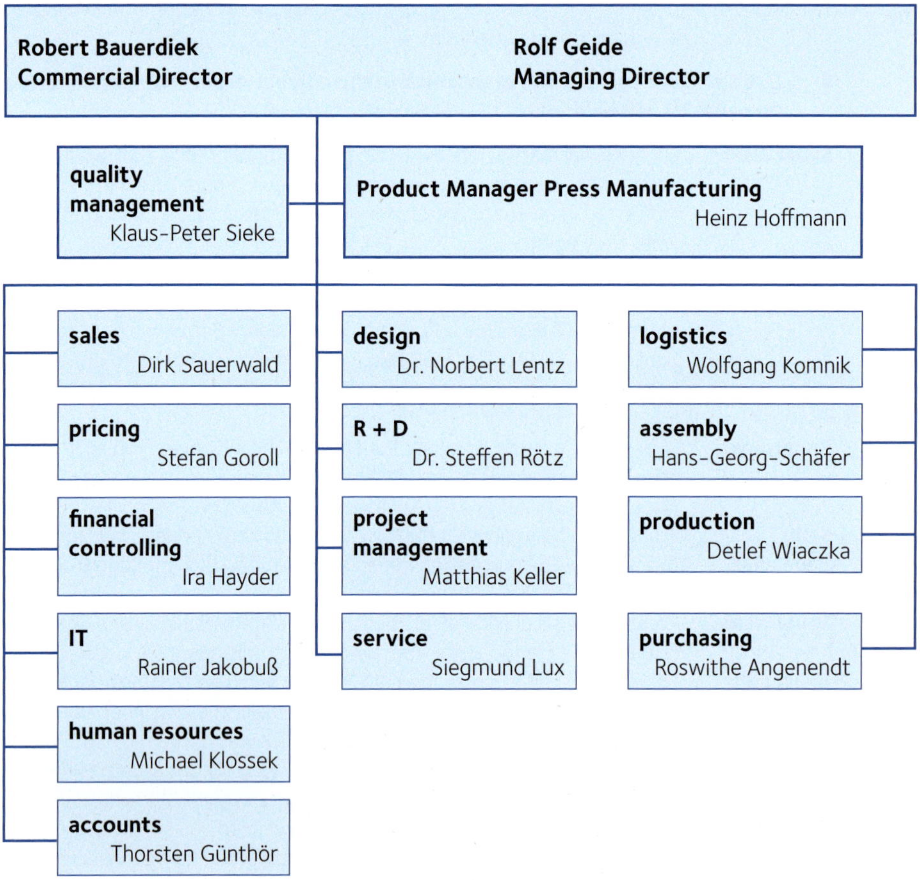

A Look at Cantec's organization chart and find the English translations of the German words in the box. Then translate the other departments into German.

Auftragsmanagement • Einkauf • Entwicklung • Geschäftsführer • Kalkulation • Kaufmännischer Leiter • Konstruktion • Logistik • Montage • Personal • Produktmanager Pressen • Rechnungswesen • Vertrieb

B Find a department for each of the descriptions below using the organization chart.

1 We work out how much the customer's order will cost.

2 We monitor how much money the company makes and spends.

3 We put the machines together here.

4 We buy the components needed for an order.

5 We find new products and improve existing ones.

6 We're responsible for employing and training people.

C **Decide whether the following statements about the organization chart are true or false. Correct the false statements.**

1. Michael Klossek buys in parts for customer orders.
2. Robert Bauerdiek und Rolf Geide are in charge of the company.
3. Dr. Steffen Rötz coordinates people, materials and equipment.
4. Thorsten Günthör deals with invoices.
5. Heinz Hoffmann visits customers all over the world and convinces them to buy products from Cantec.

6 Who are you and what do you do?

A **Use the organization chart on page 20 to find out the names and positions of these employees.**

CANTEC GmbH NEWSLETTER **ISSUE No. 42** Cantec SOUDRONIC GROUP

1 I'm responsible for the smooth running of Cantec GmbH and take overall responsibility for all decisions. I spend a lot of my time travelling and attending meetings, fairs and exhibitions, and recently gave a presentation about our company's products at a trade fair in China. Soudronic, the parent company, has subsidiaries in Europe, China, South-East Asia, the USA and Mexico.

2 I'm always on the move! My job entails visiting customers, very often in hot countries. You need patience and a lot of cross-cultural competence and understanding. Dealing with customers is a skill, and you need a good relationship with them before you can talk about a contract. That's why I recently travelled all the way to Dubai to attend a big ceremony to open two high-speed production lines supplied by Cantec.

3 My job involves preparing the company's budget a year in advance, which includes keeping an eye on the volume of orders, the turnover and profit, and making regular forecasts. It's up to me to permanently monitor and analyse the key figures and explain any deviations in our monthly financial report. I report to the Managing Director, the Commercial Director and the Group Chief Financial Officer.

4 Doing my job means taking responsibility for a whole contract. Recently, I was in charge of processing an order placed by a South African customer in Cape Town for a CAN-O-MAT machine capable of producing 250 million cans per year. My area of responsibility includes making sure that the buyer and seller keep to the contract. I'm in constant contact with the customer, which includes looking after their staff while they are being trained at our company.

5 It's my responsibility to find the right person for the job, which sometimes means training an existing employee or recruiting a new one. About 10% of our workforce are trainees, and many of them stay on and work for us after finishing vocational training college. Others come back to us after completing their university course. I enjoy working with people, but that doesn't mean I don't like working with facts and figures. That's part of my job too.

B **Find five different ways of saying "I'm responsible for …" in the newsletter texts.**

7 Working with words

A Use words or expressions from paragraphs 1–3 in exercise 6 to complete this LinkedIn profile.

Pia Hausmann's Summary

I'm …[1] for finances at HiTech Ltd, which is the European …[2] of our American …[3] company, the GlobeTech Corporation in Atlanta, Georgia. HiTech's products were recently exhibited at a major …[4] in Shanghai.
My duties at HiTech include keeping a close …[5] on spending and making …[6] about future profits. My position …[7] working with facts and figures, but I also regularly …[8] conferences and trade fairs.

B Use information from all five paragraphs in exercise 6 to complete these sentences.

Paragraph 1: This employee frequently …
Paragraph 2: This employee builds up a good relationship with a customer before …
Paragraph 3: This employee works closely with … and …
Paragraph 4: This employee is responsible for …
Paragraph 5: This employee makes sure that the company has …

C Write a profile of your own responsibilities in some of the departments you have worked in at your company. Write at least 60 words.

8 Making a flyer

KMK

Sie arbeiten in der Personalabteilung. Die Position von Dirk Sauerwald soll in den nächsten zwei Jahren neu besetzt werden, da er in Rente gehen wird. Der Geschäftsführer hat sich für die Nachfolge einen jungen, englischsprachigen Ersatz gewünscht, da immer mehr Geschäfte auf Englisch ablaufen werden.

Sie sollen im Auftrag Ihres Chefs einen Flyer auf Englisch erstellen, der an britischen Universitäten ausliegt und in dem für die Stelle geworben wird. Verarbeiten Sie folgende Informationen:

- *Stelle im Verkauf einer großen deutschen Firma*
- *Aufgabenfeld*
- *Kundenkontakt*
- *Verträge*
- *Reisen*

GRAMMAR

The *ing*-form (Gerunds)

1 I enjoy **working** with people.
2 I don't like **working** with facts and figures.
3 **Dealing** with customers is a skill.
4 I'm responsible for **finding** the right person.
5 After/Before **completing** their university course, …

- Die **ing**-Form des Verbs verhält sich wie ein Substantiv.
- Nach einigen Verben steht die *ing*-Form als Objekt (1, 2).
- Weitere Verben mit der *ing*-Form als Objekt sind *(dis)like**, *entail, hate**, *include, involve, love**, *mean, prefer, recommend, suggest* (2).
- Die *ing*-Form kann auch das Subjekt eines Satzes sein (3).
- Die *ing*-Form kann auf eine Präposition folgen (4, 5).

* Der Infinitiv kann nur auf die Verben *hate*, *like* und *love* folgen, ohne dass die Bedeutung sich ändert.

9 Practice

A Rewrite the following sentences using an expression from the box and the *ing*-form of the verb.

Example: One of my jobs is to contact clients.
My work includes contacting clients.

capable of • enjoy • ~~includes~~ • in charge of • prefer • responsible for

1 It's my job to take decisions.
I'm …

2 Our machines can produce 1,000 cans per minute.
They're …

3 It's great to go on business trips to interesting countries.
I …

4 It's my responsibility to train foreign technicians.
I'm …

5 I find it better to call customers rather than write emails to them.
I …

B Use the *ing*-forms from the box to complete this text about project management.

becoming • dealing • keeping • picking • taking • timing • training • working

Project management means …[1] with people and products. It entails …[2] everything in such a way that there are no delays. The job of a project manager involves …[3] a close eye on how an order is progressing. …[4] our customers' technicians to operate our machines is another of my many responsibilities. After …[5] them up at the airport and …[6] them to their hotel, we give them the timetable for the week. Anyone interested in …[7] a project manager shouldn't be afraid of …[8] hard!

10 Mediation

Die Cantec GmbH in Essen gehört zur Soudronic Holding AG in der Schweiz, die eine englischsprachige Website hat.

Ihr Chef sieht einen interessanten Artikel auf dieser Website und bittet Sie eine Reportage in der Mitarbeiterzeitung eine sinngemäße, zusammengefasste Übersicht auf Deutsch zu erstellen. Gehen Sie dabei nur auf die Vorteile von Metallverpackungen ein sowie auf die weiteren Schritte, die die Muttergesellschaft geplant hat. Verwenden Sie ganze Sätze und Ihre eigenen Worte.

Mozilla Firefox
Soudronic
http://www.soudronic.com
Google
Facebook Meistbesuchte... Erste Schritte Aktuelle Nachr... Lesezeichen

Green's the word

1 Ask the average consumer about their idea of eco-friendly packaging and what answers do you expect? Glass jars? PET bottles? Tetra Pak containers? One thing's for sure: most won't think of steel cans. At Soudronic, we think the time has come for manufacturers in the canmaking industry to put the record straight.

2 Consider the facts. Apart from the obvious convenience reasons for using cans, metal is a reusable material that can be recycled infinitely without losing any of its essential properties. In 2007, the EU recycled 59% of its steel cans and 58% of its aluminium drinks cans, putting it way ahead in the recycling stakes. The only metal lost is the metal consumers don't recycle. What's more, cans made from recycled material save a full 75% of the energy used to make new ones. Cans are now lighter than ever before, which means we use fewer natural resources. In short, metal packaging offers advantages that make it attractive both short and long term.

3 And these are the points taken up by the new Soudronic advertising campaign. Initially consisting of four subjects, the campaign highlights the ecological benefits of metal packaging in general. But it also shows how Soudronic's push towards downgauging and even lighter cans will further cut the industry's use of raw materials, save natural resources, and help reduce the world's carbon emissions footprint. All of which is good news for responsible customers looking to make the right environmental choices.

4 A business-to-business offensive, the new Soudronic campaign was designed to make canmakers aware of the largely unspoken – or unperceived – ecological benefits of their product. If this ultimately helps to change consumer perceptions about metal packaging, and push up recycling rates still further, Soudronic will have more than achieved its objective.

Source: www.soudronic.com/node/359

The Toyota Way

Porsche is one of the world's most profitable sports cars, but it wasn't always like that. When Wendelin Wiedeking took over in 1993, Porsche had a net loss of 122 million euros ($162 million), sales of no more than 14,000 cars, high stock levels and wasted factory space. Then they called in rival carmaker Toyota for advice on making massive changes, including fine-tuning suppliers' deliveries to make sure the factory received parts just when they were needed. Since then profits have been high, sometimes as high as 20%, and Porsche has never looked back.

Toyota's management philosophy is based on:
Challenge • Kaizen (*Improvement*) • Genchi Genbutsu (*Go and see*) • Respect • Teamwork

The 14 principles of The Toyota Way

1 Base your management decisions on a long-term philosophy, even at the expense of short-term goals.
2 Create continuous process flow to bring problems to the surface.
3 Use "pull" systems to avoid overproduction.[1]
4 Level out the workload.
5 Build a culture of stopping to fix problems in order to get quality right the first time.
6 Standardized tasks are the foundation for continuous improvement and employee empowerment.
7 Use visual control so no problems are hidden.
8 Use only reliable, thoroughly tested technology that serves your people and processes.
9 Grow leaders who thoroughly understand the work, live the philosophy, and teach it to others.
10 Develop exceptional people and teams who follow your company's philosophy.
11 Respect your extended network of partners and suppliers by challenging them and helping them improve.
12 Go and see for yourself in order to thoroughly understand the situation (*genchi genbutsu*).
13 Make decisions slowly by consensus, thoroughly considering all options; implement decisions rapidly.
14 Become a learning organization through relentless reflection and continuous improvement.

1 Materials are only supplied and used when needed.

11 Understanding the text

A Read the text and do the following tasks.

1 Give examples of inefficiency at Porsche in 1993.
2 Explain how components were supplied to Porsche before Wiedeking took over.
3 Describe how Wiedeking changed the way suppliers delivered parts.

B Find out which of the 14 principles the following statements correspond to.

1 Encourage employees to correct mistakes immediately.
2 Motivate your employees to always look for better and more efficient ways of doing their work.
3 Make sure that there are no periods of over or underactivity in the factory.
4 Plan for the future, not just for the present.
5 Always take the trouble to find out personally what is happening.

UNIT 3

A phone call to Skater Style GmbH

- Making telephone calls
- Understanding messages
- Being polite

1 Warm-up

A **What difficulties do you have when making or answering telephone calls in English? Tell your partner/group.**

B **Match the advice below about telephoning in English (1–3) to the illustrations (a–c).**

C **Which is the best piece of advice for making telephone calls in English? Why?**

D **What other advice can you offer based on your experiences of telephoning in English?**

2 The most important thing to remember when you're telephoning in English is to prepare yourself for a call. Write down the phrases you think you'll use and have these in front of you when you're making the call.

1 My advice about telephoning in English is to ask the person to repeat themselves if they say something you don't understand; it's really not that bad!

3 If a telephone call is too difficult, you can always say that the line is bad and that you'll call back. Then you can take a deep breath and start again.

> **!** *a piece of* advice or *some* advice but NOT *an* advice

2 The first phone call

06

A Listen as Tom Evans from Hoodies Ltd in the UK calls Skater Style GmbH in Germany and say what he is calling about.

Tina Skater Style GmbH. Tina Schröder. Guten Morgen.
Tom Oh, hello. Do you speak English? I'm afraid my German's not that good.
Tina Yes, of course. Tina Schröder speaking. How can I help you?
Tom Thank you, Tina. My name's Tom Evans. I'd like to speak to someone in the sales department, please.
Tina Could you tell me what it's about, please?
Tom Sure. I work for Hoodies Ltd. We're a clothing chain which sells sports and street wear. We're interested in stocking your skater clothing.
Tina Ah, OK. I'll put you through to Bernd Müller, our Sales Director. Can you hold the line for a moment, please?
Tom Yes, no problem.

Tina Hello again, Tom. I'm afraid that Herr Müller is in a meeting at the moment. Can I take a message? Or can I get him to call you back?
Tom Yes, please. He could call me back.
Tina That's fine. Could you give me your number, please?
Tom Yes, sure. Dial 0044 for the UK. Then 1342 73982. My extension is 38. So, if …
Tina Sorry, I didn't catch the last bit. Could you say it again, please?
Tom Yes. 38. If you dial that at the end of our number, you'll get right through to me.
Tina Right. I'll just read that back to you. 0044 1342 73982, extension 38.
Tom That's right.
Tina Fine, Tom. I'll let Herr Müller know that you called as soon as he comes out of his meeting. Is there anything else I can do for you now?
Tom No, thanks, that was everything. Thanks for your help. Bye now.
Tina You're welcome. Goodbye.

About an hour later, Bernd Müller tries to reach Tom Evans on the phone.

Secretary Good afternoon, Hoodies Ltd. How can I help you?
Bernd Hello. My name's Bernd Müller. I'm from Skater Style in Germany. I'd expected to reach Tom Evans.
Secretary Ah, did you call his extension?
Bernd Yes, I did.
Secretary Oh, let me just check. I'm sorry, his line is engaged; that's why you've reached me.
Bernd I see. Well, I'm returning his call from this morning. He's expecting me to call back. It's rather urgent, I believe.
Secretary OK. I'll just put you on hold and see if I can get him for you.
Bernd No problem.

Tom Hello, is that Bernd Müller?
Bernd Yes, hello.
Tom Hi, this is Tom Evans. Thanks for returning my call.
Bernd That's no problem. But … I'm sorry, Mr Evans. Hold on a moment, please. I'm calling on my mobile from our production line and it's a little loud. Just let me step in here … That's better; I should be able to hear you now. So, what can I do for you?

B **Write in your own words why …**

1. Tom wants to speak English.
2. Bernd can't take Tom's call.
3. Tom leaves his number for Bernd.
4. Bernd gets put through to Tom's secretary.
5. Bernd asks Tom to wait when he finally gets through to him.

C **Your boss would like to know what the two telephone calls were about. Summarize them for him/her.**

TIP

Addressing people on the phone

It is common for English-speaking people to use first names on the phone even if they do not know each other. If someone does this, it appears open and friendly if you do the same.

However, it is a good idea to wait until someone invites you to use their first name. While many people prefer to use first names with business contacts, some English-speakers use a more formal approach saying *Mr* ['mɪstə(r)], *Mrs* ['mɪsɪz] or *Ms* [mɪz].

If you do not know whether or not a woman is married, you should use *Ms.* She will probably tell you if she prefers to be addressed as *Mrs.* For years the expression *Miss* [mɪs] was seen as being old-fashioned, but it is slowly becoming acceptable again.

3 Important telephone phrases

A **Read the telephone conversation again and write down the English equivalents of the following phrases.**

1. Könnten Sie mir sagen, worum es geht?
2. Ich stelle Sie zu Bernd Müller, unserem Verkaufsdirektor durch.
3. Könnten Sie kurz dran bleiben?
4. Soll ich ihm sagen, dass er Sie zurückrufen soll?
5. Könnten Sie mir Ihre Nummer geben?
6. Bei ihm ist besetzt.
7. Er wartet auf meinen Rückruf.
8. Vielen Dank für den Rückruf.

B **Now match the phrases below with the phrases from the conversation which have the same or a similar meaning.**

1. Thank you for getting back to me.
2. Can I ask what it's in connection with?
3. He's probably waiting for my call.
4. I'll connect you with ….
5. Can I ask him to return your call?
6. What number can he reach you on?
7. I'll just put you on hold, if that's OK.
8. His extension is busy.

TIP

Saying telephone numbers

Say each digit separately, except for double digits.
e.g. 01233 4567899 = *oh (AE zero) one two double-three, four five six, seven eight double-nine.*

You usually say all of the numbers in a country code separately.
e.g. 0044 = *oh oh four four* (or) *zero zero four four*

country code = *Vorwahl*
extension = *Durchwahl*
mobile phone (AE cell phone) = *Handy*
landline = *Festnetz*

4 Making a telephone call

KMK

Act out this telephone conversation with a partner. The language box on page 30 will help you.

Skater Style Mitarbeiter/in

Melden Sie sich am Telefon mit Vor- und Nachnamen und mit Firmennamen.

British customer

Introduce yourself and ask if you can speak to someone in the sales department.

Fragen Sie, warum der Kunde/die Kundin anruft.

Say that you are interested in buying some of the company's clothing for your shop.

Sagen Sie, dass Sie den Anrufer/die Anruferin mit Arista Marquardt verbinden, die im Verkauf arbeitet und dass Sie ihn/sie in die Warteschleife schalten. Dann sagen Sie, dass bei Frau Marquardt besetzt ist und fragen Sie, ob er/sie eine Nachricht hinterlassen möchte.

Ask if you can leave your telephone number so that Frau Marquardt can call you back.

Reagieren Sie entsprechend und fragen Sie nach der Telefonnummer des Anrufers/der Anruferin.

Give your number: 0044 1548 7174566

Sie haben nicht verstanden. Bitten Sie den Anrufer/die Anruferin, die Nummer zu wiederholen.

Repeat your number to the employee.

Wiederholen Sie die Nummer noch einmal laut.

Thank the person you are speaking to for their help and say goodbye.

Verabschieden Sie sich.

LANGUAGE

Expressions for telephoning

Making a call
My name is .... I'd like to speak to someone in the marketing/sales/finance department, please.
Can I speak to ..., please?
Could you put me through to the ... department, please?

Saying what the call is about
I'm interested in ...
I'd like to speak to somebody about ...
The reason I'm calling is ...

Answering the phone
Good morning/afternoon/evening (,Fynton Industries Ltd). How can I help you?
Hello, ... speaking.

Asking the caller for more information
Could you tell me what it's about, please?
Can/May I ask why you're calling?

Transferring the call
I'll put you through to ...
I'll connect you with ...
Can you hold the line for a moment, please?

Explaining / Apologizing
I'm afraid that ... is in a meeting at the moment.
I'm sorry, but ... isn't in the office/ available at the moment.
I'm afraid his/her line is engaged.
Sorry, his/her extension is busy right now.
Can I get him/her to call you back?
Can I take a message?
Would you like to leave a message?
Could you give me your number, please?
What number can he/she reach you on?

Asking the caller to repeat something
Sorry, I didn't catch/understand that.
Could you say it/that again, please?
Could you spell that for me, please?
Could you read that back to me, please?

Ending a call
Is there anything else I can do for you?
Thanks for your help.
Thank you for calling.
Bye now.
Goodbye.

5 Tom and Bernd telephone again

07

A During the conversation between Tom and Bernd, the line goes dead. Listen as Bernd calls again from his office. Which of the statements best summarizes their conversation?

1 Bernd tries to get Tom to buy some of the new line of sweatshirts, but Tom doesn't seem very interested.
2 Tom expresses his interest in a new line of sweatshirts and Bernd offers to send him the details by email.
3 Tom says he's not interested in the sweatshirts which are already on Skater Style's website and that he would rather see some new designs.

B Listen again. What order are these expressions used in?

a Could I have your email address, please?
b Could you speak a little more slowly, please?
c The line just went dead.
d Let's talk again soon.

C **Bernd notes down Tom's email address, but he doesn't note it down correctly. Find and correct his mistakes in your exercise book.**

Tomivans@hoodeis_ldt.co.uk

LANGUAGE

Saying internet and email addresses

www.skaterstyle.de	*w-w-w-(dot)-skaterstyle-(all one word)-(dot)-d-e*
www.hoodies-ltd.co.uk/sales	*w-w-w-(dot)-hoodies-(hyphen)-l-t-d-(dot)-co-(dot)-u-k-(forward slash)-sales*
b_mueller@skaterstyle.de	*b-(underscore)-mueller-(with 'ue')-(at)-skaterstyle-(all one word)-(dot)-d-e*

6 Practising saying email addresses

A **How do you say each of these symbols? Match them to the words in the box.**

1 @ **2** / **3** . **4** - **5** _

forward slash • hyphen • at • underscore • dot

B **With a partner, practise saying these email addresses. Say them clearly and spell the names to your partner to make it easy for your partner to understand.**

1 yvonne.gilford@rosworth-products.com
2 jillcraig@bosworth_solutions.biz
3 vanessa_williams@tulsonsteelpipes.co.uk
4 terri-quantrill@xlogistics.co.uk

C **Now practise spelling your own private and work email addresses to your partner.**

7 Understanding answerphone messages

08

A **The next day, Tom Evans' secretary listens to an answerphone message from Bernd Müller. Look at her notes and find the three mistakes she made.**

Tom,
Bernd Müller from Skater Style left a message for you. He has sent you the pdf by email. Can you give him a call on his mobile (0049 1703 684948) so that he can give you his email address?
Janet

KMK 09

B **Hören Sie sich die anderen beiden Nachrichten auf Toms Mailbox. Notieren Sie die erforderlichen Angaben im Formular für Anrufbenachrichtigungen.**

Name:	…
E-Mail-Adresse:	…
Grund des Anrufes:	…
Telefonnummer:	…

8 Leave a message after the tone …

WEBCODE **INDMU0301**

Read the instructions below and then record your own answerphone message.

It's several weeks later and Hoodies Ltd are about to receive their first order from Skater Style. Bernd Müller writes you an email asking you to call Tom Evans to confirm the details of the order. Tom isn't in his office when you call, so you have to leave a message on his answerphone …

Betreff: **Bestellbestätigung für Hoodies Ltd**

Von: b_mueller@skaterstyle.de **Signatur:** Ohne

Könnten Sie bitte kurz bei Tom Evans in England anrufen, um die Einzelheiten zu seiner Bestellung zu bestätigen?

Die Bestellung beinhaltet 45 Sweatshirts der Serie „StreetSurf" (Nr. 54983) und 25 Sweatshirts der Serie „KoolKult" (Nr. 38928). Die Artikel werden, wie mit Tom besprochen, am 18. März FOB geliefert. Obwohl schwer zu sagen ist, wann genau die Sendung ankommt, schätzen wir, dass der mit der Lieferung beladene Lkw gegen 15 Uhr im Lager von Hoodies Ltd sein wird.

Vielen Dank
Bernd Müller

TIP

Politeness

English speakers frequently use 'extra' words to give a polite and helpful impression. If your answers are short, the person you are speaking to may feel that you are too direct and a bit rude.

Tips to help you sound more polite:

1. Always use "please" when you want the caller to do something for you such as repeat what they have just said, and "thank you" when they have done it.
2. Use expressions such as "Could you …?", "Would you mind …?", and "Would it be possible for you to …?" to 'soften' what you are asking.
3. Try to avoid giving answers with just "yes" and "no". For example:
   "Did you get my email?" – "Yes, thanks, I did."

9 Politeness on the phone

A **Complete the quiz about how to politely ask a caller to do something. Then check your answers at the bottom.**

Business English FAQs

It's normal to have to ask people to slow down or repeat something when telephoning in English. But what's the most polite way of doing it? Complete our quiz to find out how polite you are.

1 The person you are calling is speaking unclearly. What do you say?
a Sorry. Would you mind speaking a little more clearly, please?
b Sorry. Can you speak more clearly?

2 The caller is speaking too fast. What do you say?
a Sorry, speak more slowly.
b Could you speak more slowly, please?

3 The person on the other end of the line is speaking quietly. What do you say?
a Sorry, would you mind speaking up, please?
b Please speak up.

4 You want the caller to repeat themselves. What do you say?
a Would it be possible to repeat that, please?
b Say that again.

5 You want the person you are talking to to spell something. What do you say?
a Please spell that.
b Would you spell that for me, please?

Answers: 1a, 2b, 3a, 4a, 5b

B **Now look at the more polite sentences again and make a note of the 'extra' words which make them more polite.**

10 Putting politeness into action

Rephrase the sentences below to make them more polite.

1 Ask him to return my call. Would you mind ...
2 What's the reason for your call?
3 Send me an email. Could you please
4 Did you call me? – No. Sorry I didn't call you
5 Wait a moment.
6 Did you get the email I sent? – Yes.
7 Give me your email address. Would you mind giving me your ...
8 What time will he be back in the office?

11 Role-play

Read your partner file at the back of the book and the information on the Skater Style website below. Then work with a partner and act out the role-play.

Student A: turn to partner file 11 on page 117. / **Student B:** turn to partner file 2 on page 113.

Are you cool enough to wear our baseball caps?

KoolKult series – all caps in the series cost €30.00

Blue (No. 493828) SOLD OUT
Black (No. 673982)
Orange (No. 872876)
Yellow (No. 983726)

Street Style series – all caps in the series cost €24.00

Blue (No. 387197)
Red (No. 329876) SOLD OUT
White (No. 432893)
Orange (No. 887282)

Skater Style

GRAMMAR: Future tenses – the *going to*-future and the *will*-future

1 **I'll be** in the office all afternoon.
2 I have checked and you**'ll receive** the delivery next Monday.
3 **Will** she **be** in the office this afternoon?
4 We **will deliver** the consignment by 4 p.m. on Friday.
5 **I'll take a look** and see if he's in his office.
6 Kate**'s going to be** in a meeting until after 5 p.m.

- Das **will-future** wird aus *will* und der Grundform des Verbs gebildet (1–5).
- Das *will-future* wird oft für zukünftige Situationen oder Ereignisse, die mit Sicherheit eintreten werden (1, 2, 4), für Vermutungen und für spontane Entscheidungen verwendet.
- In der gesprochenen Sprache kommt die betonte Form *will* selten vor. Meistens (vor allem mit Pronomen) wird die Kurzform *'ll* benutzt (1, 2). In Fragen ohne Fragewort ist nur die betonte Form möglich (3). In der Schriftsprache ist die betonte Form üblich: die unbetonte Form wirkt dort informell (4).

- Das **going to-future** wird aus *going to* und der Grundform des Verbs gebildet (6).
- Es wird benutzt, um über Pläne oder Absichten zu Sprechen. In der gesprochenen Sprache drückt man damit auch aus, dass etwas mit Sicherheit eintreffen wird (6).

12 Practice

Use the verbs in brackets in the appropriate future form to complete the sentences.

1 OK, I … you back first thing in the morning and let you know. (call)
2 The consignment … on time because of the early-morning traffic jams. (not arrive)
3 I … him that you called and ask him to call you back as soon as he's free. (tell)
4 What time … speak to me tomorrow? (you / be able to)
5 I … you once the order has arrived and … you know if I want to order more. (call, let)
6 I … in a meeting until lunchtime but I … at 2 p.m. (be, call back)
7 I'm not sure if he's in; I … check. (have to)
8 Please tell her that I … later this afternoon. (call back)

13 Mediation

Übertragen Sie den folgenden Auszug sinngemäß in die deutsche Sprache.

Telephone greetings that customers – and employees – will love

by Mary Sandro

Many companies make their telephone greetings so long and complicated that employees hate saying them, and customers hate listening to them. But there is power in being simple. For best results, telephone greetings should be friendly, short and sound honest.

Pleasant

A friendly greeting is essential to a successful call because it creates the right emotional tone. In general, listeners tend to mirror or 'catch' the emotional states of speakers. This is a rule of communication that is true whether one is speaking to a group of 1000, a small meeting of ten, or a single customer on the telephone. In other words, people respond in the way they are spoken to. If we answer the phone in an unfriendly way, chances are the caller will be unfriendly. If we answer the phone in a friendly way, chances are the caller will be friendly, and we all know which caller is easier to work with.

One of the easiest ways to guarantee that you sound friendly and positive when answering the phone is to use the right body language. I recommend sitting on the edge of your chair, taking a deep breath and then smiling.

Sincerity

Telephone greetings have to be natural if they are to sound sincere or, in other words, honest. The key elements of a telephone greeting should be: company and department, your name, and then an offer to help.

That means that company marketing slogans or phrases such as "We're so glad you called" or "It's a lovely day here at company XYZ and even better since you called" are out. Sentiments like this just don't sound sincere and honest. And customers won't thank you for taking up their time with them.

Brevity

Keep your telephone greeting short. I've heard greetings that are so long, I feared the person answering the phone was going to run out of air just trying to say them. Excessively long greetings are unprofessional for many reasons: they don't sound pleasant or sincere because technically they are impossible to execute; employees hate them and those feelings come through; and callers hate them because they waste their time. Fortunately, if you follow the guidelines mentioned above, brevity is assured.

Source: adapted from http://www.proedgeskills.com/Customer_Service_Articles/telephone_greetings_that_custome.htm

My first mobile phone was almost the size of a brick. It also weighed about as much as a brick and, as well as making telephone calls with it, I could use the phone to hold open my office door as it recharged on the floor. It spent a lot of time there because its battery provided power for just a few hours at a time.

My new smartphone sits neatly in my hand and has more computing power under its large screen than NASA used to send the first man to the moon. I can read and send emails with it, take part in web conferences, access my company's databases, send and receive videos of product demonstrations, work on documents and, yes, make phone calls.

These small but incredible devices have a big future in business. I would even argue that they will become the business communication tool in the coming years. It's easy to see why they will make PCs obsolete: business in the globalized world is increasingly about being mobile and, in this context, smartphones leave PCs standing – on the desk.

Some people might argue that laptops, notepads and tablets are the ideal mobile IT solutions for business people. But, the point is, they're still not mobile enough. I gave up on my tablet because of the pain I got in my shoulder from carrying it around. Now everything I need fits into my jacket pocket. You might think I'm a fan of smartphones. You'd be right. In fact, the only disadvantage I can see is that they're so easy to lose. And that could be really frustrating if you've got important – and private – company data on your phone.

But this would be a small loss to companies compared to the big cost savings they would make by switching to smartphones. We might currently think of smartphones as being quite expensive, but the reality is that it would be cheaper to equip a workforce with smartphones than with a traditional IT infrastructure. So if the coolness and impressive functionality of smartphones aren't enough to convince companies to switch to them, the cost savings they promise certainly will.

14 Understanding the text

A Read the article and choose the headline which summarizes it best.

1. Why smartphones can't replace laptops and tablets
2. Why phones will outsmart PCs to become *the* business communication tool
3. Smartphones only have a future in business if they become cheaper

B Make a list of the advantages for companies of smartphones mentioned in the article.

15 Over to you

A The article mentions one disadvantage of smartphones; how many more can you think of? Discuss your ideas with a partner.

B Think of the type of jobs that people do in your company. In which of these jobs does it make most sense to use a smartphone and for which tasks?

Arranging travel to a trade fair

UNIT 4

- Making travel arrangements
- Booking a flight
- Reserving hotel rooms

1 Warm-up

A **Make a checklist like the one below of the things you have to remember to do when planning a trip. Use the photographs to help you and add your own ideas.**

Travel arrangements: checklist

1 Book train tickets

B **Compare your checklist with the person sitting next to you.**

C **Read the list (1–6) below. Then decide what the four most important items are that you should take with you on a trip abroad. Explain why to your partner.**

1 credit card
2 passport
3 map of the city you're going to
4 money
5 mobile phone
6 ticket for your flight / boarding card

2 Arranging travel to a trade fair

10

Schneider Electric GmbH makes components, connectors and terminals for power supply. The company is based in Ratingen near Düsseldorf and the company language is English.

A Christoph Eckstein calls his colleague Heather Longman to ask her to make some travel arrangements for him. Listen to or read their conversation and say where Christoph is going to and why.

Heather Morning. Heather Longman here. How can I help?
Christoph Morning, Heather. It's Christoph Eckstein from business development here.
Heather Oh hi, Christoph. What can I do for you?
Christoph A colleague and I are attending the All-Energy trade fair in Aberdeen in Scotland. Could you take care of our travel and hotel reservations, please?
Heather No problem. What are the dates of your trip?
Christoph Well, the event is on 18 and 19 May. We'd like to travel really early on 18 May.
Heather OK. When will you be returning?
Christoph Jörg would like to fly back straight after the trade fair at about 7 p.m. I'm going to stay until 20 May as I have to attend a meeting just outside Glasgow. I'd like a rental car for that. Could you take care of that booking for me too, please?
Heather Sure. Now, what about 20 May? What time would you like to depart?
Christoph I'd like to catch a flight early in the evening if possible, just after the meeting.
Heather OK. And what about your accommodation in Aberdeen?
Christoph My what?
Heather Accommodation – you know, your hotel.
Christoph Oh, I see.
Heather Is there anything special I need to know about your hotel?
Christoph No, not really anything special. But, most importantly, we'd like a hotel as close as possible to the Exhibition and Conference Centre. And I should tell you that Jörg is a smoker, so he'll need a room that he can smoke in. That's also pretty important.
Heather OK. I'll keep that in mind.
Christoph Oh, and it's not essential, but a gym and sauna would be good.
Heather Fine. And you'll need another night in the hotel in Aberdeen on 19 May, right?
Christoph That's right.
Heather Do you want to pick up your rental car early the next morning?
Christoph Yes, that would be great. What would I do without you to keep me organized?
Heather That's what I'm here for! I'll take care of all the reservations and let you know the details.

B Choose the correct sentence ending to make true statements about the conversation.

1 Christoph wants Heather to …
a … take care of travel and accommodation arrangements for a trip to a trade fair.
b … book places at a trade fair for him and his colleague.
c … change his travel arrangements for a trip to a trade fair.

2 Christoph and Jörg will be travelling together on 18 May, but …
a … Jörg will be returning alone on 19 May.
b … Christoph will be staying in Aberdeen until 21 May.
c … Christoph will be returning on 20 May for an early meeting in Ratingen.

3 Christoph will need a car to drive …
a … to the Exhibition and Conference Centre.
b … to a meeting near Glasgow.
c … from the Exhibition and Conference Centre to Glasgow airport.

4 The most important thing Heather will have to remember when choosing a hotel is that …
a … it has a gym and a sauna.
b … it has rooms for smokers.
c … it's not far from the Exhibition and Conference Centre.

5 Heather does not need to book accommodation in Glasgow because …
a … Christoph will be flying back straight after his meeting.
b … a hotel reservation has already been made for him there.
c … he has already reserved a hotel room in Glasgow himself.

C Read the conversation again and find sentences which have a similar meaning to the following.

1 Could you possibly look after the arrangements for our trip?
2 When are you planning to travel?
3 When will you be making your return journey?
4 Could you look after the reservation for me, please?
5 When do you want to leave?
6 Ideally, I'd like to fly out in the early evening.
7 I'll confirm the details with you once I've made your bookings.

LANGUAGE

Making travel arrangements

Asking for help making travel reservations
Could you take care of our travel and hotel reservations / the car rental booking for me, please?
Could you book me a flight / hotel room / rental car for …, please?

Asking for details about travel arrangements
What are the dates of your trip?
When will you be returning?
What time would you like to depart?
Is there anything special I need to know?

Giving details about when you want to travel
We'd like to travel early on …
I'm going to stay until …
I'd like to catch a flight early/late in the morning/afternoon/evening if possible.

3 Confirming the details

You are Heather Longman. Write an email to Christoph Eckstein to confirm the details.

4 Role-play: making travel reservations

Work with a partner and act out the role-play.

Student A: turn to partner file 3 on page 113.
Student B: read the partner file below.

Student B

You plan to travel to a conference in Valencia, Spain. Call your colleague to ask him/her to make travel arrangements. Be polite and make small talk with your colleague.

- Tell your colleague who is calling (own name)
- Ask your colleague to arrange your travel
- Departing: 14 October (early in the morning)
- Returning: 15 October (evening)
- Thank your colleague for their help

TIP

Times and dates

The 24-hour clock is used less frequently in English than in German, but it is often used in Britain when making travel bookings.
e.g. Departure time: 07.00 = *(oh) seven hundred (hours)*
Arrival time: 15.00 = *fifteen hundred hours*

Note, though, that while travel times are usually *written* using the 24-hour clock, when *talking* about these, people generally do not use this system and instead say:
My flight departs at seven a.m. and arrives at three p.m.

To avoid confusion it is also worth knowing that people from the US and the UK use a different system to talk about dates. People from America would read the date *07/04/20..* as *4 July*, while people from the United Kingdom would read it as *7 April*.

5 Writing the date

A Write out these dates in European form, then read them to a partner.

Example: 17.9.2022 *17 September 2022*

1 7.2.2016
2 8.12.2014
3 4.10.2017
4 1.5.1998
5 11.7.1916
6 29.11.2020

B Write out these dates from an American colleague in European form.

Example: 4.2.2011 *2 April 2011*

1 8.30.2013
2 4.18.2019
3 9.11.2025
4 3.26.1977
5 6.1.1911
6 1.3.2046

6 Making flight reservations online

Heather makes flight reservations for Christoph's return journey online.

A Look at the website and find the four mistakes in her booking. Then correct the mistakes in your exercise book.

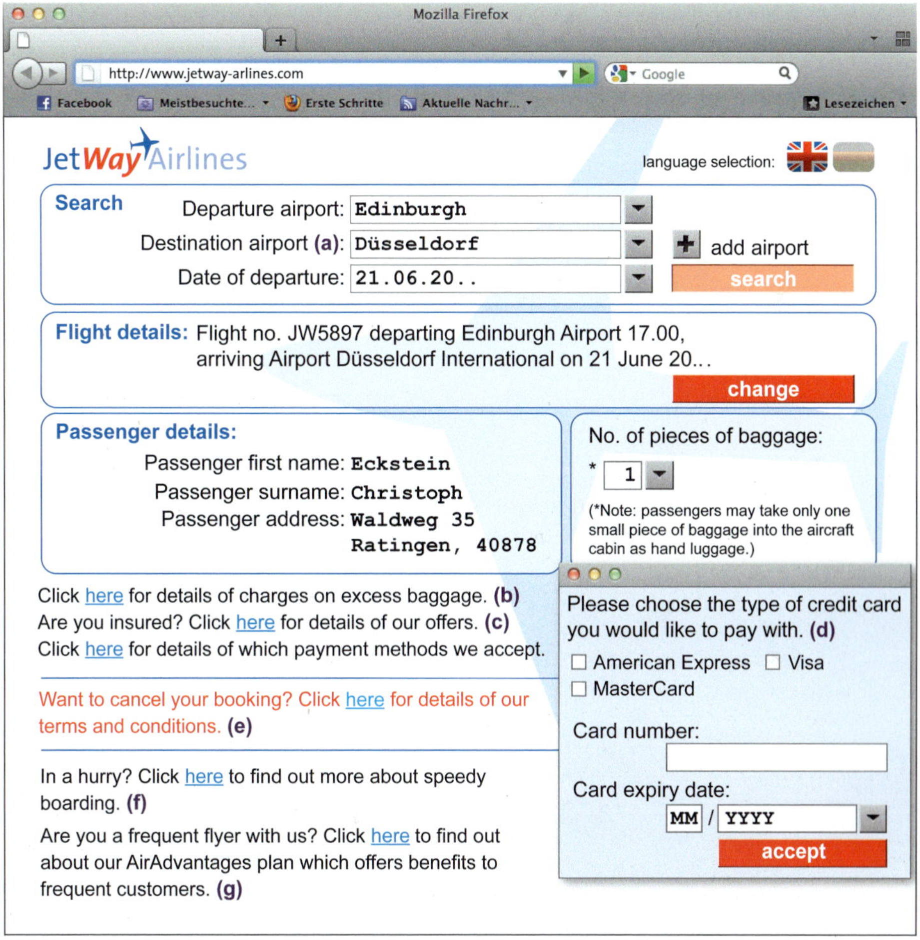

Mozilla Firefox

http://www.jetway-airlines.com

Google

Facebook | Meistbesuchte... | Erste Schritte | Aktuelle Nachr... | Lesezeichen

JetWayAirlines

language selection:

Search
Departure airport: Edinburgh
Destination airport **(a)**: Düsseldorf
Date of departure: 21.06.20..
add airport
search

Flight details: Flight no. JW5897 departing Edinburgh Airport 17.00, arriving Airport Düsseldorf International on 21 June 20...
change

Passenger details:
Passenger first name: Eckstein
Passenger surname: Christoph
Passenger address: Waldweg 35
Ratingen, 40878

No. of pieces of baggage:
* 1
(*Note: passengers may take only one small piece of baggage into the aircraft cabin as hand luggage.)

Click here for details of charges on excess baggage. **(b)**
Are you insured? Click here for details of our offers. **(c)**
Click here for details of which payment methods we accept.

Want to cancel your booking? Click here for details of our terms and conditions. **(e)**

In a hurry? Click here to find out more about speedy boarding. **(f)**

Are you a frequent flyer with us? Click here to find out about our AirAdvantages plan which offers benefits to frequent customers. **(g)**

Please choose the type of credit card you would like to pay with. **(d)**
☐ American Express ☐ Visa
☐ MasterCard
Card number:
Card expiry date:
MM / YYYY
accept

B Say where you would find the following on the screen (a–g).

1. details of the airline's customer loyalty scheme
2. information about travel insurance
3. information about how much you have to pay if your luggage weighs more than is allowed
4. the name of the airport you want to fly to
5. details of what the airline can offer you if you are not able to travel on the flight you have booked
6. details of what arrangements can be made so that you don't have to arrive early at the airport to check in for your flight
7. the area in which you enter the details of how you are going to pay

7 Finding the right hotel

Heather finds a hotel on the internet which is close to the Aberdeen Exhibition and Conference Centre.

Read the website and then do the tasks on page 43.

Mozilla Firefox
Royal Don Conference Hotel
http://royaldon.co.uk
Google
Facebook Meistbesuchte… Erste Schritte Aktuelle Nachr… Lesezeichen

The Royal Don Conference Hotel * * * *

"Where it's a pleasure to do business"

Welcome to the Royal Don Conference Hotel! The hotel is the number one destination in the area for business travellers. In fact, the car parking facilities we offer mean that you can leave your car safely with us while you stroll to the Aberdeen Exhibition and Conference Centre. Alternatively, you can make use of our shuttle bus service, which leaves from the hotel every 30 minutes.

Once a rather splendid country house, the Royal Don offers first-class, modern accommodation and business facilities to its guests. Set in eight acres of lush parkland, the hotel comprises three suites, 14 single rooms and 22 double rooms, all fully-equipped with satellite TV and en-suite bathrooms.

The Royal Don also offers three large conference rooms, each of which can accommodate up to 60 participants, as well as eight meeting rooms. Our conference and meeting rooms are fully-equipped with the latest presentation technology such as interactive whiteboards, digital projectors and cordless microphones. These facilities are complemented by our business centre which offers fax, printing and photocopying services as well as secure internet access. Wireless internet access is available to guests in all parts of the hotel. Click **here** for prices.

Checking in to the Royal Don
Guests are invited to check in from 13.00 onwards. In the event of rooms being available earlier, we will be happy to check you in.

Checking out of the Royal Don
Guests should check out by 12 noon, though later check-out times may be possible by prior arrangement.

It's not all business!
The hotel also offers a full range of leisure facilities to help you unwind after you've completed your business. These include:

- sauna
- three squash courts
- gym
- in-room movies
- The Hunting Lodge Lounge Bar
- The Club Reading Room

Dining at the Royal Don
Guests at the hotel are spoilt for choice when it comes to dining. Visit our three eateries and find out why we get star ratings in the restaurant guides.

The Auld Alliance French Bistro offers our own special blend of Scottish and French cuisines.

The Coffee Cabin Café proves that you don't have to travel to Seattle if you want to try the world's best coffee. Our cakes and pastries are also to die for!

The Fairway Restaurant offers delicious cuisine combined with romantic views over our parkland; it's just the place to entertain and impress business guests.

Guests who prefer the peace and quiet of their rooms will enjoy the full room service which we are pleased to offer. For the comfort of all its guests, the Royal Don Conference Hotel operates a strict no-smoking policy on its premises.

A **Decide which features of the hotel these symbols refer to.**

1 
2 
3 
4 
5 
6 
7 

KMK **B** **Übertragen Sie den Inhalt der Webseite in die deutsche Sprache. Beschränken Sie sich dabei speziell auf die Punkte, die für Jörg und Christoph interessant sind.**

8 Telephoning another hotel

11

A **Listen as Heather makes enquiries with another hotel in Aberdeen. Which of the following facilities are mentioned?**

1 car park
2 gym
3 squash courts
4 presentation technology
5 meeting rooms
6 room service
7 swimming pool
8 shuttle bus
9 secretarial service
10 smoking areas

B **Listen to the dialogue again and read the website for the Royal Don Conference Hotel on page 42 again. How do the facilities offered by the two hotels differ? Make notes and then tell the class.**

9 Reserving the hotel rooms

12

A **Listen as Heather calls the Royal Don Conference Hotel to make the reservations. Then say what order the following points are mentioned in.**

1 luggage
2 check-in times
3 price of the rooms
4 dates of hotel stay
5 method of payment
6 colleagues' names

B **Put the following sentences from the dialogue between Heather and the receptionist in a logical order. Then listen again to check your answers.**

Heather begins the conversation: *Two colleagues of mine are attending a trade fair in Aberdeen in May. I'd like to reserve two rooms with you.*

a	**Heather:**	What do single rooms cost?
b	**Heather:**	They'll be paying with MasterCard.
c	**Receptionist:**	When will your colleagues be arriving?
d	**Heather:**	OK, then we'll go for single rooms, please.
e	**Receptionist:**	We certainly have rooms free. Would your colleagues like to have single or double rooms?
f	**Receptionist:**	No problem. We accept MasterCard.
g	**Heather:**	They're arriving on 18 May.
h	**Receptionist:**	Single rooms cost £112 per night. Double rooms are £179.
i	**Receptionist:**	Now, can I ask how the rooms will be paid for?

10 Role-play: reserving a hotel room

KMK

Work with a partner and act out the role-play.

Student A: read the partner file below.
Student B: turn to partner file 4 on page 114.

Student A

You want to reserve a hotel room for a colleague and his wife who are travelling to Bristol in the UK for a meeting. Call the Avon View Hotel to make a reservation using your own name and the details below.

- Dates of stay: 3 nights from 22–25 September
- Accommodation required: double room (twin room also OK; single rooms not an option)
- Budget: max. £180 per double room, per night
- Payment method: Visa
- Sports facilities? Your colleague enjoys playing squash and swimming

11 Rental car reservation

Heather receives an email confirming her reservation of Christoph's rental car.

Complete the email with the words from the box.

additional • charged • collect • confirm • exceed • mileage allowance • rental period • returned • tank of fuel • vehicle

To: Heather Longman
Copy:
Subject: **Confirmation of your reservation**
From: CarPort Service Team   Signature:

Dear Ms Longman

We are delighted to …[1] your reservation of a Ford Focus for 20 May 20…

The total cost for the one-day …[2] will be £63*. This includes a daily …[3] of 100 miles. Should you …[4] this over the period of your rental, you will be billed with an …[5] charge of 17 pence per mile.

Additionally, your car will have a full …[6] when you …[7] it. Should the fuel tank not be full upon the vehicle's return, you will be …[8] the cost of refilling the tank.

Your …[9] will be ready for you to collect at our premises at the Aberdeen Exhibition and Conference Centre from 7 a.m. on 20 May. The vehicle can be …[10] to CarPort's premises at Aberdeen Airport on 20 May before 10 p.m.

We look forward to being of further service to you. If you require any further information, we will be happy to provide it.

Best regards

Your CarPort Service Team

*All prices quoted in this email include VAT.

GRAMMAR

If-sentences

if-clause	**main clause**
1 simple present	**will-future**
If you **require** further information,	we **will be** happy to provide it.
2 simple past	**would + infinitive**
If you **arrived** at the hotel at 10 a.m.,	it **would be** possible to leave your bags at reception.
3 past perfect	**would + present perfect**
If you **hadn't gone** to buy a newspaper,	we **wouldn't have missed** our flight.

- *If*-Sätze vom Typ 1 drücken eine erfüllbare Bedingung aus. Beachten Sie die Zeitenfolge: Der *if*-Nebensatz steht im **simple present**, im Hauptsatz steht das **will-future** (1).
- *If*-Sätze vom Typ 2 drücken eine möglicherweise erfüllbare Bedingung aus. Beachten Sie die Zeitenfolge: Der *if*-Nebensatz steht im **simple past**, im Hauptsatz wird das **conditional (would + Infinitiv)** verwendet (2), wobei *would* durch *could*, *might*, oder *should* ersetzt werden kann.
- *If*-Sätze vom Typ 3 drücken eine Bedingung aus, die nicht erfüllt wurde. Beachten Sie die Zeitenfolge: Der *if*-Nebensatz steht im **past perfect**, im Hauptsatz wird das **past conditional (would + present perfect)** verwendet (3).
- Steht der *if*-Nebensatz an erster Stelle, wird er vom Hauptsatz durch ein Komma getrennt.

12 Practice

WEBCODE **INDMU0401**

Complete the sentences with the correct tense of the verbs in brackets.

1. I'll take you to the airport if you … me to. (need)
2. If I … that this hotel was so far from the airport, I would have booked another hotel. (know)
3. I would call him now if I … he was still in the office. (think)
4. What will happen if we … on time? (not check in)
5. Brian would … to this conference with us if he had known it was taking place. (come)
6. If you wait and collect my bags, I … outside and order a taxi. (go)
7. We would … there on time if our taxi had been late. (not be)
8. If I … my things off quickly in my room, will I still have time to get something in the restaurant before it closes? (drop)

13 Interaktion

Work with a partner and act out the role-play.

Situation:
A client calls a large hotel in London to book a meeting room, refreshments and presentation equipment. Alex/Alice Greer answers the phone.

Eigener Name

Call the hotel to book a large conference room using the details below.

- Dates of meeting: 18–19 February
- No. of people attending: 9–13
- Refreshments required: tea and coffee (mid-morning and mid-afternoon)
- Soft drinks also available?
- Presentation equipment required: digital projector, interactive whiteboard, wireless internet access
- Price?
- Payment method: prefer Visa but also have MasterCard

Alex/Alice Greer

The details below show what is available in your hotel.

- Conference rooms available on 18–19 Feb: Autumn Room (max. 8 people)/ Winter Room (max. 15 people)
- Refreshments available: tea, coffee, water (included in room price); soft drinks cost extra
- Presentation equipment available: digital projector, wireless internet access
- Note: interactive whiteboard broken at the moment
- You will send a price offer by email
- Payment method?
- Payment options: MasterCard only (Visa causing problems recently)

14 Produktion

Sie arbeiten im Great Wellington Hotel in London. Herr Thomas Meinunger (t.meinunger_68@gmx.de) hat gerade bei Ihnen angerufen, um einen Konferenzraum für ein Meeting zu reservieren. Er hat Sie um einen Kostenvoranschlag gebeten.

Beantworten Sie seine Anfrage per E-Mail und stellen Sie ihm noch offene Fragen. Verwenden Sie die folgenden Angaben:

- Anrede und Dank für den Anruf
- Preisvoranschlag: Konferenzraum – £90 pro Tag (inkl. Tee, Kaffee und Wasser)
- Brauchen die Teilnehmer Snacks im Konferenzraum?
  - Zur Verfügung stehen verschiedene Sandwich-Sorten: Schinken und Käse / Thunfisch und Mayo / Eier und Zwiebeln / Ploughman's Sandwich
  - 10 Stück: £20; 20 Stück: £35
- Softdrinks gewünscht?
  - Cola, Orangensaft, Apfelsaft: 10 Stück – £10
- Bleiben die Teilnehmer zum Mittagessen im Hotel?
  - 2-Gänge Menü: £15 pro Person; 3-Gänge Menü: £20 pro Person
  - Speisekarte: www.greatwellingtonlondon.co.uk/menu
- Bitte um schnelle Rückmeldung, damit Sie die Gesamtkosten berechnen und die Buchung bestätigen können
- höflicher Schluss

Extra material

How to put the brakes on rising travel costs

Unlike some business costs, the cost of travel is one expense that most companies can manage better. This article offers some strategies.

...(a)

Mark Walton, business travel advisor, recommends starting with a corporate travel policy. Without clear guidelines about which flights and hotels to book, even the best employees can make wasteful decisions. For example, according to a recent survey, mid-sized companies make just 48% of their reservations online, despite the fact that this can lead to savings of 15%.

...(b)

Another strategy is to book all of your flights, hotel rooms, and rental cars through a corporate travel management agency. Such firms can help enforce your travel policy. More importantly, they provide detailed data on spending patterns that you can use to negotiate price cuts with preferred travel partners.

...(c)

To avoid expensive mistakes, it is also wise to look closely at your company's travel-expense reports. A survey carried out recently found that 22% of U.S. companies took action against employees for expense-report abuse within the previous year. Financial managers should audit at least a percentage of travel-expense claims regularly, Sushmitha Koka, a travel industry analyst, advises.

...(d)

Naturally, the best way to lower your travel expenses is for employees to travel less in the first place. For example, XRT Inc. uses web-conferencing software to replace business trips, according to Mark Adams, a product manager with the company. "We've reduced sales expenses by minimizing our need to travel to new customers to demonstrate our product," he says.

Source: adapted from: http://www.microsoft.com/midsizebusiness/businessvalue/business-travel-expenses.mspx

15 Understanding the text

A Choose the best headline for each section of the article (a–d) above.

1. Keep travel to a minimum
2. Make sure that employees know you are looking at the their travel expenses claims
3. Write clear guidelines for employees about travel costs
4. Outsource reservations to an expert provider

B With a partner, create a mind map about the approaches that companies can take to keep travel expenses down described in the text. Add your own ideas.

16 Class discussion

A The article mentions web conferencing as a way of keeping down travel expenses. What, though, are the advantages and disadvantages of travelling to meet business contacts?

B Could web conferencing ultimately replace business travel? Give reasons for your answer.

UNIT 5

An international meeting

- Preparing for a conference
- Writing emails
- Small talk

1 Warm-up

A What different types of meeting can you see here? Label the pictures (a–d) with the words from the box.

conference call • face-to-face meeting • online conference • video conference

a

b

c

d

B What types of meeting would be suitable for each of the following situations?

1 conferences in countries with extreme weather conditions
2 firing an employee
3 a job interview
4 discussions between North Sea oil workers and Head Office on land
5 technical presentations
6 weekly international team meetings

C In pairs, draw a mind map of all the factors that need to be considered before setting up each of the four types of meeting. Discuss your results with your class. Then rank the factors in order of importance for the different types of meeting.

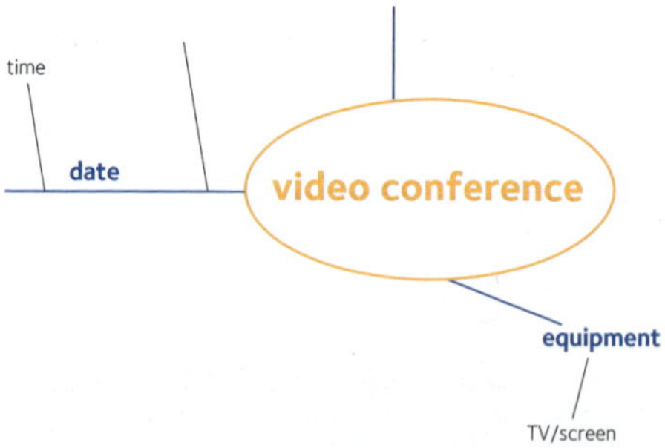

TIP

How to make a mind map

First, put your main idea in a circle in the middle of your mind map. Use a strong colour like red. Your main idea can be a word, a picture or both. Next, draw thick lines (branches) coming out from the circle, and label them with important ideas. Use a different colour for the branches. For example, if the word in the circle is video conference, the thick lines radiating out could be **blue** and labelled ***date, equipment***, etc. Next add thinner lines to each thick branch, e.g. to the line labelled ***equipment*** you could add the words *TV* and *screen*. Do this until you have filled your mind map with ideas.

2 Preparing for a conference

Sarah Bonrath is the Export Sales Director of Brewery-2-Brewery GmbH in Gelsenkirchen. Her company produces and exports brewing equipment all over the world. She organizes a video conference with colleagues from other companies in the UK, India and Singapore.
Before the video conference, Sarah writes an email to all the participants.

Read her email and do the tasks on page 50.

Kopie: Waldemar Neumann

Betreff: **Draft agenda for video conference at 9 a.m. CET on 26 June 20..**

Von: sarah.bonrath@b2b.info   Signatur: Ohne

Dear all

I hope you are all well.

You will no doubt remember that our last conference was postponed because some of the participants were unable to attend. After consulting Mr Neumann, and phoning some of you, I have scheduled our video conference for 9 a.m. CET on 26 June.
The draft agenda currently includes the following topics:

1 Presentation: Indian sales figures (Rajiv Mittal, Mumbai, India)
2 Current order situation
3 Installing and operating equipment
4 Deliveries
5 Any other business (AOB)

Please let me have any suggestions as regards changes or additions, so that I can circulate the final agenda in advance. As always, the minutes of the meeting will be emailed to you one day after the conference.

Larissa Afanasiev will unfortunately not be able to take part in the meeting as she has to attend an important conference in Moscow that day.

Best regards

Sarah

Sarah Bonrath
Export Sales Director
Brewery-2-Brewery GmbH, Gelsenkirchen, HRB 7099, Amtsgericht Gelsenkirchen
Geschäftsführer: Waldemar Neumann

A **Explain in your own words why Sarah Bonrath has written her email.**

B **Match the definitions (1–8) with the highlighted words in Sarah's email.**

1. extra points discussed at the end of a meeting
2. the first version of a document
3. a list of points to be discussed at a meeting
4. a record of all the things said or decided at a meeting
5. to go to (a meeting)
6. changed to a later date
7. arranged
8. people who take part in / attend (a meeting)

3 Finalizing the agenda

Within the next few days, each of the participants replies to Sarah's email with their suggested changes to the agenda.

Read the emails (a-c) and Sarah's email in exercise 2. Then list the points for the final agenda for the conference.

a

Subject: **Re: Draft agenda for video conference**
From: Fan Wen Fang **Signature:** None

Dear Ms Bonrath

Thank you for your draft agenda.

Please add the very important issue of customer complaints, above all as regards punctual delivery, to the agenda. Some customers have also asked about second-hand equipment, and I think this could bring in a lot of business, so please include this as well.

Best regards
Fan Wen Fang
Singapore Trading Pte Ltd

b

From: Donald Masters **Signature:** None

Dear Sarah

The agenda's fine apart from one thing. We need to discuss after-sales service because some of the microbreweries over here need repairs.

Best
Donald Masters
UK Wholesale Trading

c

From: Rajiv Mittal **Signature:** None

Dear Ms Bonrath

I am in agreement with the agenda you suggest, but would kindly ask you to include the topic of travel expenses when visiting customers under Any Other Business.

Yours sincerely
Rajiv Mittal
India Trading Services Pvt Ltd

4 Writing a reply

PAGE 134 KMK

Schreiben Sie eine zweite E-Mail von Sarah Bonrath an die Vertreter. Die folgenden Punkte sollten darin enthalten sein:

- passende Anrede (siehe die *Tip Box* unten)
- Dank für Vorschläge
- Entschuldigung für Herrn Neumanns Fehlen bei der Sitzung, der an diesem Tag an einer wichtigen Tagung in London teilnehmen muss
- voraussichtliche Dauer der Sitzung: 2 Stunden
- Liste der Tagesordnungspunkte
- Bitte um rechtzeitige Benachrichtigung bei Verhinderung
- aufgrund von Zeitmangel: nicht behandelte Themen werden auf die nächste Sitzung verschoben
- höfliche Schlussformel

TIP

How to write an email

- Make sure the subject box shows what the email is about.
- Use first names if you know the recipient well, and sign off with "Best wishes" or "Best regards". Otherwise, use "Dear Mr/Ms" (+ name) and sign off with "Yours sincerely".
- Start your email with a capital letter.
- Begin with a polite reference to a previous phone call, meeting, letter or email. If this is your first contact, introduce yourself.
- Split your email into paragraphs separated by a free line.
- Refer to any attachments to the email.
- Finish with a polite phrase.

To: "Rob Jones" <rob.jones@linkall.com>
Copy: "Bill Hampton, President" <bill.hampton@cherry-sol.com>
Subject: **"Get the world online" conference in Düsseldorf, Germany**
From: Nina Graham Attachments: brochure.pdf

Dear Rob

Many thanks for speaking at the World Aids Day meeting in South Africa last month. I also hope you had a good trip back home to Ireland and am delighted that you will be coming to Düsseldorf to be a guest speaker at Cherry Solutions Incorporated's annual convention in May.

The theme this year is "Get the world online", and I know how passionately you support internet access for poor countries and the "One laptop per child" charity. Our brochure on this year's programme is attached for your information.

Please let us know when you would be available and what your fee would be. All travel and hotel expenses will, of course, be paid for by Cherry Solutions Incorporated.

I very much look forward to welcoming you in Düsseldorf in May!

Best wishes

Nina
Chief Executive Officer
Cherry Solutions Inc.

- Include your position and the name of your company under your name.

LANGUAGE

Expressions for emailing

Starting an email
How are things?
I hope you're well / you had a good trip to …
I am writing to ask for information on …
/ book a room for … / confirm that …

Answering or forwarding an email
I was delighted to receive your email …
Many thanks for your email about … /
inviting me to …
I've just got your email / an email from … /
a phone call from …

Getting to the point
I'd / We'd / They'd like to know if/what …
I'm pleased/delighted to accept your
invitation/offer.
My plane/train arrives at …

Making requests
Please let me have some information on …
Could you tell me if/what …?
Could someone pick me/us up at the
airport?
Would you send us …?

Giving information
Please refer to the attachment for the
timetable for the visit.
Click on the link for more details / directions
to the hotel / conference centre / firm.

Closing sentence
Many thanks for your assistance/help.
Looking forward to …
I/We look forward to meeting you / your
friends.
Please let me know what your plans are.

WEBCODE **INDMU0501**

5 The video conference

13

Sarah Bonrath has a video conference with Donald Masters (UK), Rajiv Mittal (India) and Wen Fang (Singapore).

Listen to the dialogue and do the tasks on page 53.

Sarah Good morning, everybody and welcome to today's video conference. I'm Sarah Bonrath, Export Sales Director at B2B here in Germany. Since we don't all know each other, the first point, before we get to today's agenda, is introductions. Would you like to go first, Wen Fang?

Wen Fang Sure. I'm Wen Fang from Singapore Trading. I came on board six months ago, so I'm the new girl.

Sarah Thanks for that, Wen Fang. Donald?

Donald Hi. I'm Donald Masters from UK Wholesale Trading in London. I've been acting as an agent for B2B for about three years.

Sarah Thanks, Donald. Rajiv?

Rajiv Good morning. My name is Rajiv Mittal. My company is called India Trading Services Private Limited and I have had the pleasure of acting on behalf of B2B for ten years now.

Sarah Many thanks, Rajiv. Our next topic is Rajiv's presentation, so would you go ahead please, Rajiv?

Rajiv Certainly, Sarah. Thanks. My presentation is called "The upward trend of Indian sales figures" …
… To conclude, I would say that microbreweries have been extremely well received here in India.

Sarah Many thanks, Rajiv. Would anyone like to comment or ask any questions?

Donald I'd just like to say that Rajiv's done a great job!
Sarah Yes, I agree. Well done, Rajiv! OK. Let's move on to the next topic, which is our current order situation. We already know about India, so can Donald and Wen Fang now give us a brief update? Donald?
Donald As you can see from this graph, my sales are up 10% on last year.

UK sales figures
Hectolitres of beer sold

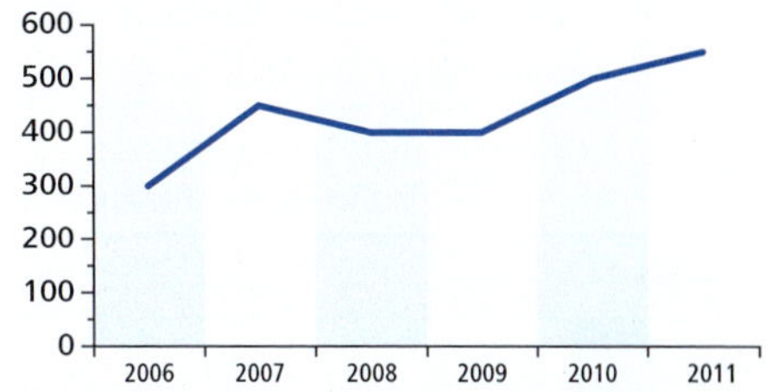

Sarah Wen Fang?
Wen Fang It's too early to tell, but they're rising.
Sarah Good. Let's move on to the next point on our agenda, shall we, which is second-hand equipment. I'm pleased to say that we have some here in Germany. We'll be posting a list on our website next month.
Wen Fang Thank you, Sarah. My customers will be very pleased.
Sarah Good. The next point is deliveries. How are things going here? Are there any issues?
Wen Fang Could I just say that my customers expect deliveries to be punctual and not two or three days late?
Sarah Is that what you meant by complaints in your email, Wen Fang?
Wen Fang Yes, that's right.
Donald Can I come in on that, Sarah?
Sarah Go ahead, Donald.
Donald I thoroughly agree with Wen Fang. We can't have late delivery. It's bad for business.
Sarah OK. I'll pass that on to our logistics department. Any other complaints? No? All right, so delivery has been covered ... and complaints have been covered, too, which is point number 6 on the agenda. We've decided to postpone point number 7, which was going to be installing and operating equipment, so our next point today is after-sales service.
Rajiv Wouldn't it be better to spend just a few moments on installing and operating equipment, Sarah?
Sarah I see your point, Rajiv, but we can't really do much without the report from our service department. As soon as it's been written, I'll put it on the agenda. Can we move on to after-sales service? Is that all right? Good, would you go ahead please, Donald?
Donald Yes certainly, Sarah ...
Sarah ... Right. Let's wrap up the meeting with AOB shall we? I just have one final point here – travel expenses when visiting customers. I've checked with the finance department and they'll get back to you, Rajiv. Is that all right?
Rajiv That's fine, Sarah.
Sarah Well, that would seem to be it. You'll be getting the minutes by email tomorrow. Many thanks for joining us today and goodbye to everybody.

A Put the points on the agenda (1–9) in the correct order. Which point cannot be discussed?

1 after-sales service
2 AOB
3 complaints
4 current order situation
5 deliveries
6 installing and operating equipment
7 introductions
8 Rajiv's presentation ("The upward trend of Indian sales figures")
9 second-hand equipment

B Listen again and answer the following questions about the dialogue.

1. Which agent has been working for B2B the longest?
2. What is the sales situation in the UK?
3. Who wants to buy second-hand equipment?
4. Why does Sarah decide to postpone talking about installing and operating equipment?

C Find expressions in the dialogue to match the following headings.

starting the meeting • introducing yourself • asking someone to speak • asking for reactions • asking to speak/interrupting • agreeing • disagreeing • finishing the meeting

LANGUAGE

Describing trends

Upward movement		Horizontal movement		Downward movement	
to rise/grow to go up to increase	from … to … by …%	to keep stable to remain constant to even out	at …	to fall/drop to go down to decrease	from … to … by …%

Adverbs to indicate a degree of change

small change	medium change	large change
negligibly, slightly	significantly, considerably	sharply, dramatically

Indian sales figures over past 12 months
Hectolitres of beer sold (608)

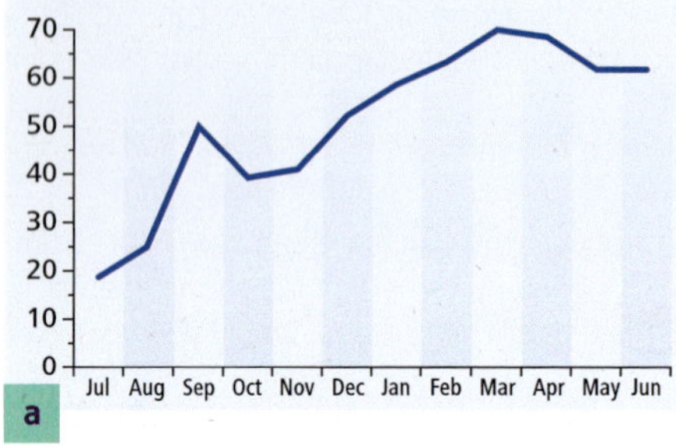

Indian sales figures previous year
Hectolitres of beer sold (338)

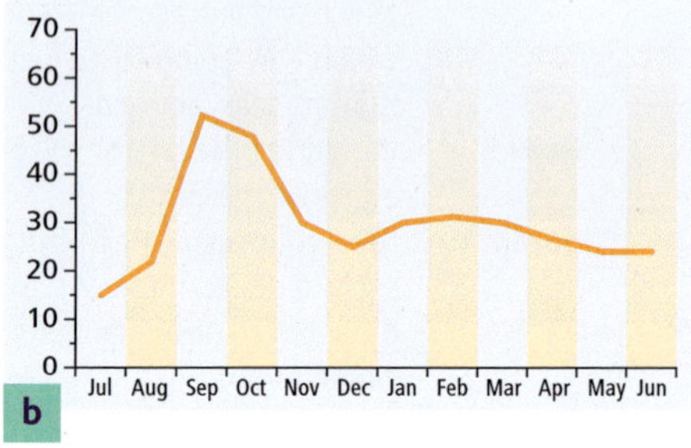

6 Describing sales figures

Look at line graph a and complete the text with the words from the box. Then describe line graph b in your own words.

at • between • decrease slightly • drop negligibly • from • grow considerably • increase slightly • remain constant • rise sharply • to

As you can see from this chart, in July last year, the sales figures stood …[1] 18 hectolitres. Between July and August, they …[2] and then …[3] by September. After that, between September and October, they …[4] from 50 …[5] 39 hectolitres. …[6] October and March, however, the sales figures …[7]. Then they …[8] from March to April, and again …[9] April to May. Between May and June, however, they …[10] at 62 hectolitres.

GRAMMAR

Question formation

1 **Has** he **gone** for lunch yet?
2 **Are** you **married**?
3 **Can** I **give** you any more information?
4 Who **installs** the equipment?
5 You knew. – **Did** you **know**?
6 Why **was** the meeting not **organized** earlier?

- Fragen werden im Englischen grundsätzlich mit einem Hilfsverb gebildet.
- Fragen mit den Hilfsverben *have/has/had*, *will* und *would* (1), mit einer Form von *be* (2), mit Modalverben (3) (Ausnahmen: Modalverben mit *to*, z. B. *want to*) und Fragen mit einem Fragewort, das Subjekt oder Teil des Subjekts ist (4) werden **ohne** das Hilfsverb *do* gebildet.
- Sollte kein Hilfsverb vorhanden sein, benutzt man eine form von *do* (*do/does/did)* (5).
- Fragen mit Fragewörtern beginnen mit *when, where, how, why, who, which* usw. (4, 6).

7 Practice

Write questions to match the following answers.

Example: Mr Winter works in the exports department. *Where does Mr Winter work?*

1 Mrs Jones is waiting at reception.
2 The director has brought the report.
3 No, we don't. We only have five sales representatives.
4 The meeting will be at 3 p.m.
5 The press officer met the managing director in the lift.
6 He phoned his secretary because his train was late.
7 No. Our brochures are only in English.
8 The managing director owns three houses.
9 He spent €500 on a business trip last weekend.
10 She flies to New York three times a year.

8 Making small talk with a visitor

14

Marco Kowalski is a trainee industrial business management assistant at Brewery-2-Brewery. Today his company has sent him to Düsseldorf Airport to collect Jane Seymour, the training officer from the Watermill Brewery in Cumbria, UK.

A **Read the tip box an page 56. Then listen and write down the things Marco *shouldn't* have said or asked.**

B **Listen again and make a list of the topics and questions mentioned which are suitable for small talk.**

C **Use the table in the tip box on page 56 to structure a smalltalk conversation with a partner. Choose two or three smalltalk topics from the box below.**

cars • celebrities • computers • culture • entertainment • fashion • food and drink • hobbies • music • sport • the weather • TV programmes

TIP

Making small talk

Native speakers of English always begin a meeting with a few minutes of small talk. It is considered impolite to leave it out. For this reason, it is important to understand how small talk works. Small talk is not about information; it is about creating a good atmosphere, so it is important to give more than just a short answer to a small-talk question, and, above all, to show interest in the other person by asking questions too. Always make sure you ask your partner the same question he or she has just asked you.
Try to avoid topics such as politics, religion, health and salaries, as they are usually not suitable topics for small talk.

Holidays

Person A

1 Question
- Did you have a nice holiday last year?

4 Answer
- Yes, thanks. We went to Italy.

6 Comment
- Yes, I love the heat.

Person B

2 Answer
- Yes, we did. We went to Spain.

3 Same question to Person A
- Did *you* have a nice holiday last year?

5 Comment
- I see we both like hot countries.

9 Role-play: discussing plans for a visit KMK

Next year four trainees from the UK will be coming to Germany to shadow some employees at your company. Jane/Jack Seymour, their training officer, comes to discuss the details of the visit.

Use the agenda and the partner files at the back of the book to act out a meeting about the details.

English trainees' visit 20..
Meeting with Jane/Jack Seymour
Thursday, 27 September 20.., 9.30 a.m.

Agenda

1 Introductions
2 Date of visit
3 Accommodation for trainees
4 Return visit
5 AOB

Student A: turn to partner file 6 on page 114.
Student B: turn to partner file 12 on page 117.
Student C: turn to partner file 5 on page 114.

Student D

You are a trainee at your company (own name).
- Take the minutes of the meeting (see page 57)
- Inform the others of how you plan to send the minutes and when they will receive them

10 Taking the minutes

15

The English trainees from the Watermill Brewery in Cumbria, UK have just spent a week at Brewery-2-Brewery GmbH in Gelsenkirchen. Today is the last day of their stay, and they are at a meeting with German trainees to review their experiences and plan their next visit.

Matthias Beling writes the minutes of the meeting with the English trainees but makes five mistakes. Listen to the recording. Then find and correct his mistakes in your exercise book.

Brewery-2-Brewery, Gelsenkirchen, Germany
Meeting with English trainees from the Watermill Brewery in Cumbria, UK – Minutes

21 September 20..

Attendees:
Andrea Kegelmann, Training Officer at Brewery-2-Brewery,
Emma Jones (English trainee), Tony Harding (English trainee),
Sevda Yildiz (German trainee), Matthias Beling (German trainee)

Item 1
Review of the week
Tony Harding said the English trainees had very much enjoyed the week, especially the visit to the football match.

Emma Jones agreed and added that she now understands much better how people work in Germany and is glad she speaks German.

Matthias Beling and Sevda Yildiz said their English had improved because they spoke English to the English trainees all week.

Tony Harding said he was unable to start work at 6 a.m.

Item 2
Visit to the UK next year
Emma Jones asked if the German trainees would like to take part in a marathon in Cumbria next year to collect money for children with learning disabilities. She will be taking part in the marathon with Tony Harding. Matthias Beling and Sevda Yildiz both wish to run in the marathon.

Emma Jones said Jane Seymour would like to know whether the German trainees would prefer homestay or guest house accommodation. They decided that the German trainees would stay at a guest house with Wi-Fi.

Sevda Yildiz suggested that a similar charitable event for the local community should be organized in Germany.
This topic will be included on the agenda at next month's board meeting.

Everyone agreed the visit had been a great success.

AOB
None

11 Interaktion

Work with a partner and act out the role-play.

Situation

Mr/Mrs Kumar, a sales representative from New Delhi in India, has come to Germany to meet members of the export sales department of a brewery in Essen, which exports beer all over the world. The main reason for his/her trip is to give the employees a presentation on the Indian sales figures (see graphs below) for the last two years. When he/she arrives at the company, one of the members of the export sales department greets him/her and takes him to their office for a chat before the meeting.

Eigener Name

You work in the export sales department of the brewery in Essen. You meet Mr/Mrs Kumar at reception when he/she arrives and take him/her to your office for a chat. Use the following points to structure your conversation:

- Small talk
- Topic of presentation?
- Any time for sightseeing?
- Recommend local sights
- Offer to get information (internet)
- Describe German food
- Suggest some restaurants
- Invent extra details
- End conversation politely

Mr/Mrs Kumar

You are Mr/Mrs Kumar from India. One of the members of the export sales department picks you up at reception and takes you to their office for a chat. Use the following points to structure your conversation.

- Small talk
- Topic of presentation: description of sales figures (graphs)
- Free Saturday (flight on Sunday)
- Local sights?
- Opening hours of … (museum, gallery)?
- Directions to … (hotel, company, etc.)?
- Ticket for … (event)?
- Typical German food?
- Restaurants locally?
- Invent extra details
- End conversation politely

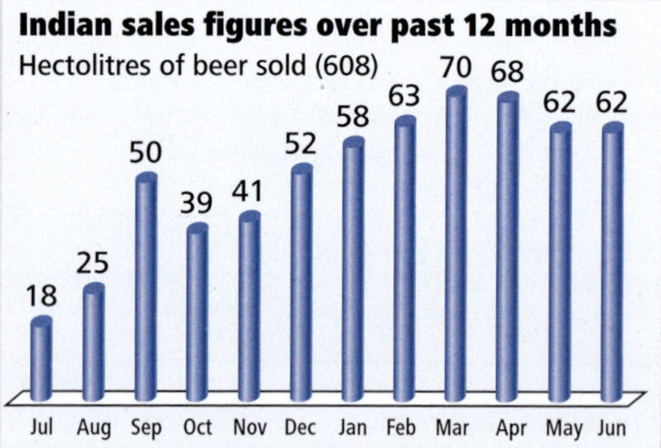

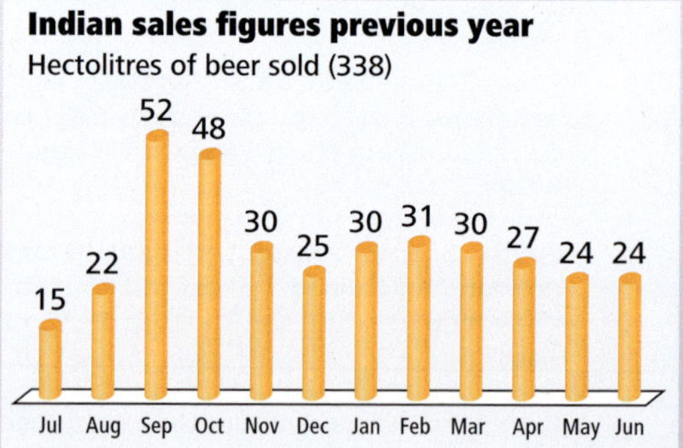

Facebook · Meistbesuchte... · Erste Schritte · Aktuelle Nachr... · Lesezeichen

I hate meetings and they stink

Extract from Dannielle Blumenthal's blog

I have had this happen to me SO many times.

I'm sitting in a meeting, and something is going on. Not something like an actual thing, but a tense, negative, or unproductive social dynamic between two people or within the group. I must be like the Terminator of sociology, because I can actually sense these situations, like in the movie where the heat-seeking goggles glowed red when there were humans around.

Bad vibes like this are why I usually hate meetings. Particularly because people are generally averse to working out conflict openly, so I have to watch it and not talk while it's actually going on. Just sit there and have to wait it out till it's over and I can be real again.

Here are some examples:

1. **asserting, without explanation, that an idea will definitely not work**
2. **completely ignoring a suggestion and going on to the next person**
3. **making the "Are you crazy?" face**
4. **rolling eyeballs behind someone's back**
5. **responding to idea with blank stare / silence**
6. **ganging up on someone (meeting their suggestion with two "No's")**
7. **laughing at someone's ideas**
8. **standing up and leaving the meeting without explanation**
9. **going into "deep chair slouch"**
10. **closing eyes**

True, sometimes I find myself entertained by the goings-on. Sometimes I hear things that are funny, or the group gets along and there are decent jokes. There is always some gossip that's not too bad. Meetings can be educational as well, seriously. But more often than not, as soon as they get into full swing, I feel like I am nine years old again and watching a big family dinner degenerate.

Please don't start writing comments about how YOUR place of work has fantastic meetings and how you feel bad for me, OK? It's not about any particular agency; I've been around for more than a dozen years, both in government and outside it, and they all generally stink. As soon as you call it a 'meeting' and whip out the leather portfolios and play business card roulette, group dynamics start going into motion and the pain begins.

Source: abridged from: http://www.govloop.com/profiles/blogs/i-hate-meetings-and-they-stink

12 Understanding the text and further discussion

A Answer the following questions on text.

1. What does the blogger spend most of her time doing at meetings?
2. Describe briefly what happens at the meetings the blogger describes.
3. What positive things does she mention about meetings?

B In groups, choose two of the following points and discuss them.

1. What rules of behaviour should be followed at meetings?
2. How can you make a meeting less boring?
3. Describe some meetings you have attended and explain why they were good or bad.

UNIT 6

Production processes at Schaeffer AG

- Understanding production processes
- Identifying methods of production
- Writing a press release

1 Warm-up

a

b

A Work with a partner and decide where these descriptions of the various stages of production go in the flowchart below.

a The product is packaged and shipped to distributors or direct to the customer.
b The product's functionality and features are developed based on the market research.
c Any changes that are necessary in the production methods to manufacture the product are made.
d The product is manufactured in the company's production facilities.
e The company carries out market research and decides what to produce based on demand in the market.
f Raw materials needed to manufacture the product are ordered from suppliers.

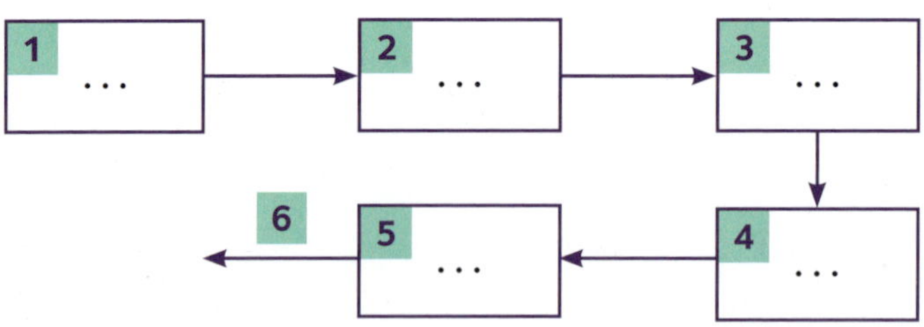

B Which stages of production are shown in the photographs?

C Can you think of any other steps that are not mentioned here? Which ones?

D Does your company do things differently? In what ways? Discuss with a partner.

2 A modern and innovative manufacturing company

Schaeffer AG specializes in the manufacture of front panels and housing units for a wide range of electrical devices. The company is based in Berlin and is in partnership with Front Panel Express LLC, which is based in Seattle, USA.

A Read as Kai Schaeffer, a senior manager for Schaeffer AG, introduces Tony Doyle, a new business administration trainee from Seattle, to his company. Then say what Tony wants to learn about.

Kai So, Tony, you said that you have a few questions about Schaeffer AG.

Tony Yes, right. I learned quite a lot about modern manufacturing ideas at college and obviously a lot of companies use these ideas, so I wanted to ask a few questions about that.

Kai OK, well ... fire away.

Tony I'm interested in lean manufacturing ... you know, cutting down waste in areas like production, waiting time, inventory and scrap. I wanted to ask to what extent you use these ideas here.

Kai Well, as you know, our main customers are electronics companies which want short production runs of front panels either for prototypes they're developing, or for products which will only be produced in small numbers. So, we gear our production exactly to what our customers want. If they want five front panels or if they want 200, that's exactly what we produce.

Tony So, what we produce is linked very closely to customer orders.

Kai That's right. I think that could be described as "lean".

Tony OK, I see.

Kai We never over-produce, so we avoid waste in that way. By the way, this system is also called "batch production".

Tony Ah ... that's interesting.

Kai Another example of lean manufacturing is the fact that we put product design in customers' own hands. As you know, our customers use our Front Panel Designer software to design their own front panels. This means that we don't have to spend time discussing design issues with customers. That would be quite costly for us.

Tony Yes, and I suppose the way that the customers' designs are input straight into the CNC, eh, Computer Numerical Control machines, is also pretty innovative.

Kai Right, yes. I mean, obviously there is a monitoring stage before the CNC machines start on a job, during which we check the technical feasibility of the customer's design, but our automated order system allows customers to feed their designs straight into our manufacturing plant.

Tony OK, right.

Kai And we use computer automation in other ways too to ensure that production runs as efficiently as possible. For instance, the Enterprise Resource Planning or ERP software we use automates a lot of activities, such as ordering raw materials from our suppliers. So, Schaeffer AG is a modern, innovative company. We use very streamlined, modern business processes here.

Tony Yes. It is kind of impressive ...

B According to Kai, how are computers used to make production more efficient?

C Read again and decide whether the statements (1–6) are true, false or not mentioned. Correct the false statements.

1. Tony wants to go to college to learn about modern manufacturing ideas.
2. Schaeffer AG's customers are mostly electronics companies.
3. Schaeffer AG's customers often want front panels for electronic devices that will be made in small numbers.
4. Customers who don't want to use Front Panel Designer can get personal help to design their front panels.
5. Customers' designs are put straight into the CNC machines without being checked.
6. The company doesn't use any other software in its production.

3 Working with words

The words in the box are from the dialogue. Use them to complete the sentences.

automate • feasibility • gear • monitoring • plant • production run • raw materials • scrap

1. The company decided to … production to making those products that could be produced most cheaply and easily.
2. Last year, Pullman Ltd invested in a new … to make production faster and more efficient.
3. We aim to … as much of our production as possible, so we want to invest in robot production technology very soon.
4. The product costs much more to manufacture than we originally thought; we didn't look carefully enough at the … of making it before we started production.
5. They use high-cost … such as titanium in their products. That's why they're so expensive.
6. We carry out … at various stages of production to ensure that quality standards are being met.
7. If we invest in this new plant, we will be able to cut our costs on each … .
8. … materials not used during production are stored in this area until they are collected and taken away.

4 A summary

In your own words, summarize what you have learned about Schaeffer AG's production processes using the vocabulary from exercise 3.

5 Methods of production

A Match the approaches to production (1–10) to their descriptions (a–j).

1	global sourcing	**a**	buying raw materials from around the world
2	mass production	**b**	also called "unit production"; a single unit is made to the individual specifications of the customer
3	batch production	**c**	purchasing raw materials from the country a company is based in
4	just in time (JIT)	**d**	avoiding having large amounts of raw materials inventory by arranging for suppliers to deliver materials shortly before they are needed on the production line
5	job production	**e**	arranging for a business activity to be carried out by another company
6	outsourcing	**f**	purchasing one type of raw material from several suppliers
7	single sourcing	**g**	manufacturing products in large numbers using automation to keep costs down
8	make or buy	**h**	buying one type of raw material from one supplier
9	multiple sourcing	**i**	assessing whether it is better to produce an item in-house or purchase it from a supplier
10	domestic sourcing	**j**	manufacturing small numbers of a product according to a customer's specifications

B Look at the three cartoons below. Which approaches to production do they show?

a

b

c

C Now decide which of the methods in exercise A best describes the approach to production taken by Schaeffer AG.

6 Production processes at Schaeffer AG

Kai Schaeffer and Tony Doyle make their way to the production unit at Schaeffer AG.

A Before listening to the dialogue, match the words on the left (1–8) to their German definitions (a–h) on the right.

1	inventory	**a**	aufgefüllt
2	shop floor	**b**	verpackt in
3	replenished	**c**	Fertigungs- bzw. Produktionsbereich
4	by hand	**d**	Luftpolsterfolie
5	surplus paint	**e**	Durchlaufzeit, Bearbeitungszeitraum
6	packaged in	**f**	überschüssige Farbe
7	bubble wrap	**g**	von Hand, manuell
8	turn-around time	**h**	Bestandliste

16

B **Listen to the dialogue and put the photographs in the order in which they are mentioned.**

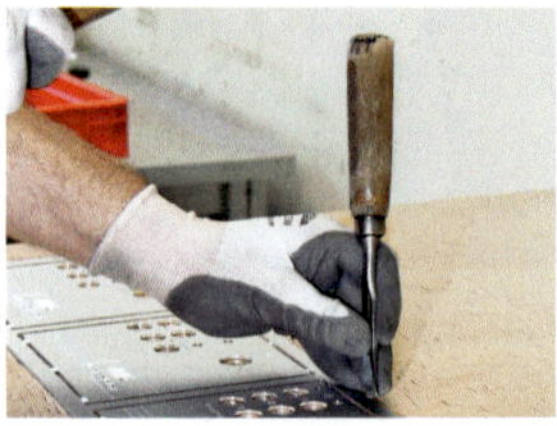

a mounting area

b packaging and shipping

c warehouse

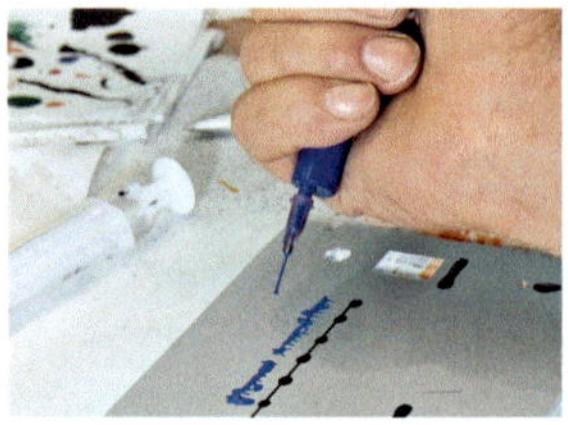

d finishing shop

e CNC milling machines

C **Listen again and choose the correct sentence ending to make true statements about production at Schaeffer AG.**

1 Schaeffer AG doesn't use just in time (JIT) as …
a … the system is too expensive for the company.
b … it could result in the company not being able to get enough raw materials at the right price at certain times.
c … they have a big enough warehouse to store six months' worth of raw materials.

2 The Enterprise Resource Planning (ERP) software …
a … keeps track of the amount of raw materials being used and orders fresh supplies.
b … ensures that the right raw materials go to the production area for a particular job.
c … inputs customer orders into the CNC milling machines.

3 Schaeffer AG has not automated the finishing stage because …
a … it would be too expensive to do so.
b … the required quality could not be guaranteed by automation.
c … the company hasn't thought about it yet.

4 Schaeffer AG employees carry out …
a … one quality-control check of each front panel.
b … two quality-control checks of each front panel.
c … three quality-control checks of each front panel.

7 Over to you

PAGE 131 WEBOCDE INDMU0601

Collect materials on the production process in your company and prepare a short presentation.

8 Manufacturing acronyms

Use the internet to find out what these common manufacturing acronyms stand for and how the systems and ideas they describe work. Say which of the systems are used in your company.

1 TQC **2** CAM **3** BTO

9 Schaeffer AG looks forward to another good year

A **Read the press release issued by Schaeffer AG to publicize its successes. Then say what kind of publication you think the text is aimed at.**

Press release

(For publication after 31 December 20..)

Schaeffer AG looks forward to another good year

The manufacturer of customized front panels and housing units for the electronics industry, whose operations are based in Berlin, is looking forward to building on its successes of the past 12 months in the New Year.

Growing customer numbers

"We've had a very solid year," said board member and son of the company's founder, Kai Schaeffer. "We've increased our customer base to over 10,000 customers. The result has been a significant increase in our production and we're anticipating building on this success in the New Year."

... (a)

Schaeffer AG, which began life as a manufacturer of amusement machines in 1961, later moved on to specialize in producing scientific measuring instruments. The company adopted its current business model in 1998 when it realized the market potential for front panels manufactured to customers' individual specifications. In the same year, the first version of Front Panel Designer, the CAD software which allows Schaeffer's customers' designs to be transferred directly to the company's CNC machines, was launched.

... (b)

Since then, the Front Panel Designer has been under constant development. Kai Schaeffer explains, "Our intention is to make the software as comfortable for customers to use as possible. This year we have introduced new features which fulfil this by improving the user interface and enabling customers to specify the use of aluminium sheeting with a thickness of more than 4 mm in their designs."

The latter feature will accommodate the introduction of a new range of raw materials out of which customers can choose to have their front panels constructed, including natural and raw aluminium.

The core business of the company is the production of customized front panels on the ten CNC milling machines dedicated to the purpose. They guarantee that production volume meets customer demands for rapid production and delivery.

... (c)

Schaeffer AG now plans to expand its product portfolio to include a new product line of digitally printed aluminium signs. According to Kai Schaeffer, "We have identified the market opportunity in this area and have invested in plant which will allow us to produce high-quality, digitally printed signs for our customers."

B Answer the following questions on the text in your own words.

1. Who are Schaeffer AG's main customers?
2. What has the increased customer base meant for the company?
3. When did the company start concentrating on its current products? Why?
4. What has the company introduced in the last year?
5. What plans does Schaeffer AG now have for its product range?

C Work with a partner and write sub-headings for sections a–c of the text.

10 Key words

A Match the expressions (1–10) with the highlighted expressions in the text.

1. made
2. activities
3. machinery
4. range of products
5. made-to-order
6. main focus
7. expanded
8. to stipulate
9. type of product
10. quantity

B Now use six of the highlighted expressions to complete the sentences below.

1. In the past, Schaeffer's … included scientific measuring instruments as well as amusement machines.
2. The main … used in the manufacture of front panels at Schaeffer AG are the ten CNC milling machines.
3. The … of Schaeffer AG's partner company in the USA are based in Seattle.
4. The company specializes in providing customers with … front panels for electronic devices.
5. Before it could introduce a new …, Schaeffer AG had to invest in new printing technology.
6. Schaeffer have recently increased the range of materials from which their products can be … .

11 Mediation

KMK

Sie arbeiten bei der Schaeffer AG als Auszubildender. Ihre Abteilung plant für das bevorstehende Jubiläum einen Messeprospekt zu veröffentlichen.

Verwenden Sie den vorliegenden Text als Informationsquelle und stellen Sie in Stichworten auf Deutsch wichtige geschichtliche Meilensteine aus der Vergangenheit sowie den Ausblick auf zukünftige Projekte zusammen.

12 Writing a press release about your company

PAGE 135

Write a press release about your company. Include details of what the company manufactures, where it is based, its history and what its plans are for the future.

GRAMMAR

The passive – Grammar for describing processes

1 This is where all the materials that we need for our production **are stored**.
2 A lot of companies **have been shut down** in the last few years.
3 The company **was founded** by Kai Schaeffer's father in 1961.
4 Starting next March, more products **will be developed** by our new researchers.
5 This ensures that our stock of raw materials **is** constantly **being replenished**.
6 How long does it take for a front panel **to be produced**?
7 You'll also hear this system of production **referred to** as "batch production".

- Durch den Gebrauch des Passivs wird das Prädikat hervorgehoben. Das Passiv wird daher oft verwendet, wenn die beschriebene Handlung wichtiger ist als der Handelnde. Der Gebrauch des Passivs gibt die Möglichkeit, den Handelnden wegzulassen, wenn die Angabe nicht wirklich wichtig ist (1, 2, 4).
- Das Passiv wird mit der entsprechenden Form von *be* + Partizip Perfekt (3. Form) des Vollverbs gebildet. Wie im Aktiv können alle Zeiten gebildet werden. Die Kriterien für deren Gebrauch sind dieselben wie im Aktiv (1–4).
- Die Verlaufsform (*be* + *ing*) kann im Passiv sinnvoll nur im *present* oder im *past* gebildet werden (5).
- Infinitivkonstruktionen mit dem Passiv sind ebenfalls möglich (6).
- In Passivkonstuktionen mit Verben der Wahrnehmnung wie *see*, *hear* usw. wird *be* manchmal unterdrückt (7).
- „Von“ und „durch“ werden undifferenziert durch *by* ausgedrückt (3).

13 Practice

KMK

Ihr Chef beauftragt Sie, einen Kurzbericht auf Englisch vorzubereiten. Verwenden Sie Ihre Notizen und schreiben Sie eine Zusammenfassung der Entwicklungen, die in der Produktionsabteilung stattfinden.

Betreff: Aktuelle Entwicklungen in der Produktionsabteilung

Für: Versammlung der Geschäftsführer von Forrester Ltd, 14. März 20..

- *Die Produktionstechniken wurden in den letzten drei Quartalen ständig weiterentwickelt.*
- *Teilweise war das auf die Einführung einer neuen Produktpalette im letzten Quartal zurückzuführen.*
- *Neue Produktionsanlagen, die die Verpackungskosten senken, wurden gesucht.*
- *Diese werden nächstes Quartal gekauft und werden bis Ende des Jahres installiert sein.*
- *Als Resultat wurden die Lagerkosten um 12% gesenkt.*

Recent developments in the production department for meeting of the board of directors, 14 March 20..

– *Production techniques have been under constant development at Forrester Ltd in the last three quarters. …*

14 Rezeption: Leseverstehen

Quality control versus quality assurance

These days, all kinds of manufacturing companies operate in a global marketplace. This means that they have to compete directly with companies from all over the world to win and satisfy customers. One way of doing this is to focus on ensuring that their products are of the best possible quality. That is the reason why quality control (QC) and quality assurance (QA) have become such popular buzzwords in manufacturing. However, there can be confusion about how these approaches differ even in companies with a lot of experience of focusing on quality. Here's a quick explanation.

Quality assurance

The best way of thinking about QA is that it takes place before a product has been manufactured. Basically, it refers to all of the activities that go into ensuring that a product at the required standard of quality can be made in the first place. So QA includes, for instance, ensuring that supplies of raw materials at the right quality are secured and that plant on a production line is set up so that it can produce at the required quality level. QA would also include the setting up of the monitoring processes which take place under QC.

Quality control

If QA is about making sure that systems are in place to manufacture a product of a certain quality before the production line starts operating, QC is about confirming that the products which roll off the production line are up to standard. In the main, this is carried out by inspection and testing of products to make sure that the required quality has been met. Depending on the product – and the production method in use – approaches will differ. A company involved in the mass production of, say, washing machines will test a sample of products (perhaps every twenty-fifth washing machine). A manufacturer which uses job or small batch production on the other hand may inspect each individual product.

Once the difference between QA and QC is clear to companies, they will also be able to see that the two approaches do not exclude each other; just because you use one approach, doesn't mean that you shouldn't use the other. Indeed, the best way to guarantee quality in production is to have both systems in place.

Stellen Sie fest, welche der Aussagen (1–4) hinsichtlich vorstehenden Textes richtig oder falsch sind und begründen Sie kurz Ihre Entscheidung auf Deutsch. Beantworten Sie anschließend die Verständnisfragen (5–8) in Stichworten auf Deutsch.

1. Firmen müssen nur Wettbewerb aus dem eigenen Land fürchten.
2. QA und QC werden noch nicht sehr häufig verwendet, um Qualität in Firmen zu gewährleisten.
3. Die Unterschiede zwischen den beiden Herangehensweisen werden im Allgemeinen von den Firmen verstanden.
4. QA ist eine Methode, die produzierten Waren zu überprüfen, um sicherzustellen, dass sie die erforderliche Qualität besitzen.
5. Welche Faktoren sollten in einem QA-System integriert sein?
6. Wird QC von QA beeinflusst? Wenn ja – warum? Wenn nein – warum nicht?
7. Wie unterscheidet sich die QC-Herangehensweise kleiner Unternehmen von der großer Produzenten von Massenwaren?
8. Warum sollten Betriebe sowohl QA als auch QC einführen?

Outsourcing – in or out?

Large numbers of companies in Europe outsource "non-core" activities to contractors, often based in other countries. This is seen as a way of cutting costs and allowing managers the chance to concentrate on their core business. Now, however, there is a trend in the other direction as companies bring these activities back in-house. This article looks at why one company finally decided that outsourcing is out – and that insourcing is the only realistic approach.

Craig Andrews is Managing Director at Eastik Engineering Ltd. In 2002, his company made what he saw as a radical decision to outsource the manufacturing of some of its components to another company based 200 miles away from the company's base in London.

Andrews explains: "We identified several components which we thought it would be better to have manufactured elsewhere. The main reason was cost savings. But we also wanted to free up the time which we spent managing the production of the components."

At first, the arrangement with the company Andrews sub-contracted to seemed very promising. It agreed to the quality standards demanded by Eastik but still promised to cut production costs by 25%. However, it didn't take long before problems arose.

"We started to get complaints that our products did not work as well as they had in the past. When we looked into it, we found that our sub-contractor was cutting corners when it came to quality. We were starting to lose customers, so the savings we made by outsourcing was worth nothing," according to Andrews.

At first Andrews invested time in sorting out the quality problems his sub-contractor was having. However, after two years, he decided that he was spending more time monitoring his sub-contractor's activities than he was running his own company.

"We brought the manufacturing of all our components back in-house in 2005. We thought, "OK, the price of making the components is going to rise again, but at least we have control of quality."

"I must admit that the story of the disaster we experienced with outsourcing isn't the worst I've heard. Several companies I know have really had their hands burned by outsourcing parts of their production to India or China where quality assurance issues can be really difficult to solve. But my experience was enough to teach me that, while it's acceptable to outsource the management of our staff canteen, outsourcing what are really core manufacturing activities is really not an option," said Andrews.

15 Talking about outsourcing

A Read the text above and then, in your own words, explain ...

1 why companies generally outsource to other companies.
2 what Eastik Engineering decided to do in 2002 and why.
3 how things went in the beginning and why people started to complain.
4 what decision Andrews made after two years and why.

B Work with a partner and discuss the following questions.

1 Which activities does your company outsource?
2 Has your company experienced problems with outsourcing? Which problems?
3 What benefits to your company are there in outsourcing?

UNIT 7

Andres Industries AG markets a new product

- Talking about marketing strategies
- Understanding consumer questionnaires
- Discussing competitive analysis

1 Warm-up

A Match the photographs (a–d) to the descriptions of the four marketing activities below (1–4).

a

b

c

d

1 carrying out research among potential customers to find out what they need
2 representing the company at a trade fair
3 planning which media to use for advertising
4 analysing how big the potential market for a product is

B What other marketing activities can you name? Make a list.

C Have you ever been involved in any of the marketing activities in exercise A for your company? Which ones?

I've been involved in …

I was once asked to …

2 Andres Industries AG's new product

Andres Industries AG is a small, Berlin-based company which produces specialized computers and other devices for industrial companies, as well as carrying cases for these devices. Recently, the company started producing a prototype of a protective case called the Case for iPad.

A Read as Simon Prince, a marketing student from the UK who is doing work experience at the company, talks to company CEO Björn Andres about the marketing of the case. Then explain what area of work Simon will be involved in during his work experience.

Björn So, Simon, it's great that you've come to us at this point as we're going to be working on our new Case for iPad.

Simon I'm glad to hear I'm going to be working on that! With all the marketing hype for the iPad, the case is certain to be a success.

Björn Yes, the iPad has sold very well. That definitely means a big marketing opportunity for us. And we've started getting enquiries about the case from people who saw the prototype at CeBit. So it's all systems go now! But we're still unsure of exactly how we're going to market our case and what price it should retail at. We'll have to sort out these issues well before our launch campaign starts.

Simon OK. So tell me. What would you like me to do?

Björn Well, I'm going to be leading our marketing campaign, so you'll be reporting to me.

Simon Great.

Björn I'm going to need you to help me with, basically, everything.

Simon OK.

Björn The first thing I need you to do is some competitive analysis, which will be part of our market research. Unfortunately, we're not the only players in this market, and several other companies, some of them quite big brand names, are developing cases for the iPad right now. I need you to monitor them and find out exactly what it is they're offering and at what price point they plan to sell it.

Simon OK. And I suppose I should be doing this on an ongoing basis in the next few months.

Björn Exactly. I'll need you to make a database of competitive products which you update every two weeks or so.

Simon OK, no problem. I'll be able to get all that information on the internet.

Björn Exactly. Now, your next important task will be to carry out some market analysis of who's bought the iPad and what they do with it. This information could have a big impact on how we develop our case and which features we build into it in the future. Now, we don't have the resources to carry out extensive market research into consumer uptake of the iPad. However, there are several online forums started by iPad users. I'd like you to monitor these for any patterns emerging in the way that people use the device. That way, I think we'll be able to identify specific target groups which we can aim our marketing at.

Simon No problem. We might not have a lot of money to carry out much market research, but can I suggest that we include a consumer questionnaire with the cases so that our customers have the chance to feed back to us what they want to do with their iPads and why they've bought our case?

Björn That's a great idea. Could you get straight onto that?

Simon Absolutely. I'll start it immediately and you can have a look at it, say, first thing tomorrow morning.

Björn Fine. There is one other thing I would like you to be involved in, and that's planning our advertising campaign for the case. The market data that you collect will have a direct impact on the kind of advertising we do, so it would be great if you could help out there too.
Simon I'd love to. But first, I have to start gathering that data, so …
Björn So, you'll need another coffee and the password to your PC.
Simon Exactly.

B **Complete the statements about the dialogue in your own words.**

1 It's a good time for Simon to be doing his work experience at Andres Industries because …
2 Simon will carry out competitive analysis by …
3 To carry out market analysis he will …
4 Simon suggests finding out about people who buy the case by …
5 Björn wants Simon to help with advertising since …

C **Read the dialogue again and the "To do" list below, which Simon writes after the meeting. He makes five mistakes. Find and correct them in your exercise book.**

First meeting with Björn Andres – To do list

- *Make a database of competitive products by other companies making cases for the iPad, and update every month.*
- *Carry out market analysis of who's bought the iPad and how long they have been using it, e.g. by phoning and asking customers.*
- *Write a consumer questionnaire to include in the case by this afternoon.*
- *Help plan the marketing campaign for the case.*

3 Marketing terminology

A **Find two-word expressions in the dialogue and match them to these definitions.**

1 marketing activities focussed on getting a product onto the market
2 examination of the activities of other companies in the same market
3 names used by companies to identify their products clearly in the marketplace
4 goods produced by other companies in the same market
5 customers' buying patterns
6 specific set of consumers in a marketplace
7 set of questions designed to obtain specific information from customers
8 planned series of promotional activities designed to encourage consumers to buy a product

B **Find all the collocations which include *marketing* or *market* in the dialogue and write them in word spiders. Then write definitions for the expressions. The tip box on page 73 will help you.**

TIP

Collocations

Spotting collocations (or word partnerships) is a valuable skill which can help you to enrich your word power. If you come across word combinations while reading which you think might be set collocations, you can use the internet to confirm whether this is the case. Simply type the two words into a search machine to find out how many instances of the words being used together you can find.

WEBOCDE **INDMU0701**

4 Results from the consumer questionnaire

On page 74 is the summary report of the results of Simon's consumer questionnaire. Read it and then do the tasks below.

A Based on the evidence provided by the report, decide which of the following questions were asked in the questionnaire.

1 How did you find out about the Case for iPad?
2 How long have you had your iPad?
3 Which type of advertising influences your purchasing decisions most?
4 Why did you decide to buy the Case for iPad and not another similar case?
5 Where do you make most use of your iPad?
6 What is your annual salary?
7 How many hours a day do you use your iPad?
8 Do you use your iPad while taking part in a particular pastime?

B Find the English equivalents of these expressions in the text.

1 Kaufentschluss
2 Antwortquote
3 Anzeichen
4 die Befragten
5 überwältigende 70 %
6 Teil (der Befragten)
7 Großteil
8 Werbemittel

KMK

C Stellen Sie fest, welche der nachfolgenden Aussagen (1–4) hinsichtlich des Textes richtig oder falsch sind und begründen Sie Ihre Antwort. Beantworten Sie anschließend die Verständnisfragen (5–8) in kurzen Stichworten auf Deutsch.

1 Die Anzahl der Teilnehmer, welche den Fragebogen zurückgesandt haben, zeigt wie zufrieden sie mit den neuen iPad-Etuis sind.
2 Der Großteil der Kunden hat die Etuis über das Internet gekauft.
3 54 % aller Kunden ist im Internet auf das Produkt aufmerksam geworden.
4 Die große Mehrheit der Kunden, welche den Fragebogen zurückgesandt haben, benutzt ihr iPad bei der Ausübung von Hobbys und Aktivitäten im Freien.
5 In welchem Bereich soll ein Großteil der Werbemittel für Segler investiert werden?
6 In welchem anderen Bereich sollte die Firma mehr Geld investieren und warum?
7 Warum wurde der Fragebogen versandt?
8 Wie viel soll für Zeitungen, die sich auf spezielle Hobbys konzentrieren, ausgegeben werden?

Interim report on results of consumer questionnaire related to the Case for iPad

10.1 Summary

In order to discover more about the purchasing decisions of our customers, questionnaires were included in the product's packaging. Of the 763 customers who bought the product, 342 completed the questionnaire. This response rate of 44.8% is exceptionally high, and may be an indication of customer enthusiasm.

Statistical breakdown of results:

- Of the respondents, 76% found out about the product on the internet, 19% saw it in a shop, and 5% learned about it in a newspaper or magazine.
- 54% of respondents said that they are most influenced by internet advertising, 32% by print advertising, and 14% by advertising in other media.
- 16% of respondents said that they make most use of their iPad on the way to work, and 14% use it most at home. The iPad is used by a massive 70% of respondents while engaged in an outdoor hobby. Of these, 64% use their iPads for navigation purposes while sailing, 19% for the same purpose while walking, and 17% while rock climbing.
- 24% of respondents have salaries between 30,000–50,000 euros per year, 39% have salaries between 50,000–80,000 euros annually, and 37% earn more than 80,000 euros per annum.

10.2 Conclusions

Given that a 70%-segment of respondents use their iPads while pursuing outdoor hobbies, it would be reasonable to conclude that they are attracted to our product due to the protection it offers their iPad in outdoor conditions. Moreover, since 76% of respondents came across our product on the internet, and 54% say they are most influenced by online advertising, it could be concluded that the bulk of our limited advertising spend should be concentrated on online advertising.

10.3 Recommendations

In order to target the largest segment of our customers (i.e. hobby sailors) most effectively, efforts should be made to identify websites aimed specifically at sailors which offer the best potential ROI for advertising.

Given that a significant segment of respondents read newspapers and magazines, efforts to generate editorial coverage of our product in print media should be increased.

A limited amount of the advertising budget could be targeted at hobby-specific magazines, such as those aimed at sailors and walkers.

LANGUAGE

Saying and writing numbers and figures

German	English	Written as words
763	763	*seven hundred and sixty-three*
1.600	1,600	*one thousand six hundred*
145.000	145,000	*one hundred and forty-five thousand*
1.000.000	1,000,000	*one million*
1.000.000.000	1,000,000,000	*one billion (eine Milliarde)*
44,8	44.8	*forty-four point eight*

In English, a 'point' is used for decimals and a comma is used to separate blocks of three digits.

5 Saying figures

With a partner, take it in turns to read the figures in the box out loud.

0.5 • 39.6 • 679 • 4,833.5 • 78,301 • 190,000 • 307,962 • 8,932,765 • 296,237,134

GRAMMAR

The passive (2) – Making a report sound official

1. The iPad **is used** by 70% of respondents while engaged in an outdoor hobby.
2. 54% of respondents said that they **are influenced** by internet advertising.
3. Questionnaires **were included** in the product's packaging.
4. The questionnaire **will be enclosed** in the Case for iPad packaging.
5. Effort **should be made** to identify websites for hobby sailors.
6. A limited amount of the advertising budget **could be targeted** at press advertising.

- Das **passive** wird oft verwendet, wenn man auf einer unpersönlichen Art und Weise über Fakten, Vorgänge und Zahlen berichtet.
- Das *simple present passive* wird mit *am/is/are* + Partizip Perfekt (3. Form) des Vollverbs gebildet (1, 2).
- Das *simple past passive* wird mit *was/were* + Partizip Perfekt gebildet (3).
- Das *will-future passive* wird mit *will* + *be* + Partizip Perfekt gebildet (4).
- Das *passive* mit Modalverben (*can, could, have to, must, should* usw.) wird mit dem Modalverb + *be* + Partizip Perfekt gebildet (5, 6).

6 Practice

A Use the verbs in brackets to make sentences in the passive. Select an appropriate tense for each sentence.

1. 500 respondents … how they use their iPads. (ask)
2. 26% of respondents said that they … by TV ads more than by online advertising. (influence)
3. 2.5 thousand questionnaires … to existing customers next week. (send)
4. 36% of iPads … without protective cases. (use)
5. 17% of new mobile phones … within the first year. (lose)
6. 20% of advertising spend … print media. (should aim at)

B Rewrite these sentences using the appropriate form of the passive.

1 We will ask visitors at our stand next year what they think of the case.
2 Ben and Peter added several questions to the questionnaire after the meeting yesterday.
3 74% of customers use their iPads for listening to music.
4 The app makes the job of navigating on open water much easier.
5 Our new advert provides customers with advice about where to buy the case.
6 The report states that we should make more effort to reach customers through press coverage.

7 Competitive analysis

17

Listen as Simon updates Björn about his research into their competitors' activities.

KMK

A Beantworten Sie die folgenden Fragen in kurzen Stichworten auf Deutsch.

1 Warum hat Simon so viel Zeit mit der Wettbewerbsanalyse verbracht?
2 Warum finden Simon und Björn das Dokumentenfach des ersten Etuis merkwürdig?
3 Welche anderen Eigenschaften des ersten Etuis finden sie merkwürdig und warum?
4 Weshalb zweifelt Simon an, dass das zweite Etui wasserfest ist?
5 Welche Schritte fordert Björn als nächstes?

B Use the words and expressions from the box to complete the sentences from the dialogue. Listen again to check your answers.

allows • combine • come in • constructed from • features • includes • offers access to • retails at

1 It's … leather-look material and … a hand strap to make it easier to carry.
2 The case also … a sleeve which you can keep paper documents in.
3 Our case … you to use your iPad fully at all times.
4 It … 120 euros.
5 It's a carrying case which … all iPad functions but doesn't feature a carrying strap.
6 The defining feature of cases in this category is that they … unusual colours and materials.
7 The cases … a sporty look with practical functionality.

LANGUAGE

Verbs for talking about products

The case **is constructed from** water-resistant plastic.
It **includes** a carrying strap.
Our case **allows** you to use your iPad anywhere.
The case **comes in** a full range of colours, and **features** a shoulder strap.
It **combines** full functionality **with** style.

8 An advert for the Case for iPad

A **Use words from the language box on page 76 to complete the advert. Then use the same words to describe one of your company's products.**

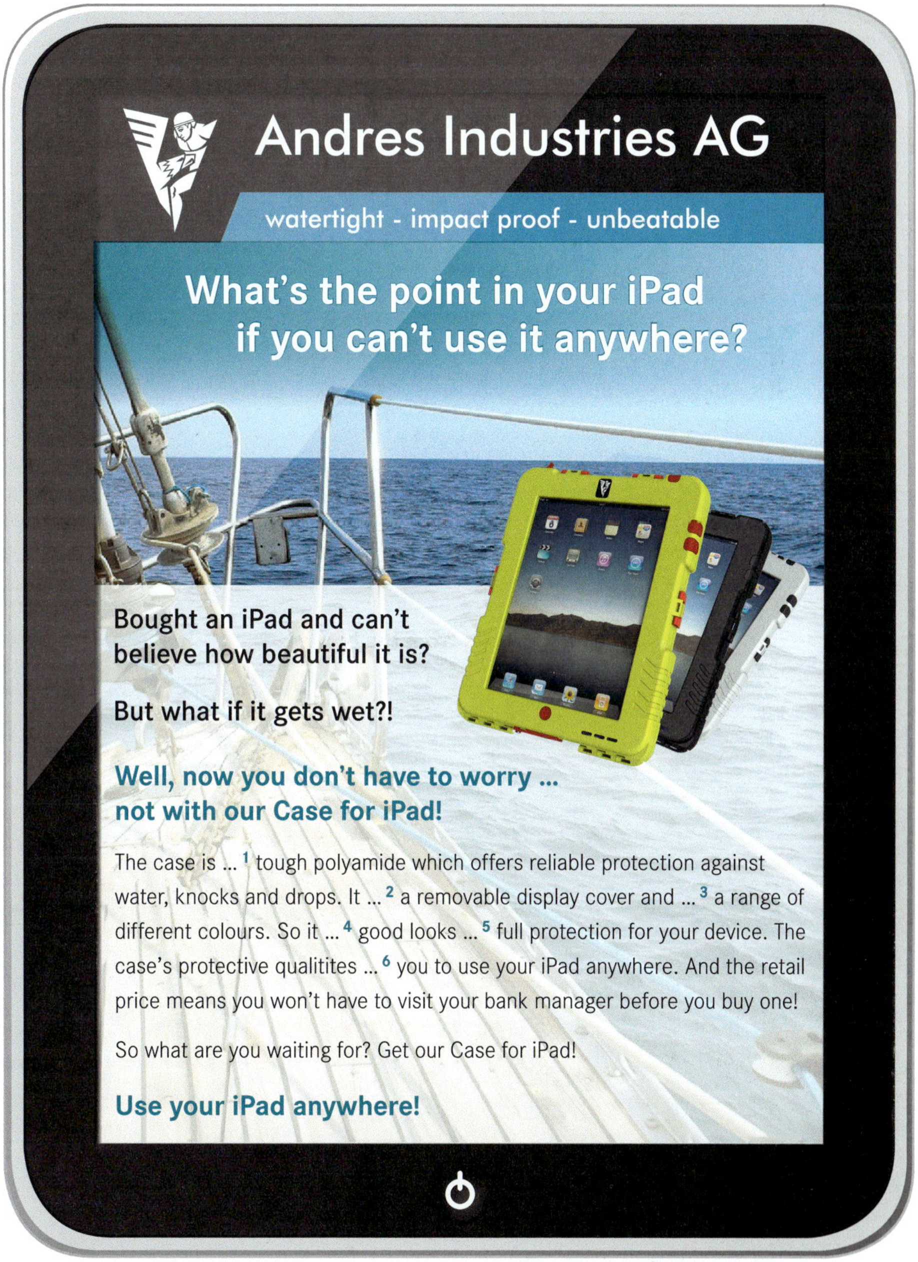

B **Read the complete advertisement and decide whether it is more likely to be aimed at magazines for general iPad users or specialist outdoor hobby magazines.**

9 Mediation

Sie vertreten einen kranken Kollegen in der Marketingabteilung. Dort finden Sie Informationen zum Konzept der 4Ps. Erstellen Sie für sich selbst zum Verständis eine tabellarische Übersicht auf Deutsch, wie die einzelnen Ps beschrieben sind und geben Sie je ein Anwendungsbeispiel an.

Stirring up the 4Ps to create the right marketing mix

When these elements are combined by marketeers, the end product is referred to as the marketing mix. To obtain a successful marketing mix, the four elements have to be combined in the right way to appeal to customers. It might be unproductive, for instance, to distribute a well-designed product which is on offer at an appropriate price through inappropriate distribution channels.

It's crucial to get this P right if you're going to enjoy success and sell enough to return a profit. The **product** has to be designed in the light of market research which establishes what customers are likely to buy. It also has to be designed after careful examination of what the competition is offering. Ideally, the product has to feature a unique selling point which differentiates it from the competitive products.

This P is another crucial element of the marketing mix. There would be little point in carefully thinking through the design of a product, how to pitch it to potential customers, and where to make it available to them if you get the **price** wrong and ask them to pay too much for it. Depending on what kind of product you're offering, and to which market segment, it may also be possible to get the price wrong by setting it too low. Those in a position to buy exclusive, high-quality goods, for instance, may not respond well to being asked to pay what they consider a low price.

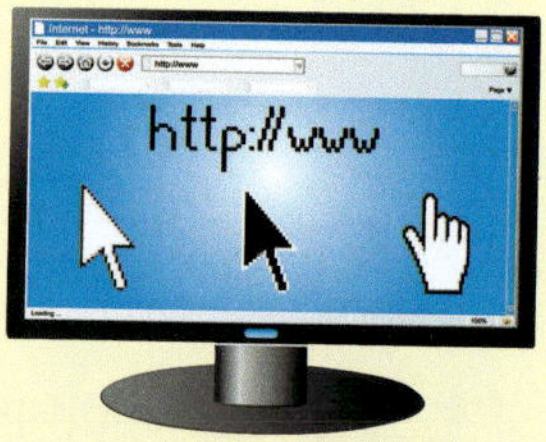

This P refers to **place**, otherwise known as the distribution channel. The question here is, are you going to sell your product, for example, through retail shops, direct to customers door-to-door, by means of mail order catalogues, or on the internet? It's crucially important to make the product available to customers via the right distribution channels if you're going to sell it in satisfactory quantities.

The type of **promotion** that you carry out to market a product will play an important role in its success. Promotion includes, of course, advertising in all its forms and the public relations efforts that you engage in, as well as the personal approaches of the sales people whose job it is to sell the product.

Marketing: The Future

Where it's all heading

For most companies, marketing is a straightforward business. You have a product and you know which markets you want to aim it at. You hire an advertising agency to develop an ad campaign for you. Then you hire a media buying agency which helps you decide where to place your ads and then buys space for you. And then you sit back and wait for customers to buy your product.

But if the previous paragraph summarizes how you understand the marketing process (particularly the part of it which involves communicating with potential customers), you may need to think again.

That's because there are several new approaches to marketing which are becoming increasingly important. Get up to speed with two of these by reading on.

Viral marketing

One of the key motivations behind this new form of marketing is the cost of buying advertising space in traditional media. With the arrival of the internet, marketeers discovered people's willingness to pass on marketing messages to friends online, providing the message was packaged in an interesting way. The cost savings in this are clear.

Viral marketing messages can take the form of videos, photos or soundclips which people send on to contacts for their entertainment value. It's often not made clear that a product is actually being sold through these messages, and many people who post a viral marketing video on their social networking site would be surprised that they have passed on an advertisement. Nevertheless, the technique has been proved to work, and a company which markets successfully in this way will guarantee a "buzz" for its product.

Guerilla marketing

The idea behind guerilla marketing is to change the form in which marketing messages are presented, and to get them out of conventional advertising media. The technique, now being used by large companies, aims at presenting marketing messages in a form that people do not expect to see them.

Guerilla marketing campaigns can take many forms and include, for example, putting your message on crudely produced (but cool) stickers, or hiring groups of actors to play out a scene in public spaces which conveys your marketing message.

Even if these approaches to marketing are too unconventional for many companies, they offer significant cost savings over more conventional approaches. For this reason alone, they are certain to be used by increasing numbers of companies.

10 Understanding the text and further discussion

A **Make a mind map featuring the ways in which viral and guerilla marketing are different from conventional forms of marketing.**

B **With a partner, discuss which of these methods you could imagine your company using. Then suggest a concrete idea about how they might be used.**

UNIT 8

Ritter Starkstromtechnik deals with an enquiry

- Dealing with enquiries and orders
- Writing an offer
- Making an appointment

1 Warm-up

A How does the sales/procurement department of your company get orders for its goods and services? Rank the ideas below in order of importance and add more ideas of your own.

B In groups of three or four, write a short explanation of how an order at your company is processed from procurement to completion.

Refer to *Unit 2, Roles and responsibilities* for the names of company departments. Use the expressions: *first, next, after that, then, finally*

Example: *First, one of our representatives visits …*

C Compare your results with those of other members of your class. Do all the companies process orders in the same way?

D Look at the list of documents below. Then say (a) who issues each of the documents (the supplier or the customer) and (b) which order they come in.

a delivery note
b order acknowledgement
c quotation (offer)
d sales enquiry
e invoice
f purchase order

2 Ritter Starkstromtechnik receives an email

Ritter Starkstromtechnik GmbH & Co. KG in Wilnsdorf sells electrical equipment to a large number of customers both inside and outside the EU. Every year it exhibits its products at trade fairs all over Europe. After the Hanover Trade Fair, it receives the following email.

A Read the email and say why it has been sent and what its purpose is.

B Find phrases in the email for the following headings.

1 source of address
2 description of Silvassa Industries
3 requirements
4 references

> Dear Mr Nordstern
>
> I was most impressed by the equipment you showed me on your stand at the Hanover Trade Fair last month, and note from your company's website that you sell a wide range of switchgear. As you may remember, my company, Silvassa Industries India Ltd, is a rapidly-growing mining company near Mumbai with subsidiaries all over India and beyond, and with many long-standing customers in Europe.
>
> We are currently installing new equipment at one of our sites and would therefore welcome a quotation for your SCC-D-48 short circuit switch, including details of your terms of delivery and payment. We would require delivery within 8 weeks.
>
> Should you require references, please refer to our website for a list of our major customers who will be pleased to supply you with any information you may require.
>
> If your product meets our requirements, we will be in a position to place substantial orders in the future.
>
> Yours sincerely
>
> Sanjeev Khurana
> Sales Representative
> Silvassa Industries India Ltd

3 Writing an enquiry

PAGE **123 & 135** KMK

Sie sind Mitarbeiter/in der Konrad Installation & Co. KG (Luisenstr. 17, 44225 Dortmund). Sie haben erfahren, dass die niederländische Firma Tools International BV, (Melbournestraat 33, Rotterdam 3047 BJ), hochwertige Werkzeuge liefert, die im Angebot sind.

Verfassen Sie ein Schreiben (E-Mail oder Brief) mit dem folgenden Inhalt an die niederländische Firma.

- Datum, Anrede, Betreff
- Ansprechpartner: Mr Edwin van Dijk, Verkaufsleiter
- Empfehlung von Ms Jackie Miles von der Firma Bauerkamp GmbH in Magdeburg
- Vorstellung Ihrer Firma als eine der führenden deutschen Elektroinstallationsfirmen mit Niederlassungen überall in Deutschland
- Anlass der Anfrage: Firma expandiert und benötigt neue Werkzeuge zu guten Preisen
- Bitte um Zusendung eines Katalogs sowie einer aktuellen Preisliste, einschl. aller gewährten Rabatte
- Bitte um Angabe der Liefer- und Zahlungsbedingungen: frühester Liefertermin?
- Referenzen auf Wunsch erhältlich
- bei günstigen Konditionen und hervorragender Qualität größere Aufträge möglich
- höfliche Schlussformel

4 Ritter sends out an offer

PAGE 123

Ralf Nordstern sends an offer for the SCC-D-48 short circuit switches to Sanjeev Khurana at Silvassa Industries India Ltd.

Read the offer and do the tasks on the next page.

RITTER Starkstromtechnik GmbH & Co. KG,
Essener Str. 10a, 57234 Wilnsdorf, Germany [1]

RITTER Starkstromtechnik

RN/MB [2]
05 May 20.. [3]

Silvassa Industries India Ltd [4]
Solitaire Business Centre
20th Floor
Andheri-Kula Road
MUMBAI
400 093
INDIEN

Attn. Mr Sanjeev Khurana, Sales Representative [5]

Dear Mr Khurana [6]

Offer for SCC-D-48 short circuit switches [7]

Many thanks for your enquiry dated 02 May 20.. . Our company manufactures a wide range of switchgear, and has many satisfied customers both inside and outside the EU. We offer tailor-made solutions to customers' specifications. To download more information, please visit our website at www.ritter-starkstromtechnik.de. A brochure on the SCC-D-48 short circuit switch is enclosed for your information. [8]

As regards the goods requested, we are pleased to submit the following quotation:

SCC-D-48 short circuit switch, with pneumatic drive, without cover at €12,722.00 each

Our price is quoted FCA Wilnsdorf (Incoterms® 2010) and our usual terms of payment for an initial order are letter of credit or cash with order. Regular customers may be granted preferential terms. Delivery is made within approx. 3 months after receipt of order. This offer is valid until 30 June 20.. .

We hope our offer is to your liking, and look forward to doing business with you.

Yours sincerely [9]
RITTER Starkstromtechnik GmbH & Co. KG

[10]

Ralf Nordstern [11]
Export Sales Department

Enc [12]

A Match the words in the box with the parts of the business letter (1–12).

attention line • body of letter • complimentary close • date • enclosure(s) • inside address • letterhead • reference initials • salutation • signatory's name • signature • subject line

B Answer the following questions about the offer.

1 Who in Silvassa Industries is the letter addressed to?
2 What does Ralf say about the products that Ritter Starkstromtechnik produces?
3 What has Ralf sent Sanjeev along with the letter?
4 Where can Sanjeev find further information about Ritters' products?
5 How should Silvassa Industries pay for the order?
6 Compare the offer from Ritter with Sanjeev's original enquiry. Which of the terms might Silvassa Industries have a problem with?

C Find the English equivalents of these expressions in the business letter.

1 zu Händen von
2 Angebot
3 Anfrage
4 im Anhang
5 Preisangebot
6 Zahlungsbedingungen
7 Dokumentenakkreditiv
8 Lieferung

5 Writing an offer

PAGE 123 & 136

Use the layout and the expressions in the offer to Silvassa Industries India Ltd on page 82 and the phrases on page 136 to write the following offer.

You work in the export department of Mertens KG (Stahlstr. 60-90, 77108 Donaueschingen). Your company has been manufacturing high-grade German steel cutlery for the past 50 years and enjoys an excellent reputation all over Europe. Use the points below to write an offer (email or letter) to Mrs Margaret Wilkinson (m.wilkinson@scc.org), Purchasing Director at Sheffield Cutlery Co. (90 Brightside Lane, Sheffield S9 2RW, UK).

- Date, salutation, subject
- Source of address: Ulm Chamber of Commerce
- Brief description of your company
- Current catalogue and price list enclosed / attached to email
- Samples available on request
- Prices quoted CPT British airport
- Terms of payment: CWO for an initial order; terms will be reviewed if regular orders are placed
- Delivery: three to four weeks after receipt of order
- Polite ending

6 Taking a message

KMK

18

Heute ruft ein Kunde bei Ritter Starkstromtechnik in Wilnsdorf an, um mit Herrn Ralf Nordstern zu sprechen. Da er außer Haus ist, nimmt seine Kollegin Janina Petrovic das Gespräch entgegen.

A Hören Sie sich das Gespräch an und füllen Sie die Telefonnotiz aus.

Anrufer (Name, Firma, Stadt, Land):	...
Kontaktdaten:	...
Grund des Anrufes: ...	
Ergebnisse des Anrufes: ...	

B Listen again and complete the following sentences from the phone call.

1. When would ... you?
2. ... about Tuesday, 5 June ... 9 a.m.?
3. Just let me see if he's ... .
4. I'm sorry, but I've already got an ... then.
5. I'm afraid not. He's ... up until 4.00 p.m.
6. Yes, that's ... with me.

7 Arranging an appointment

Next week Ralf Nordstern will be in Norway for two days to work on Ritter's booth at the ELIADEN Electrical Engineering Trade Fair in Lillestrøm. One of Ritter's potential customers is the Norwegian energy company Statkraft Energi AS. Ralf phones the Vice President of Procurement, Ms Ellen Forfang, to invite her to visit his company's booth and also to ask her out for dinner. In Lillestrøm there is a well-known Italian restaurant (Fratelli's) and a very popular Chinese restaurant (Chi restaurant).

Use the partner files at the back of the book and the language box below to agree on a day and time to meet.

Student A: turn to partner file 10 on page 116. / **Student B:** turn to partner file 7 on page 115.

LANGUAGE

Making an appointment

Suggesting a time
When would suit you?
Would Thursday be possible/convenient for you?
How about 12 o'clock on Monday?
Are you free on Tuesday at 10 a.m.?

Responding
Let me just check my diary.
Just let me see when I'm free/available.
Yes, that's fine/OK with me.
I'm sorry, but I've already got an appointment then.
I'm busy then until 4.00 p.m.
I'm afraid not. I'm tied up all day.
Unfortunately, I'm not available on ... .

Suggesting an alternative
Could we arrange something else?
What about Tuesday? Preferably in the morning/afternoon/evening.

TIP

Incoterms® 2010

In international trade, the eleven Incoterms® 2010 Rules (**in**ternational **co**mmercial **terms**) are used in contracts of sale to define the rights and obligations of the buyer and seller as regards risk, transport, insurance, packing, customs duty and documentation. They are terms of delivery.

8 The Incoterms® 2010 Rules (terms of delivery)

WEBCODE **INDMU0801**

Study the Incoterms FCA, CPT and DAT and the illustration on page 124. Then decide which of the three Incoterms rules is required in each of the cases (1–4) below.

FCA – FREE CARRIER (... named place of delivery): Multimodal transport
The seller is not responsible for the main carriage of the goods. The seller delivers the goods at his own expense, in the customary packing, cleared for export to the carrier selected by the buyer. The seller provides the commercial invoice and, if requested, a certificate of origin at the buyer's expense. If the goods are collected at the seller's premises, the seller loads the goods. The seller bears the risks until the goods are in the custody of the first carrier. After that, the buyer bears all the costs and risks of transporting the goods to the destination.

CPT – CARRIAGE PAID TO (... named place of destination): Multimodal transport
The seller pays for the main carriage of the goods. The seller delivers the goods, in the customary packing, cleared for export to the carrier which he nominates. The seller bears the risk until the goods have been delivered into the custody of the first carrier. The seller pays the transport costs for the goods, excluding transport insurance, up to the named destination. The buyer is responsible for insuring the goods for the main carriage and pays all import duties and taxes.

DAT – DELIVERED AT TERMINAL (... named terminal at destination): Multimodal transport
The seller pays for carriage of the goods in the customary packing, cleared for export to the named terminal at the destination by the carrier which he nominates. He bears the risk until the goods have been delivered to the named terminal. The seller is responsible for unloading the goods at the place of destination. The buyer pays all import duties and taxes.

1 A German exporter is willing to take the goods to Hamburg and pay for them to be transported to his customer in New York, but is not prepared to have them insured for this part of the journey or for unloading at their destination.

2 An Irish buyer in Dublin buys goods from a German supplier in Frankfurt am Main, and wishes the seller to bear all the costs and risks of transport to Dublin, including unloading. He is prepared to pay Irish import duties and taxes.

3 A German exporter in Mülheim an der Ruhr is not prepared to pay for transport of the goods from his factory to Guangzhou Airport in China. However, he is willing to clear them for export and to load them onto a lorry when they are collected by the buyer's freight forwarder.

4 An Australian importer buys goods from a German supplier in Munich and wants the price to include transport to Melbourne. The Australian company is prepared to insure the goods between Munich and Melbourne, but wishes the seller to find a freight forwarder and deal with all other formalities in Germany.

9 Negotiating better terms

PAGE **126**

A Sanjeev Khurana calls Ralf Nordstern. Read their conversation and say why he is calling.

Ralf Ritter Starkstromtechnik. Sie sprechen mit Ralf Nordstern. Was kann ich für Sie tun?

Sanjeev Good morning, Ralf. It's Sanjeev Khurana from Silvassa Industries in India.

Ralf Hello, Sanjeev. Nice to talk to you again. How are things?

Sanjeev Fine, thanks. And you?

Ralf It's very nice here today – nice and sunny. Did you get my offer?

Sanjeev Yes, thanks. I got it yesterday. Since then I've spoken to our Purchasing Director and he has suggested a few changes, including a different Incoterm because he doesn't want to have to look for a freight forwarder in Germany.

Ralf I see. Well, at the moment the Incoterm is Free Carrier Wilnsdorf, so what does he suggest?

Sanjeev DAT Mumbai.

Ralf Let me just check my price list … Delivered at Terminal Mumbai. Well, DAT would be more expensive than FCA because we would have to pay for transport and bear the risk all the way to Mumbai.

Sanjeev Yes, I know, but we took delivery of an FCA consignment from France last week and had to arrange transport all the way to India. It was a lot of work, so we would rather you did that. How much more would it cost?

Ralf DAT would cost you approximately 15% more.

Sanjeev I see. And what about import clearance – I mean customs duties and taxes in India?

Ralf You would pay for that but we, the seller, would pay for unloading in Mumbai. How far are you from Mumbai?

Sanjeev We're not far. Only about 90 miles.

Ralf In that case, you could send your own lorry to Mumbai to pick up the switches.

Sanjeev Yes, we can do that. I think DAT is much better in this case.

Ralf And what was the other suggestion?

Sanjeev It's about payment. I rang our bank a few hours ago, and they gave us the charges for payment by letter of credit. It's very expensive for us. We would prefer documents against payment instead.

Ralf D/P … Well, we haven't done business with you before, and with documents against payment we wouldn't have a guarantee of payment, which is what we would have with a letter of credit or cash with order.

Sanjeev Yes, I understand, but as we haven't done business with your company so far, either, we would prefer not to have CWO, because that would be a risk for us too. Would it help if we provided references?

Ralf Yes, that would certainly help. Has your company dealt with suppliers in Europe before?

Sanjeev Yes, we have, and I'm sure Armstrong Electrics in London will give us a good trade reference, and so will ABB in Cottbus. I talked to the Export Sales Director of ABB at the electrical engineering fair in Norway a few months ago, and he promised to give us a trade reference too.

Ralf Well, in that case, I'll look at the terms of delivery and payment again, and as soon as we have those references, I'll send you a new offer.

Sanjeev Good. I'll pass them on to you, and as soon as we have your new offer, you'll hear from us immediately.

Ralf Great! Anything else I can do for you, Sanjeev?

Sanjeev Yes, I was wondering if you could deliver any quicker than three months?

Ralf Three months is standard delivery time, I'm afraid.
Sanjeev OK, I think that will still be within time.

B **Match the highlighted words in the dialogue with the following terms and definitions.**

1 tax paid on goods entering a country
2 CWO
3 without delay, straight away
4 an idea that you want other people to think about
5 not exactly, more or less
6 money paid for a service
7 an event at which companies show their goods
8 permission to let goods enter a country

C **Read the dialogue again and answer the following questions.**

1 Why does the Purchasing Director want to change the Incoterm?
2 What was the original term of delivery?
3 How much more does DAT cost than FCA?
4 Who pays import clearance and customs duties with a DAT delivery?
5 What is the disadvantage of documents against payment for Ritter?
6 What must Sanjeev do now to get better terms?

!
- I've been in Berlin ~~since~~ **for** three weeks.
- I started working here ~~for~~ two weeks **ago**.

GRAMMAR

Present perfect and simple past

1 Since then **I've spoken** to our Purchasing Director.
2 We **haven't done** business with your company so far.
3 **Has** your company **dealt with** suppliers in Europe before?
4 He **has suggested** a few changes.
5 I **got** your offer yesterday.
6 **Did** you **get** my offer?
7 We **didn't want** to arrange transport.
8 I **talked** to the Export Sales Director a few months ago.

- Das **present perfect** wird verwendet, wenn der im Satz angegebene Zeitraum bis in die Gegenwart andauert (*unfinished time*) (1–4), dies wird durch Zeitadverbien wie *before, ever, since then, so far, up to now, yet* ausgedrückt (1–3).
- Es wird auch verwendet, wenn keine Zeit angegeben wird (4).
- Es bezieht sich auf Ereignisse oder Handlungen, deren Ergebnisse in der Gegenwart sichtbar, spürbar oder von Bedeutung sind (4).
- Das *present perfect* wird mit *have/has* + Partizip Perfekt (3. Verbform) gebildet.

- Das **simple past** verwendet man, um abgeschlossene Handlungen und Ereignisse in der Vergangenheit auszudrücken (*finished time*) (5–8).
- Bestimmte Zeitadverbien stehen oft in Verbindung mit dem *simple past*, z. B. *last week, two years ago, yesterday* (5).
- Bei regelmäßigen Verben wird das *simple past* durch das Anhängen von *-ed* an den Infinitiv gebildet (8). Das *simple past* wird mit der 2. Form von unregelmäßigen Verben gebildet (5). Fragen und Verneinungen werden mit *did/didn't* + Grundform gebildet (6, 7).

10 Practice

A **Decide whether these expressions of time are about *finished time* (simple past) or *unfinished time* (present perfect). None of them are about the future.**

at seven o'clock • at Christmas • ever • in 2000 • in February • in the spring • just • last month • never • on Friday • on my birthday • this morning • this week • today • two years ago • since 2010 • yesterday • yet

B **Complete these sentences using the present perfect or the simple past.**

1. We … all the contracts yet. (not receive)
2. She … two contracts last week. (receive)
3. They … many orders this month. (not have)
4. We last … a new order five days ago. (get)
5. … it yet? (you / see)
6. Our new computer … three times. (break down)
7. It … last week. (not break down)
8. It … this week. (break down)
9. I … our new sales manager. (just meet)
10. He … at the company since Monday. (be)

11 A problem with the order form

A **Compare the order form with the terms that Ralf and Sanjeev agreed upon in exercise 9. What is wrong with the order?**

B **Write a short email to Ralf Nordstern to apologize for the mistake and to rectify the order.**

Dear Mr Nordstern

Order for short circuit switches

On the basis of your offer dated 20 June 20.., we now wish to place the following order in line with the negotiated terms:

Article:	Short circuit switch
Type:	SCC-D-48
Quantity:	10
Unit price:	€12,722.00
Total price:	€127,220.00
Terms of delivery:	DAT Mumbai (Incoterms® 2010)
Terms of payment:	CWO
Delivery:	By 30 September 20..
Shipping:	Kühne + Nagel (AG & Co.) KG, Wilnsdorf

We look forward to receiving your confirmation of order and advice of dispatch.

12 Interaktion: Anfrage

Führen Sie ein Telefongespräch mit Hilfe folgenden Ablaufes.

Situation
Ein/e Mitarbeiter/in in der Verkaufsabteilung der Firma Best Buy Großhandel GmbH in Dortmund erhält einen Anruf von Jack/Jacqueline Jones, der/die bei Crown Sports Supplies im UK arbeitet.

Best Buy Mitarbeiter/in

Jack/Jacqueline Jones

Best Buy Mitarbeiter/in	Jack/Jacqueline Jones
Melden Sie sich am Telefon mit Vor- und Nachnamen und mit dem Firmennamen.	
	Stellen Sie sich vor und sagen Sie, dass Sie sich für Turnschuhe interessieren.
Fragen Sie nach dem Modell der Turnschuhe.	
	Sie hätten gerne die Cool Runner 400 in weiß und pink.
Sagen Sie, dass weiß nicht mehr hergestellt wird, dafür aber silbergrau.	
	Sie sind mit silbergrau einverstanden und fragen nach dem Preis.
Informieren Sie den Kunden / die Kundin, dass die Turnschuhe 12,– € pro Paar kosten.	
	Fragen Sie nach einem Musterstück.
Sagen Sie, dass Musterstücke nicht geliefert werden.	
	Sie sind enttäuscht. Fragen Sie nach den Lieferbedingungen.
Die Lieferbedingungen sind: EXW Dortmund.	
	Fragen Sie nach dem Preis für DAP Exeter.
DAP Exeter würde ca. 10 % mehr kosten.	
	Fragen Sie nach Rabatten.
Geben Sie folgende Informationen: ab 100 Paar gibt es Rabatt von 5 %.	
	Fragen Sie nach den Zahlungsbedingungen.
Sagen Sie, dass die Zahlungsbedingungen Kasse bei Auftragserteilung beinhaltet.	
	Fragen Sie nach der Lieferzeit.
Sagen Sie, dass die Lieferung nach Auftragseingang ca. 7 Tage dauert.	
	Bedanken Sie sich.
Fragen Sie den Kunden / die Kundin, ob er/sie einen Auftrag erteilen möchte.	
	Sagen Sie, dass Sie sich ggfs. melden werden.
Danken Sie für das Gespräch und verabschieden Sie sich.	
	Verabschieden Sie sich.

13 Understanding a confirmation of order

Study the document and do the tasks below.

RITTER Starkstromtechnik GmbH & Co. KG,
Essener Str. 10a, 57234 Wilnsdorf, Germany

RITTER Starkstromtechnik

Confirmation of order – contract number 10600674

Item	Quantity	Part	Details	Net unit price (€)	Total (€)
1	4	Short circuit switch	AD-D-38.5	€7,500.00	30,000.00
2	4	Control box	G7 1130	€2,500.00	10,000.00
3		Delivery FCA Germany (Incoterms® 2010)			550.00
				Total order value	**€40,550.00**

Delivery: 3 months after approval of drawing (enclosed) and payment

Terms of delivery: FCA (named place of delivery) (Incoterms® 2010)
Place to be in Germany and nominated by buyer

Shipping documents: Commercial invoice / packing list / certificate of origin / export documents / operating manual / test reports / technical drawing

Payment: Payment in advance against commercial invoice (enclosed)

Guarantee: 18 months after commissioning or 24 months after delivery, whichever is earlier

Changes: All changes must be made in writing and confirmed by both parties (fax, email, letter)

Confidentiality: Any information of a commercial or technical nature exchanged either verbally or in writing between the two parties to this contract is to be kept in the strictest confidence and may not be disclosed to any third parties, unless this is explicitly agreed in writing by both parties to this contract.

Arbitration:
After both parties have signed this contract (or confirmed this contract by email), it will become valid.

Signatures:

1. Decide whether the goods have been delivered or not. Explain your answer.
2. Find out where the goods will be collected.
3. Name the Incoterm rule used here and, with the help of the information on pages 124–126, explain (a) who will provide export documentation and (b) who will pay for transporting the goods to their destination.

14 Over to you

Get permission to bring in some of the documents used for export by your company. Find out what the documents are called in English and explain when they are used.

A problem at GEM Foods

UNIT 9

- Receiving and replying to complaints
- Dealing with payment problems
- Writing reminders

1 Warm-up

A **Describe what the problem is in each of the illustrations (a–d). The words in the box will help you.**

damaged in transit • delayed consignment • error in invoice • faulty goods • incomplete consignment • wrong consignment

B **In pairs, talk about some problems that you have experienced, either in your private or working life. Then tell your partner how you solved these problems.**

Examples: *waiting for a repair man, phoning a call centre about a problem, losing your purse or wallet*

2 An accident at work

A Read as Marc Schmidt from GEM Foods in Hanover calls Clive Haynes at Laker-Moss Biscuit Machines in the UK to discuss a problem they have encountered. Then say what the problem is.

Clive Good morning. Laker-Moss Biscuit Machines. How can I help you?
Marc Hi, Marc Schmidt here from GEM Foods in Hanover. Is that you Clive?
Clive Yes, it's me. Hello, Marc. What can I do for you?
Marc We have a major problem here with one of our high-speed mixers.
Clive Oh dear. That's never good. What's the problem?
Marc Well, one of our new apprentices reversed a fork lift into the machine and now the doors won't close, and the mixer is damaged as well. It was a big mistake to let him drive it, because he's only just passed his test.
Clive Hmm, that sounds like a major set-back for your biscuit production line. We'll have to get our engineers to fly out to repair it. Although, thinking about it again, if the doors and mixer need to be replaced, as you say, then it will be easier for them to drive over because the new parts will be too heavy to transport by air.
Marc Well, we can't produce any more biscuits until it's fixed. How soon can your engineers get here?
Clive I'll have to talk to Carol Jackson; she's in charge of that department. I can get back to you later on this morning if that's OK with you?
Marc Yes, fine, but it's really urgent. We have to have that machine repaired as soon as possible because we have orders to fulfil and deadlines to keep to.
Clive Don't worry. I'm sure the engineers will be there with you, at the latest, the day after tomorrow. You're one of our best customers, so we don't want to let you down.

Clive calls Marc back about an hour later.

Marc Schmidt, hallo.
Clive Hi Marc, it's me again, Clive.
Marc Ah, Clive. That was fast. I didn't expect you to get back to me quite so quickly, although I'm delighted that you have.
Clive Well, as I said earlier, we do go the extra mile for our best customers.
Marc So, what news do you have for me?
Clive I've arranged for two of our best engineers to take the night ferry over. They should be with you by half nine tomorrow morning. The earlier they get to work, the sooner you will be able to restart biscuit production.
Marc That's great Clive, thanks. I really appreciate it. We really can't afford all of these delays.

B Answer the following questions about the dialogue.

1 What needs to be repaired?
2 Which transport methods are discussed?
3 Why can't the engineers go by air?
4 Why does Clive arrange things so quickly?
5 When are the engineers due to arrive?
6 Why does Marc need the machine fixed so quickly?

C **Match the words and phrases below to the highlighted words in the text which have a similar meaning.**

1 broken
2 to complete
3 manufacture
4 mend
5 a delay
6 repaired
7 responsible for
8 serious
9 error

D **Now use the words from exercise C to complete the following sentences.**

1 I'm often accused of making …; it's really unfair, because I'm still learning how to do the job.
2 My printer isn't working; it's a … disaster, because I can't print out any orders!
3 A faulty conveyor belt has caused a huge … to our production this week. We'll never … 50,000 packets of biscuits by Friday.
4 We'll have to call the technicians in to … the … belt.
5 I was late home again last night. We have to work overtime because we need to … lots of urgent orders.

TIP

Times

When making arrangements to meet, it is best to use a.m. for times in the morning (usually before twelve o'clock midday), and p.m. for times in the afternoon (after twelve o'clock midday), in the evening or at night. "Half past eleven" in English means 11.30 but *halb elf* in German means 10.30. So, if you plan to meet an English speaker at half past the hour, it is best to say "nine-thirty", "ten-thirty", or alternatively "half *past* nine", "half *past* ten", etc. in order to avoid confusion.
You only say 'o'clock' when the time is eight o'clock, nine o'clock, ten o'clock, etc. and never say ~~ten o'clock a.m.~~ or ~~ten o'clock p.m.~~

3 An angry answerphone message

19

Read the tip box and listen to or read the message that Marc leaves on Clive's answerphone the next day. Then discuss with a partner what might have gone wrong.

4 Role-play: getting the time right

KMK

Work with a partner and act out the role-play.

Student A: read the partner file below. / **Student B:** turn to partner file 8 on page 115.

Student A

Your boss at GEM Foods has asked you to call your English-speaking visitor to confirm the details for an upcoming meeting.

- Introductions and small talk
- The visitor asks for the following information:
  - Herr Schlorff will pick the visitor up from the airport
  - Hotel: MidCity Hotel / Meeting: conference room at GEM Foods
- The visitor **must** arrive at the company next Thursday by 8.30 a.m. (at the latest)
- Meeting begin: 9 a.m. promptly
- During your conversation you realize that a mistake has been made regarding the day and the time of the meeting. Try to confirm the day and time of the meeting.

GRAMMAR

Adjectives and adverbs

1 We have a **serious** problem on our production line.
2 It is **usual** for employees in the factory to wear overalls.
3 The blades were **badly** damaged.
4 The consignment arrived **early**.
5 The goods were packaged **well**.
6 It is **extremely** loud on the production line today.

Adjektive und Adverbien sind im Deutschen meistens in der Form identisch. Das ist im Englischen nicht der Fall.

- Adjektive beschreiben Substantive (1) und Pronomen.
- Adverbien beschreiben Verben (3–5) oder Adjektive (6).
- Die meisten Adverbien werden durch das Anhängen von *-ly* an das Adjektiv gebildet (3). Ausnahmen bilden Adjektive auf *-ic*. Die dazugehörigen Adverbien werden durch das Anhängen von *-ally* gebildet: *basic – basic**ally**; careful – careful**ly**; easy – easi**ly**; terrible – terri**bly***. (Eine Ausnahme von dieser Regel ist das Adjektiv *public*, welches zu *publicly* wird.)
- Einige wenige Adverbien haben dieselbe Form wie das Adjektiv: z. B. *early, fast, hard, high, late, long, low, right, straight, wrong* (4).
- Zum Adjektiv *good* gehört als Adverb *well* (5).

5 Practice

A Choose the correct word in italics.

1 Bobby McShane is a *young/youngly* apprentice.
2 He was given *exact/exactly* instructions on how to operate the forklift.
3 Unfortunately he didn't follow them *proper/properly*.
4 No-one was *bad/badly* hurt in the accident, but Bobby knew afterwards that he had not made a *good/well* impression.
5 Clive's engineers were able to fix the problem *easy/easily*.

WEBCODE **INDMU0901**

B Complete the sentences with the correct form of the word in brackets.

1 The men loaded the … parts into the lorry while it was raining …. (heavy)
2 No-one was … injured. The accident was not …. (serious)
3 The colleagues in our department all work … together; we have a very … reputation in the company. (good)
4 John always drives …; he is a … driver. (fast)
5 It is always … in the factory, so factory workers have to speak …. (loud)
6 You can never be too … with sharp blades, so we always tell our apprentices to clean sharp mixer blades …. (careful)

6 Dissatisfied customers

Once the engineers from Laker-Moss arrive at the factory, they discover that some of the parts were damaged in transit. In situations like this, a letter or an email of complaint is sent to the company responsible.

A Use the phrases (a–h) below to complete these two emails of complaint.

a has caused us considerable inconvenience

b at your earliest convenience

c at your expense

d I was most upset to discover

e As you are aware

f I am writing to express my dissatisfaction

g We need new replacements as soon as possible

h that production has had to be halted

1

An: c.haynes@l_m_biscuit.co.uk
Kopie:
Betreff: **Damaged parts**
Von: marc.schmidt@gem.de Signatur: Ohne

Dear Clive

…[1] that due to badly packaged cartons, some of the replacement parts that your engineers brought this morning are unusable. When the consignment was opened, we found that water had seeped in and that some of the door panels were beginning to go rusty. …[2] because our chocolate biscuit production has been stopped. I intend to return the parts to you …[3].

Please let me know your thoughts on this matter …[4].

Yours

Marc Schmidt
Production Director

2

An: b.pentland@aircon.co.uk

Kopie:

Betreff: **Leak in celling**

Von: andreas.schneider@gem.de Signatur: Ohne

Dear Bryan

…[5] with the poor service we have experienced from your company.

…[6], we have already had several problems with the air-conditioning system that was fitted in our new extension for the Fruit In Jelly Pots production line. Now water has started to leak through the ceiling again, which has meant …[7]. We have urgent orders to fulfil and this ongoing issue …[8].

We expect you to react to this situation as soon as possible.
I look forward to hearing from you.

Yours sincerely

Andreas Schneider
Head of Maintenance

B **Read the emails again and then discuss with your partner which department in the company they were sent from and what they concern.**

7 Replying to complaints

Use the information on the post-it notes below to reply to the emails in exercise 6 in English. The language box on page 97 will help you.

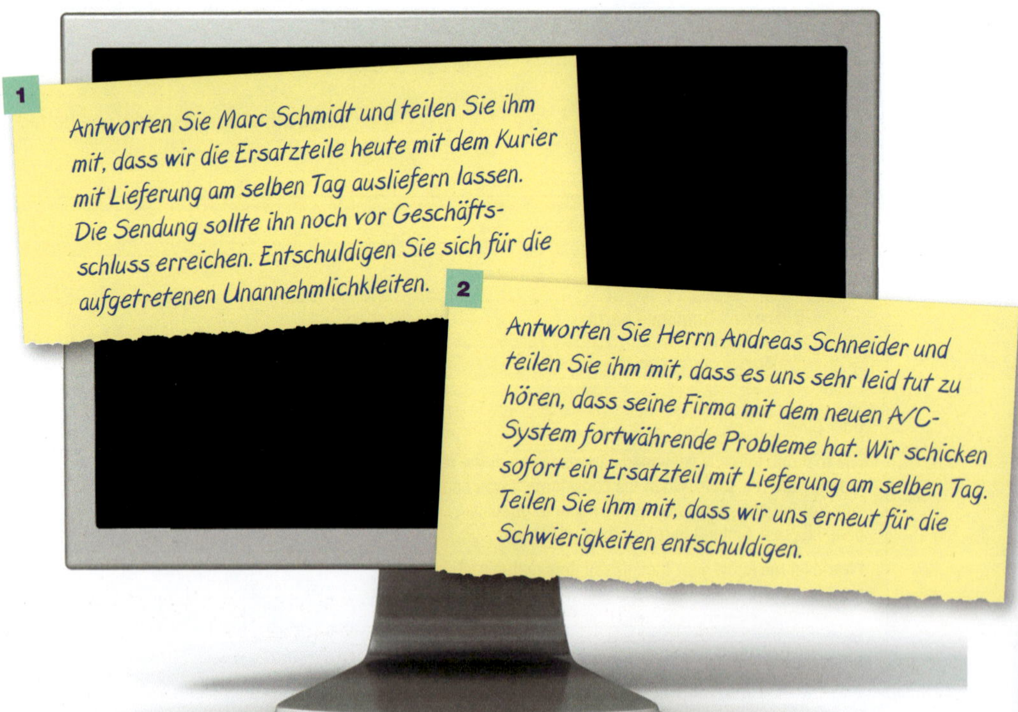

LANGUAGE

Apologizing

I am/We are (extremely) sorry to hear that …
I/We would like to apologize for …
The delay is/was due to …
The damage resulted from …
It was due to circumstances beyond our control.
Please accept my/our sincere apologies.
Please accept my/our apologies for any inconvenience caused.

8 Writing a complaint

KMK

Andreas Schneider, Chef der Reparaturabteilung von GEM ist immer noch unzufrieden mit Bryan Pentland von der Firma Aircon. Er gibt Ihnen den Auftrag in seinem Namen, umgehend an Herrn Pentland ein Fax zu schreiben. In der *Language Box* (unten) finden Sie hilfreiches Vokabular.

Datum: 14.07.20..

Schreiben Sie an Bryan Pentland und sagen Sie ihm, dass eins der Austauschteile, die er geschickt hat, fehlerhaft ist – es geht ständig kaputt. Fordern Sie ihn auf, das Ersatzteil A/C TGD7521b sofort mit einer Lieferung, die noch am selben Tag hier eintrifft, zu senden. Das fehlerhafte Ersatzteil hat ernsthafte Probleme in der Produktion verursacht. Erinnern Sie ihn daran, dass das System immer noch unter Garantie steht. Machen Sie ihm deutlich, dass die gesamte Situation sehr unbefriedigend ist.

LANGUAGE

Language of complaints in writing

I am writing with reference to …
I am writing to complain about/express my dissatisfaction with …
There seems to have been an error/mistake made concerning …
I/We would like to remind you that the … is still within its warranty period.
This has caused us considerable inconvenience.

9 Dealing with payment problems

Months later, Laker-Moss is still waiting for payment for the work that was done at GEM Foods in Hanover. The total amount due on invoice GEM892011 is £15,000.

Work with a partner and do the tasks below.

1. Explain what action you think Laker-Moss should take. Give reasons for your answer.
2. Think of some reasons why the invoice has not yet been paid.
3. Consider why some companies do not pay their bills on time.
4. Find out if your company has a prompt payment policy.

10 May I remind you that ...

A **Read the correspondence below between Margaret Blackwell, Accounts Manager at Laker-Moss, and Heinrich Schulz, Accounts Manager at GEM Foods. Then explain (a) how long the invoice is overdue and (b) the reason for the delay in payment.**

Laker-Moss Biscuit Machines plc
Minn Street
Stamford
PE9 7RZ
Tel: 0044 (0)7133 482909

7 August 20..

GEM Foods GmbH
Steinkamp
Hanover 30855
GERMANY

Attn. Mr Schulz, Accounts Manager

Dear Mr Schulz

Re: GEM892011

I am writing in connection with the attached unpaid invoice for work done at your premises.

As it is now two months since we completed the work, we would be grateful if you could let us have payment without delay.

We are very concerned that you have not paid this invoice. Please contact us at your earliest convenience.

Yours sincerely

M. Blackwell

Margaret Blackwell
Accounts Manager

GEM Foods GmbH
Steinkamp
Hanover 30855
Germany

12 August 20..

Laker-Moss Biscuit Machines plc
Minn Street
Stamford
PE9 7RZ
UNITED KINGDOM

Attn. Ms Blackwell, Accounts Manager

Dear Ms Blackwell

Re: GEM892011

Thank you for your letter of 7 August 20.. concerning the attached overdue invoice.

I have instructed our accounts department to pay the full amount into your company's bank account today. I really must apologize for not transferring the due amount until now. We recently installed a new software system and somehow your invoice was overlooked.

With apologies once again.

Yours sincerely

H. Schulz

Heinrich Schulz
Accounts Manager

B **Explain to your partner what a reminder is.**

C **Match the phrases (1–5) to the highlighted words and phrases in the letters.**

1. failed to notice that something should have been done
2. immediate payment
3. a document giving details about services that have been done but that have not yet been paid for
4. a payment that should have been paid before now
5. when it suits you

11 Writing a reminder

Margaret Blackwell sends a written reminder to another customer, Mr Watson. Arrange the parts of her letter (1–7) in the correct order.

1 Yours sincerely

2 I am afraid that if we have not received your payment within the next seven days, we will have to instruct our solicitors to take legal action.

3 Would you please settle the outstanding amount of £590 within the next seven working days at the latest.

4 **Invoice no. GEM652012**

5 Dear Mr Watson

6 Margaret Blackwell
Accounts Manager

7 Further to our conversation earlier today, I am writing in connection with the unpaid invoice for replacement parts sent to you some six weeks ago.

LANGUAGE

Writing a reminder

I am/We are writing in connection with the above unpaid invoice for work done at your premises.
I/We would like to draw your attention to invoice no. X.
Would you please settle your account by 1 October 20.. at the latest.
We insist on payment within five working days.
If we have not received your payment within the next seven days, we will have to instruct our solicitors to take legal action.

12 Rezeption: Hörverstehen

20

A Margaret Blackwell ruft einige Kunden an, die ihre Rechnungen noch nicht ganz bezahlt haben. Hören Sie aufmerksam zu und vervollständigen Sie die folgende Tabelle.

	1. Anruf	2. Anruf	3. Anruf
Kundenname	…	…	…
Rechnungsnummer	…	…	…
Letzter Zahlungstermin	…	…	…

B Stellen Sie fest, ob die folgenden Aussagen richtig oder falsch sind. Begründen Sie Ihre Antwort.

1 GEM Foods zahlt normalerweise Rechnungen pünktlich.
2 Herr Schulz bei GEM kann leider gerade nicht bei Ihrer Anfrage helfen, da er gleich in die Kantine geht.
3 Laker-Moss bietet bei frühzeitiger Zahlung einen Discount von 15 % an.
4 Fresssh GmbH hat 15 % zu wenig bezahlt.
5 Frau Baker bei Nibbles Ltd ist nur heute nicht im Büro.
6 Margaret Blackwell entscheidet sich dafür, Clare Jones zurückzurufen, da es sonst zu lange dauert.

C Beantworten Sie diese Verständnisfragen in kurzen Stichworten auf Deutsch.

1 Wann hat Herr Schulz versprochen, die Rechnung zu bezahlen?
2 Wie hoch war die erste Rechnung von Fresssh GmbH?
3 Wann hat Frau Ohler vor, Frau Blackwell zurückzurufen?
4 Wieviel Geld schuldet Nibbles Ltd Laker-Moss Biscuit?

13 Produktion

Frau Jones von der Firma Nibbles Ltd hat den Betrag, den Margaret Blackwell in Rechnung gestellt hat, noch nicht bezahlt. Margaret bittet Sie, Frau Jones eine Zahlungserinnerung zu entwerfen.

Ihre Aufgabe besteht darin, die Anrede sowie den Brieftext einschließlich Betreff zu formulieren. Bitte schreiben Sie vollständige Sätze und berücksichtigen Sie in Ihren Brief folgende Punkte:

- Datum, Anrede, Betreff
- Schreiben Sie, dass Frau Jones sicherlich nur vergessen hat, die Rechnung zu begleichen, da Sie sonst immer pünktlich bezahlt hat.
- Informieren Sie Frau Jones, dass eine Zahlung innerhalb der nächsten 5 Arbeitstage dringend notwendig wäre, um die guten Geschäftsbeziehungen weiterhin zu erhalten.
- Informieren Sie die Kundin, dass man die Sache an ein Inkassounternehmen weiterleiten müsste, falls bis dahin keine Zahlung eintrifft.
- Formulieren Sie einen geeigneten Schlusssatz.

Using social media to deal with complaints

Many people believe that the internet is an ideal medium through which to express their dissatisfaction with a company's products or services. Often customers communicate this way in addition to complaining directly to the company concerned, because that way complaints are usually dealt with much more quickly. As such, more and more companies are monitoring social media websites so that they can respond quickly to customer complaints, and in some way limit any bad publicity they may receive. But once a complaint is made, it is often too late for a company to practise damage limitation.

Dave Carroll, a member of a Canadian folk group, has been in a real life David and Goliath battle with United Airlines over a broken guitar on YouTube. Whilst sitting on a plane, Dave said that he saw some guitars being thrown to the ground by baggage handlers.

When Dave arrived at his destination, he found out that his Taylor guitar had been badly damaged. This was despite the fact that it had been carefully packed in a padded, double case.

So, Dave made a claim for compensation, but was told by the airline that his claim was submitted too late, because it had been made after their standard 24-hour claim-deadline period had expired. Dave corresponded with the airline by letter and email for around nine months trying to resolve the issue, but eventually he got so fed up that he decided to write a song and make a music video about his experience.

The song he wrote is called *United breaks guitars*. Within one day of it being posted on YouTube, United Airlines contacted Dave to try to resolve the matter. After a short period of time, the video had received over 10 million hits. In the meantime Dave's career took off.

Much to the embarrassment of United Airlines, the story behind the song was reported by the media all over the world. As soon as United Airlines became aware of the issue, they said they would pay the repair costs for Dave's guitar, and give him some free flight vouchers. Dave, however, told United Airlines to give the money to charity.

As a result of this, United Airlines said they would be changing their customer-service policy. Dave still chooses to fly with United Airlines, even though on a later flight they lost his luggage!

14 Understanding the text and further discussion

A Complete the following statements about the text.

1. Consumers choose to use social media to make complaints because …
2. Before his flight took off Dave saw …
3. Dave's claim for compensation was …
4. Dave chose to write a song because …
5. In the end, United Airlines offered …, but …

B In groups, choose one of the following points and discuss it further.

1. What are some of the advantages of using social media to make complaints?
2. What are some of the disadvantages for companies when their customers use social media to complain about faulty goods and/or bad service?

UNIT 10

Applying for a job abroad

- Understanding job advertisements
- Writing CVs and cover letters
- Preparing for a telephone interview

1 Warm-up

a

b

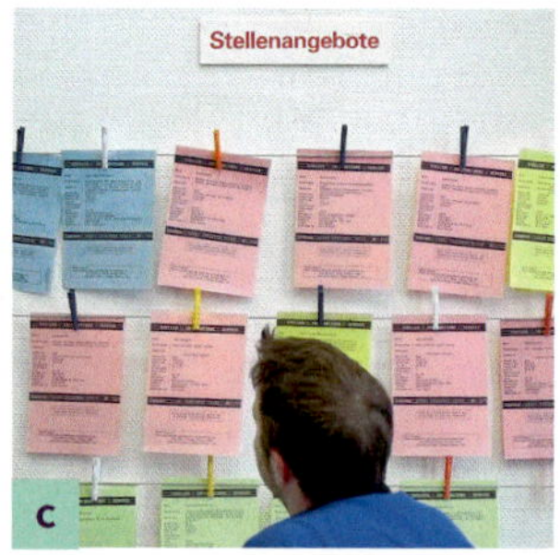

c

A **What do you need to think about before looking for a job? Look at the photos and the language box for help.**

B **How do you look for a job in …**

1 Germany? **2** abroad?

C **How did you find your job?**

LANGUAGE

Applying for a job / an internship / a work placement

source of job
- job centre (BE)
- employment centre (AE)
- recruitment agency
- advertisement
- on the internet
- in a publication (newspaper/magazine)

job application
- CV/curriculum vitae (BE)
- résumé (AE)
- certificate(s)
- reference(s)
- an applicant
- to apply for …
- a post/position/job as …
- a work placement/an internship

2 Advice about job hunting

Sebastian Hartmann is a trainee at RWE in Essen. He plans to work abroad after finishing his traineeship and today he is talking to his friend Jessica Bell on Skype about job applications.

A Read their conversation and then say why Jessica is so stressed.

Jessica Hi, Sebastian.
Sebastian Hi, Jess. How are things?
Jessica Let's just say I'll be feeling a lot better this time tomorrow!
Sebastian Oh?! Why's that?
Jessica I'm stressed out at the moment. I've got my interview tomorrow and I'm afraid they'll ask me horrible questions I can't answer!
Sebastian They will, but I'm sure you're well prepared, Jess. What sort of job is it?
Jessica It's an IT job at PetroChem. I was very surprised I was short-listed for the job.
Sebastian They must have liked your application. Can you give me any tips? I want to apply for some jobs abroad soon myself, and I'd like to make my application more attractive.
Jessica Well, over here most employers use a recruitment agency. The agency publishes advertisements on its website, selects the best applications, and sends them to the employer.
Sebastian Oh really! Can't you just write to the employer directly?
Jessica You can, but companies get so many applications for a job these days that they prefer to get a recruitment agency to make a short-list for them.
Sebastian Is that how you got your interview tomorrow?
Jessica Yes, that's right, but first I got expert advice from the college careers advisor, and she told me I had to tailor my CV to each job I applied for. I then registered with some recruitments agencies, looked at the advertisements, and researched the companies thoroughly before I started writing my CV. Each time I found an interesting job, I looked at every word of the description and made sure my profile fitted exactly what they wanted.
Sebastian I'm sorry but I'm not quite sure what you mean by 'profile'.
Jessica A British CV has a section called "Profile" at the beginning. It's the part of the CV you see first, and in it you show that you are the perfect person for the job. If your profile's good, the recruitment agency reads the rest of the CV. If it isn't, they bin it. In Britain they look at your CV for about 20 seconds. That's how much time you've got to make a good impression.
Sebastian So you need a really good photo and good paper too, I suppose.
Jessica There's no photo on a CV here because that could prejudice the employer and most communication is by email, so the paper is less important than the layout – just keep it simple.
Sebastian Well that's very different from Germany.
Jessica Oh really? The hardest thing about my CV was getting all the important facts onto two pages. I had to choose the right headings and sell myself. Anyway, I've got three interviews now.
Sebastian Wow, that's great! Listen, I don't want to keep you, so good luck tomorrow!
Jessica Thanks. Bye.
Sebastian Bye.

B **Complete the following sentences about the dialogue in your own words.**

1 Sebastian tries to reassure Jessica that …
2 We know that there are still other applicants for the job Jessica wants because …
3 Sebastian would like Jessica to …
4 Sebastian was surprised to hear that …
5 Jessica was advised to …
6 The "profile" section of a British CV is …

3 Understanding job advertisements

A **Read the job advertisement for Energy International plc and then complete the statements with a, b or c.**

1 The job is in …
a Germany.
b England.
c North America.

2 The pay is about £ 25,000 …
a per month.
b per project.
c per year.

3 The person employed will …
a help the team leader.
b be the team leader.
c work in Germany.

4 The person employed will …
a translate complaints.
b deal with complaints.
c make complaints.

5 The person employed …
a must have experience of customer services.
b needn't have experience of customer services.
c will receive training in customer services.

6 The job advertised is …
a never stressful.
b always stressful.
c sometimes stressful.

Energy International plc –
safe solutions in a fast-moving world

German-speaking Customer Services Specialist

Location	London, UK
Salary	£23,000–£27,000 per annum
Sector	Customer services
Job type	Permanent

Job description: duties include
– Supporting sales team and team leader for German market on a day-to-day basis
– Dealing with customer enquiries
– Ensuring accurate order processing from order to invoice
– Resolving complaints quickly and efficiently

Person specification
– Customer services experience essential
– Good MS Office knowledge essential
– Excellent spoken and written English
– Fluent German speaker
– Excellent soft and teamwork skills
– Confident and calm under pressure
– Learns and adapts quickly
– Builds rapport with customers and staff

Submit your application to
Ms J Winters, Recruitment Manager,
Energy International plc, Century House,
99 Prince William Street

B **Match the highlighted words in the job ad to their German equivalents.**

1 erforderlich
2 selbstbewusst
3 gute Beziehungen
4 Reklamationen
5 Aufgaben
6 fließend
7 Rechnung
8 Bewerbung

GRAMMAR

Comparatives and superlatives

1 My working hours are **shorter** than yours, but Paul's are the **shortest**.
2 Jane's boss is **happier** than mine, but Zara's is the **happiest**.
3 I hope I feel a lot **better** after my job interview tomorrow.
4 He wore his **best** clothes to the interview.
5 I always feel **worst** the night before an interview.
6 The layout of your application is just **as important as** the content.
7 For me, a job in sales is **more attractive than** a job in financial controlling.

- Einsilbige Adjektive werden mit *-er* und *-est* gesteigert (1).
- Zweisilbige Adjektive, die auf *-y* enden, werden auf ähnliche Weise gesteigert, wobei auf die Schreibweise zu achten ist (2).
- Zweisilbige Adjektive, die nicht auf *-y* enden, und längere Adjektive werden mit *more/less* und *most/least* gesteigert (7).
- Einige Adjektive haben unregelmäßige Steigerungsformen (3–5).
- Vergleiche bildet man mit *as … as* (so … wie) (6), und *than* (als) (7).

4 Practice

Employer	Kwikpak Ltd	Energy International plc	Parker IT Services
Working hours per week	40 (45-minute paid break)	38 (30-minute unpaid break)	42 (45-minute paid break)
Hourly rate	£18	£20	£25
Overtime pay	Time off (or) 25% for first five hours 50% for any longer	Time off (or) 25% for first two hours 50% for any longer	Time off (or) 50% more per extra hour
Holiday days p.a.	20	25	30

Read the table and then complete the sentences with the comparative or superlative of the adjectives from the box.

attractive • bad • few • generous • good • healthy • high • long • low • short

1 Working hours at Parker IT Services are … at Energy International.
2 Working hours at Kwikpak Ltd aren't … at Energy International.
3 A paid lunch break is … an unpaid one.
4 Lunch-break arrangements are … at Energy International.
5 The hourly pay rates at Kwikpak Ltd are the … .
6 Overtime pay at Kwikpak is … at Energy International. Parker IT Services have the … overtime pay.
7 Doctors say that taking time off work is … getting payment for overtime.
8 Parker IT Services have the … holiday arrangements, whereas employees at Kwikpak Ltd are given the … holiday days per year.

5 Writing a CV

WEBCODE **INDMU1001**

Sebastian applies for the job at Energy International plc and models his CV on Jessica's.

A **Use Sebastian's CV and the Skype dialogue in exercise 2 to list the differences between a British and a German CV.**

B **Which differences surprise you? Explain why to your partner.**

Sebastian Hartmann
Cranger Str. 251, 45891 Gelsenkirchen, Germany
Landline: 0049 209 36549931 Mobile: 0049 176 3960024
Email: sebastian.hartmann@linkall.de

PROFILE

Final year commercial trainee about to obtain a professional qualification from the Essen Chamber of Commerce as an Industrial Business Management Assistant. Offering problem-solving skills, able to work both independently and in a team, and deliver results under pressure. Seeking to use existing skills and education in sales and customer services with opportunities for development.

KEY ACCOMPLISHMENTS

- Member of winning team in trainees' Team Project Management Competition at RWE AG
- Optimized intranet webpages for RWE trainees
- Played a key role in organizing a programme for Norwegian trainees visiting RWE

KEY SKILLS

Professional
- Accountancy, Business Studies, Human Resources, Economics
- Excel, Microsoft Word, PowerPoint

General
- Experienced in planning and coordinating projects during traineeship and at school
- Native speaker of German
- Fluent written and spoken English
- Excellent command of written and spoken French

PROFESSIONAL TRAINING

Aug 2009 – present **Trainee Industrial Business Management Assistant**
RWE AG, Essen, Germany

- 2 ½-year dual system traineeship programme
- Block release attendance of Gelsenkirchen Vocational Training College
- Subjects taken: Business Studies, Accountancy, IT, Commercial English, Business Processes

EDUCATION

June 2009 **German Higher Education Entrance Qualifications *(Abitur)***
Max-Planck Gymnasium (grammar school), Gelsenkirchen, Germany (2000–2009)

- Final grade: 2.0 (merit)
- Major subjects: English, Physics
- Minor subjects: German, French, Mathematics, Social Studies, History, Biology, Sport, Literature
- Awarded Appolinaire Prize in French

WORK EXPERIENCE

June 2010	**Commercial Services, University of York, UK** Gained valuable professional and personal insights into English working life and culture
July 2008	**Gelsenkirchen City Utilities** Became skilled in face-to-face and telephone interaction with corporate and private customers

HOBBIES & INTERESTS

Climbing, skiing, reading, music, travel

PERSONAL DETAILS

Date of birth:	26 January 19..
Nationality:	German
Marital status:	Single
Driving licence:	Full driving licence

REFERENCES

Available on request

TIP

Sell yourself

You should use as many positive statements in your CV as possible; each one should boost your application.
To boost his image, Sebastian uses two positive headings in his CV (*key accomplishments* and *key skills*) and a number of positive words and expressions such as *offering, able to, optimized, troubleshooter, boosted, experienced in*, etc.
Remember: *"Your application is a product with a price tag. Make sure it sells."*

6 Language for CVs

A Use the words from the box to complete the following profile.

awarded • boosted • challenging • experienced in • key • optimized • powerful • wide

Profile
Team player ...[1] working in many different fields. Able to find solutions in ...[2] situations. Offering a ...[3] range of skills and abilities. ...[4] sales by 50% last year. Played a ...[5] role in setting up the company's intranet. Developed a ...[6] online tool to deal with FAQs. ...[7] order procedures resulting in greater efficiency. ...[8] a Grade A for a Fair Trade project in final year of traineeship.

B Match the CV headings (1–9) with the meanings (a– i).

1	profile	**a**	what you do in your free time
2	key accomplishments	**b**	your qualifications from school, further and higher education
3	key skills	**c**	the temporary jobs you have had
4	professional training	**d**	age, nationality, etc.
5	education	**e**	the section of the CV in which you say who you are, what you can do and what you want to do
6	work experience	**f**	the most important things you have done so far
7	hobbies & interests	**g**	people who think you will do the job well
8	personal details	**h**	the job you have learned to do
9	references	**i**	your most important abilities

7 Sebastian's cover letter

Use the expressions (a–j) to complete Sebastian's cover letter.

a Although I have been offered
b I look forward to
c became proficient in
d has confirmed my interest in
e I am a native speaker of
f I am available for interview
g I was extremely interested
h it has taught me to
i I quickly adapted to
j Vacancy for

Sebastian Hartmann
Cranger Str. 251
45891 Gelsenkirchen
Germany

16 April 20..

Ms J Winters
Recruitment Manager
Energy International plc
Century House
99 Prince William Street
EC4V 4DD
LONDON
ENGLAND

Dear Ms Winters

…[1] **customer services specialist with fluent German**

…[2] to read your advertisement for a fluent German speaker in customer services, since this precisely fits my career plans.

…[3] German and first became interested in the energy sector when I did a four-week work placement at Gelsenkirchen City Utilities in Germany during the summer vacation in 2008. Before my traineeship at RWE, I completed a further work placement in the Commercial Services department of the University of York, where I enjoyed the hands-on approach to delivering services and …[4] spoken English. …[5] the new English-speaking working environment and enjoyed it immensely.

My traineeship at the RWE energy company …[6] the field of energy provision, and enabled me to use my skills in working with people, both as a team player and service provider. In particular, …[7] be customer-focused and get the best out of a team within a tight time frame, which helped my team to win the Team Project Management Competition for Trainees.

…[8] a permanent contract at RWE, I wish to make use of both my professional and linguistic skills and feel sure that the vacancy at your company would be ideal for me.

…[9] at any time except for the first two weeks of June when my final examinations take place. My CV is enclosed for your consideration, and …[10] hearing from you at your earliest convenience.

Yours sincerely

Sebastian Hartmann

Sebastian Hartmann

Enc

LANGUAGE

Writing a cover letter

Showing interest and suitability

I was extremely interested to see/read your advertisement for the post of …
I wish to gain experience in … / make use of my foreign language skills.
I feel sure that your company/organization has the post I am looking for.
I believe I am particularly suited for the post advertised because …

Describing your skills

As a native speaker of French/German/Spanish/English, …
I am fluent in (spoken and written) …
I have a good knowledge of …

Talking about previous experience

Before/After my traineeship, I completed a work placement at … in the … department.
My experience/traineeship at … has confirmed my interest in …
My traineeship has enabled me to use/develop my skills in …

Expressing availability for an interview / the job

I am available for an interview immediately / at short notice / at a week's notice / as from …
I would be able to start work any time after …
I very much look forward to hearing from you at your earliest convenience.

8 Tailoring your application

A **Tailor your own CV to fit the vacancy advertised by Recruitnet. It is at Kwikpak Ltd. Make sure you use positive language to boost your image and most of the headings in Sebastian's CV.**

B **Use the contact details and the expressions in the language box above to write a cover letter to Kwikpak Ltd in the form of a letter or an email to accompany your CV.**

Our client has an excellent opportunity for a German-speaking credit controller to join their team reporting to the office manager. Your duties for this role will include general administration, resolving account queries, making credit decisions regarding the dispatch of goods and chasing customers for overdue monies whilst building rapport with both customers and internal branch staff. The job would ideally suit a good team player able to work well under pressure. The successful candidate must be fluent in both written and spoken German. If you are a fluent German speaker send us your CV. We promise to respond within 48 hours.

Contact details: Mrs Deborah Sharples, Human Resources Director, Kwikpak Ltd, 40 Tanners Drive, MILTON KEYNES, MK14 5BW, ENGLAND,
email: deborah.sharples@kwikpak.co.uk.

9 Choosing the right candidate

21

Jennifer Winters, Head of Human Resources at the British company Energy International plc, carries out telephone interviews with candidates applying for the job of German-speaking Customer Sales Representative.

A Listen to the interviews and complete the table below.

	Interview 1	Interview 2	Interview 3
Name	*Tobias Klein*	*Bianca Tiemeyer*	*Sebasatian Hartmann*
Present employer?	*Atlas Machinery in Frankfurt*	*Tiemeyer Import/ Export in Dortmund*	*RWE in Essen*
Strengths?	*- good at work and school* *- team ...1*	*- good at English* *- ...2* *- honest* *- hard-working*	*- teamwork* *- taking the ... 3* *- working independently* *- ...4*
Weaknesses?	*- forgets important things*	*- ...5* *- own standards too high*	*- lack of ...6*
Why this job?	*- wants to work in Manchester*	*- thinks she is best ...7* *- would like to work ...8*	*- has the necessary skills* *- link with Germany* *- likes working in UK*
Future plans?	*- wants a ...9* *- wants to be independent and free*	*...10*	*- wants to develop in job, gain experience and study in evenings*
Own questions?	-	*- would like some help with ...11*	*- ...12*

B In your exercise books, add another column to the table with the heading 'Interview 4 – Me'. Then fill in your own answers to the interviewer's questions.

Interview 1	Interview 2	Interview 3	Interview 4 – Me

C Explain why you think each applicant is suitable/unsuitable for the job.

10 Interaktion

Work with a partner and act out the role-play.

Situation
There is a job vacancy at Energy International plc. Jennifer/John Winters, Head of Human Resources, calls an applicant for a telephone interview. Take turns to act out each role with the help of the points below.

Jennifer/John Winters

- Introduce yourself.
- Suitable time for phone call?
- Ask the candidate to talk about their CV.
- How would the candidate describe themselves?
- How would the candidate's colleagues describe him/her?
- Is the candidate a team player? Examples?
- Hobbies?
- Strengths and weaknesses?
- Reason for deciding to train as …
- Expectations of the job?
- Why should this particular candidate be chosen?
- Questions?

Applicant

- Introduce yourself.
- Say that this is a suitable time for phone call.
- Talk about your CV.
- Describe yourself from your own point of view and from that of your colleagues.
- Give examples of how you are a team player.
- Describe your hobbies.
- Describe your strengths and weaknesses.
- Give reasons for choosing this career.
- Describe what you expect from the job.
- Justify why you should be chosen for the job.
- Ask any questions you may have.

Virtual job-hunting: Technology fills situations vacant

By Rory Cellan-Jones, Technology correspondent, BBC News

Ready for your close-up? Graeme Anthony's video CV got him the job he was looking for.

Looking for a job – or trying to find a new employee? Then prepare for a technological revolution. New tools, many of them related to the explosion in the use of social media, are transforming the recruitment world.

Until recently, the process of seeking a job followed a familiar routine – scan the newspaper recruitment pages, or visit an agency, then despatch your carefully prepared CV (or resume if you're American) in all directions. Now though, those who want to stand out in a crowded job market are resorting to more sophisticated approaches. A search on YouTube throws up plenty of examples of the new breed of job-seeker, promoting themselves with video offerings. Among them is Graeme Anthony, who needed to get a new job in PR in a hurry when he moved from Manchester to London. His YouTube C.V.I.V. – curriculum vitae interactive video – is simple but effective. He sits behind a table pitching his skills, and then links appear to more videos giving greater detail. "It brings me to life in a completely new way," he explains, "It shows off my personality in a way a paper CV can't. It's got the wow factor."

It worked. When London's Frank PR agency saw the video, Graeme was quickly invited for an interview, and got the job. Graham Goodkind, chairman and founder of Frank PR, says he's surprised that so few candidates resort to hi-tech tricks. "It's always amazed me in this day and age, that when things are moving so quickly from a technological point of view, CVs and resumes are really the same as they were 10, 15 or even 20 years ago. So this really opened up our eyes to how it really could be done, and we wanted to meet the guy straight away."

Source: abridged from: www.bbc.co.uk/news/business-12194581

11 Understanding the text

Do the following tasks based on the text.

1. Outline the traditional method of looking for a job.
2. Describe how Graeme Anthony looked for a job.
3. Explain what he means by the "wow factor".
4. Describe Graham Goodkind's reaction when he saw Graeme Anthony's video CV.

12 Videos about yourself

Graeme Anthony made six videos of himself, each 1–3 minutes long. He also used background music. In groups of three to four, make a series of videos of each group member. Use Graeme Anthony's ideas or your own ideas to structure your videos.

Video 1 – About me / **Video 2** – Contact / **Video 3** – Introduction / **Video 4** – Portfolio / **Video 5** – Timeline / **Video 6** – Skills

File 1: Unit 2, Exercise 3A, page 18

Student A:

Use the floor plan on page 17 and the language box on page 18.
Ask your partner for directions to the people in column A.
Give your partner directions to the people in column B. Begin like this:

Student A: Excuse me. Do you speak English?
Student B: Yes, I do. How can I help you?
Student A: I'd like to …

A	B	
Person you wish to see	**Person**	**Office**
Ms Angenendt	Mr Bauerdiek	Commercial Director, spare parts sales
Mr Geide	Mr Gönthör	accounts
Mr Goroll	Ms Hayder	financial controlling
Mr Hoffmann	Mr Klossek	human resources
Mr Komnik	Dr Lentz	design
Mr Lux	Ms Raue	project management
Mr Sauerwald	Mr Sieke	quality management

File 2: Unit 3, Exercise 11, page 34

Student B:

You work for Skater Style in the sales department. You receive a phone call from a customer in the UK who would like to order some baseball caps from you.

- Details of the order?
- Reference to website on page 34 to see availability of items
- Suggest alternatives if items not available
- Take order
- Order will be sent out tomorrow
- Thank the customer

File 3: Unit 4, Exercise 4, page 40

Student A:

You are responsible for making travel reservations for your colleagues.
A colleague calls you. Answer the phone using your own name and offer your help.
Be polite and make small talk with your colleague.

You require the following information:

- Destination
- Departure date
- Return date

You will take care of the reservations and pass on the details.

File 4: Unit 4, Exercise 10, page 44

Student B:

You are a receptionist at the Avon View Hotel in Bristol in the UK. Take a phone call and make a reservation using your own name and the information below.

- Rooms available: single room: 22, 23, 24 September; double room only available: 22, 23 September; twin room: 23, 24 September
- Prices: single room: £100 per night; double room: £170 per night; twin room: £90 per person, per night
- Payment methods available: Visa / MasterCard
- Hotel facilities: squash court (closed for repairs), small gym, swimming pool and sauna

File 5: Unit 5, Exercise 9, page 56

Student C:

You are a trainee at your company (own name).

- Introductions and small talk
- Exams in Germany in June
- September best for English trainees' visit
- Room in your house (sister – own flat)
- Can take boy or girl trainee
- Promise to ask friends, family, workmates to find three more families
- German class tests and exams in summer
- Soon after Easter best for visit to UK
- Own ideas

File 6: Unit 5, Exercise 9, page 56

Student A:

You are the training officer at your company (own name). You lead the meeting.

- Introductions and small talk
- Welcome the visitor (Ms Jane / Mr Jack Seymour from the Watermill Brewery in Cumbria, UK)
- Number of English students coming?
  - Age?
  - Knowledge of German?
- Arrival date?
- Preferred accommodation (host family / guest house / hotel)?
- German side will find accommodation
- Date of return visit to UK?
- Will send minutes to all participants
- AOB?
- Finish/Close the meeting

File 7: Unit 8, Exercise 7, page 84

Student B:

You are Ms Ellen Forfang. Read your diary and try to agree on a day and time to meet Ralf Nordstern.

Appointments diary: Ellen Forfang, Statkraft Energi AS

Monday
6 a.m. – 7 a.m.: Personal trainer – jogging
8 a.m. – 9 a.m.: Working breakfast – 1 hour
11 a.m. – 12 p.m.: Meeting with board of directors
12.30 p.m. – 13.30 p.m.: Lunch
3 p.m. – 6 p.m.: Factory visits

Tuesday
6 a.m. – 7 a.m.: Personal trainer – gymnastics
12 p.m. – 1 p.m.: Lunch
5 p.m. – 6 p.m.: Meeting with Finance Director
8 p.m.: Gunner's birthday party

File 8: Unit 9, Exercise 4, page 94

Student B:

You are Giles/Gemma Atkinson from the UK and will be attending a meeting at GEM Foods in Germany next week. Someone from GEM calls you to confirm the dates and times of the meeting.

- Introductions and small talk
- Find out: who will pick you up at the airport/which hotel you'll be staying in/where the meeting will be held
- According to your notes you must be in the conference room next Tuesday by 9.30 a.m.
- Mistake regarding the day and the time of the meeting – you have written in your notes that the meeting begins at 9 o'clock, but you don't arrive until 9.30 a.m.
- Try to resolve the issue

Confirm the day and time of the meeting you have been invited to attend.

File 9: Unit 2, Exercise 3A, page 18

Student B:

Use the floor plan on page 17 and the language box on page 18.
Ask your partner for directions to the people in column A.
Give your partner directions to the people in column B. Begin like this:

Student A: Excuse me. Do you speak English?
Student B: Yes, I do. How can I help you?
Student A: Can you tell me where I can find ..., please?

A	B	
Person you wish to see	**Person**	**Office**
Mr Bauerdiek	Ms Angenendt	purchasing
Mr Gönthör	Mr Geide	Managing Director
Ms Hayder	Mr Goroll	pricing
Mr Klossek	Mr Hoffmann	press design
Dr Lentz	Mr Komnik	logistics
Ms Raue	Mr Lux	service
Mr Sieke	Mr Sauerwald	sales

File 10: Unit 8, Exercise 7, page 84

Student A:

You are Ralf Nordstern. Read your diary and try to agree on a day and time to meet Ellen Forfang.

Terminkalender: Ralf Nordstern, Ritter Starkstromtechnik

Montag
11.00 – 12.30: Gespräch mit Knut Frøshaug, Trondheim Energi AS
13.00 – 14.00: Mittagessen mit Dr. Havermeier, Europower AS
Dienstag
8.00 – 9.30: Geschäftsfrühstück mit Autronica Fire and Security (ca. 1 Stunde)
10.00 – 12.30: Gespräch mit Scandinavian Electric AS
13.00 – 14.00: Mittagessen
15.00 – 16.00: Vortrag Qualitätsmanagement
17.00 – 19.30: Verhandlungen mit Fjordkraft AS

File 11: Unit 3, Exercise 11, page 34

Student A:

You work for a clothing chain in the UK. Call up Skater Style to order some baseball caps. Ask to be put through to the right person.

The baseball caps you are interested in ordering are:

- 30 KoolKult caps – 10 in blue (No. 493828), 10 in black (No. 673982) and 10 in yellow (No. 983726).
- 60 Street Style caps – 25 in blue (No. 387197), 15 in red (No. 329876), 20 in orange (No. 887282).

You would like to have the colours in the quantities specified above; if this is not possible, you are prepared to compromise as you would like the order to be delivered as soon as possible.

File 12: Unit 5, Exercise 9, page 56

Student B:

You are Jane Seymour, Training Officer at the Watermill Brewery in Cumbria, UK.

- Introductions and small talk
- Thanks for allowing students to shadow
- 4 trainees to come to Germany
  - 2 boys, 2 two girls, 18+
  - No knowledge of German
- Good dates: June or September next year?
- Homestay accommodation preferred – chance to experience family life in Germany
- German visit to UK: just before or just after Easter the following year?
- Own ideas

Business documents

1 Certificate of origin

1 Consignor
The Black Horse Co Ltd
Ache Road
Moorgate, LONDON

No. PQ 74459 | ORIGINAL

2 Consignee
The Importing Co Ltd
Queensway
New York, United States of America

3 Country of Origin
European Union - United Kingdom

EUROPEAN UNION

4 Transport details (Optional)
Ship - Filly Noir

5 Remarks

CERTIFICATE OF ORIGIN

6 Item number, marks, numbers, number and kind of packages; description of goods			7 Quantity
10 Cases	Horse New York 1 - 10	Power Units	310 kilos

8 THE UNDERSIGNED AUTHORITY CERTIFIES THAT THE GOODS DESCRIBED ABOVE ORIGINATE IN THE COUNTRY SHOWN IN BOX 3

THE HERTFORDSHIRE CHAMBER OF COMMERCE AND INDUSTRY

Place and date of issue; name, signature and stamp of competent authority

Hatfield

....

....
The Hertfordshire Chamber of Commerce and Industry

2 Irrevocable letter of credit

Advice for the beneficiary

NAME OF ISSUING BANK
ABC Bank Plc, International Division,
1, Broadway, London EC27

Irrevocable documentary credit

Number 62340

Place and date of issue
London 15th April 1998

Place and date of expiry
at counters of advising bank 31st August 2011

Applicant – Playtime Toys Limited, Blisset Street, London W36	Beneficiary – The Orient Toy Company, Cornwall Road North, Hong Kong
Advising Bank – Bank XYZ, Duke Road, Hong Kong Ref. No. –	Amount – HK$ 9,000 (Hong Kong Dollars nine thousand)
Partial Shipments: [ ] allowed [X] not allowed Transhipment: [ ] allowed [X] not allowed	Availability: [ ] by sight payment [X] by acceptance [ ] by negotiation [ ] by deferred payment at against the documents detailed herein
Shipping/despatch/taking in charge from/at Hong Kong for transportation to: Heathrow Airport, London	[X] and beneficiary's draft at 90 days sight on Bank XYZ, Duke Road, Hong Kong

INVOICE IN THREE COPIES ALL ORIGINALLY SIGNED certifying that the goods are in accordance with Playtime Toys Limited Order Number 51 dated 4.2.1998.

AIR WAYBILL evidencing goods dispatched to Playtime Toys Limited London W36 marked "Freight Paid".

PACKING LIST IN TRIPLICATE

We are informed that insurance is being arranged by our principals.

DESCRIPTION OF GOODS

Plastic toy cars

CFR Heathrow Airport, London.

Documents to be presented within 21 days after the date of issuance of the transport document(s) but within the validity of credit.

We hereby issue the Documentary Credit in your favour. It is subject to the Uniform Customs and Practice for Documentary Credits (2007 Revision International Chamber of Commerce, Paris, France, Publication No. 500) and engages us in accordance with the terms thereof. The number and the date of the credit and the name of our bank must be quoted on all drafts required. If the credit is available by negotiation, each presentation must be noted on the reverse of this advice by the bank where the credit is available.

ABC Bank Plc, International Division
1, Broadway, London EC27

This document consists of signed page(s)

3 Commercial invoice

The Black Horse Co Ltd
Ache Road
Moorgate, London

The Importing Co Ltd
Queensway
New York
United States of America

Invoice No: 6789

2	15 HP "Power Units" @ £345.00 each		
	Total value ex works	£690.00	
	FOB Charges plus Insurance Premium	£127.00	
	Sea Freight Charges	£ 90.00	
Marks & Nos.	Total CIF NEW YORK	STG£907.00	
Horse New York 1 - 10	Goods manufactured in UK by A. Power Co. Ltd. Power Road, Peterborough UK		
	Total No. of pieces: 10 cases Net Weight: 292 kilos Gross Weight: 310 kilos Cube: 1.35 cubic metres Despatched per vessel - Filly Noir		
	Certified True & Correct for THE BLACK HORSE CO LTD		

4 Bill of lading

Bill of Lading for Combined Transport shipment or Port to Port shipment

Shipper
P&O NEDLLOYD LTD
BERTH 204/205/206
WESTERN DOCKS,
SOUTHAMPTON

B/L No.: PONLBHX23009678
Reference: LGM0099535

Consignee or Order (for U.S. Trade only: Not Negotiable unless consigned 'To Order')
YUSIF BIN YUSIF FAKHRO
P.O.BOX 214
MANAMA
BAHRAIN

Notify Party/Address (It is agreed that no responsibility shall attach to the carrier or his Agents for failure to notify (see clause 20 on reverse))
YUSIF BIN YUSIF FAKHRO
P.O.BOX 214
MANAMA
BAHRAIN

Place of Receipt (Applicable only when this document is used as a Combined Transport Bill of Lading)
SOUTHAMPTON

Vessel and Voy. No.
OOCL FREEDOM OFM0234

Place of Delivery (Applicable only when this document is used as a Combined Transport Bill of Lading)
PORT OF MINA SULMAN
STATE OF BAHRAIN

Port of Loading
SOUTHAMPTON

Port of Discharge
BAHRAIN

Undermentioned particulars as declared by Shipper, but not acknowledged by the Carrier (see clause 11)

Marks and Nos; Container Nos;	Number and kind of Packages; Description of Goods	Gross Weight (kg)	Measurement (cbm)
POCU0432963 SEAL: 000204	1x20'GP CONTAINER SAID TO CONTAIN		
	20 C/S FCL/FCL	6240.0000	
TEST DATA TEST DATA TEST DATA	TEST DATA FOR REMOTE BILL PRINTING FREIGHT COLLECT SHIPPERS LOAD, STOW & COUNT SHIPPED ON BOARD PER OCEAN VESSEL OOCL FREEDOM AT SOUTHAMPTON ON XXXXXXXXXXXXXXXX FOR P&O NEDLLOYD LIMITED		

TOTAL: PART OF 1x20' CONTAINER(S) ONLY

FREIGHT AND CHARGES:

ORIGIN INLAND HAULAGE CHARGE	P	HAI
ORIGIN TERMINAL HANDLING/LCL SERVICE CHARGE	P	HAI
OCEAN FREIGHT	C	BAH
DESTINATION TERMINAL HANDLING/LCL SERVICE CHARGE	C	BAH
DESTINATION INLAND HAULAGE CHARGE	C	BAH

* Total No. of Containers/Packages received by the carrier	Movement	Freight Payable at
1 PART	FCL/FCL	KANOO, BAHRAIN

Received by the Carrier from the Shipper in apparent good order and condition (unless otherwise noted herein) the total number or quantity of Containers or other packages or units indicated in the box above entitled "*Total No. of Containers/Packages received by the Carrier" for Carriage subject to all the terms and conditions hereof (INCLUDING THE TERMS AND CONDITIONS ON THE REVERSE HEREOF AND THE TERMS AND CONDITIONS OF THE CARRIER'S APPLICABLE TARIFF) from the Place of Receipt or the Port of Loading, whichever is applicable, to the Port of Discharge or the Place of Delivery, whichever is applicable. If the acknowledged tally is of Containers, this indicates that the Container has been packed and sealed by the Merchant at his premises without the Carrier being represented and able to check or verify either the tally of Goods or the stowage, which are consequently unknown to him (See Clause 8). The Merchant accepts that, except by special arrangement or pursuant to Clause 9 hereof, Containers are not weighed by the Carrier at any time. If the Carrier so requires, before he arranges delivery of the Goods one original Bill of Lading, duly endorsed, must be surrendered by the Merchant to the Carrier at the Port of Discharge or at some other location acceptable to the Carrier. In accepting this Bill of Lading the Merchant expressly accepts and agrees to all its terms and conditions whether printed, stamped or written, or otherwise incorporated, not withstanding the non-signing of this Bill of Lading by the Merchant. Without prejudice to the generality of this reference, attention is drawn, inter-alia, to Clause 12 (Shipper's/Merchant's Responsibility), 19 (Dangerous Goods) and 24 (Law & Jurisdiction). 0/t2 IAP 8/t2

Number of Original Bills of Lading	Place and Date of Issue	
2/TWO	PONL BIRMINGHAM 23/09/00	IN WITNESS of the contract herein contained the number of originals stated opposite has been issued, one of which being accomplished, the other(s) to be void.

EXCESS VALUATION: REFER TO CLAUSE 7(3) ON REVERSE SIDE (U.S. TRADE ONLY).....

*** ORIGINAL ***

This Bill of Lading has been printed remotely via the Internet, at the customer's premises.

5 Documentary credit

Deutsche Bank
Musterstadt Branch
P.O. BOX 222777
D-12345 Musterstadt

DOCUMENTARY-CREDIT ISSUANCE
PAGE 1 OF 2

Ihre Nr./Your No.	
Unsere Nr./Our No.	7770550128IA

	Währung/Currency	Betrag/Amount
+05%/-05%	EUR	45.130,00

TELEX : 888833
SWIFT : DEUTDEDE987
PHONE : 0123/456-789 MEIER

PER SWIFT ERLEDIGT
14. FEB 2003

PUSAN BANK
P.O. BOX 5555

SEOUL
KOREA, SUED

BY ORDER OF

FREIZEIT & WELLNESS GMBH
STADTGARTEN 15
D-12345 MUSTERSTADT

WE ISSUE OUR IRREVOCABLE DOCUMENTARY CREDIT IN FAVOUR OF
SUN FUN & WIRELESS LTD.
7TH FLOOR, DONGWOO BLDG.
123 YEOKSAM-DONG, KANGNAM-KU
SEOUL, KOREA 987654
FOR AN AMOUNT OF EUR 45.130,00
AMOUNT IN WORDS
****** ****** ****** ****** ****** FOUR** FIVE** ONE*** THREE* ZERO**
DECIMAL PLACES, IF ANY, AS STATED ABOVE.
UP TO AN AMOUNT OF 05 PERCENT MORE OR 05 PERCENT LESS
AVAILABLE WITH US
BY DEFERRED PAYMENT AT 30 DAYS AFTER BL-DATE.
THE FOLLOWING DOCUMENTS ARE TO BE PRESENTED:

1) SIGNED COMMERCIAL INVOICE 1 ORIGINAL AND 3 COPIES
2) PACKING LIST IN 3-FOLD CONFIRMING THAT ALL PACKING INSTRUCTIONS AS PER APPLICANT'S LETTER DATED 11. FEB 2011 HAVE BEEN COMPLIED WITH
3) FULL SET (3-3) OF CLEAN ON BOARD SHIPPING COMPANY MARINE BILLS OF LADING ISSUED TO ORDER, BLANK ENDORSED, MARKED: FREIGHT PREPAID TO HAMBURG AND NOTIFY APPLICANT WITH FULL ADDRESS.
4) INSPECTION CERTIFICATES ACC. EN13456-4.2B FOR EACH ITEM SHOWING THE FIGURES OF THE ACTUAL ROPE-DIAM, THE ACTUAL BREAKING LOAD AND THE CHEMICAL ANALYSIS OF THE ROPING WIRES

CERTIFICATE OF ORIGIN
EVIDENCING SHIPMENT OF THE FOLLOWING GOODS:
XYZ AS PER ORDER SPECIFICATION NO. 24681359
QUALITY AISI 124 / ...... = 18.000 M +/- 5 PCT,
QUALITY AISI 236 / ...... = 114.000 M +/- 5 PCT.
DDP 20359 HAMBURG

Dokumenten-Akkreditive unterliegen den Einheitlichen Richtlinien und Gebräuchen für Dokumenten-Akkreditive, Revision 2007, ICC
Documentary credits are subject to Uniform Customs and Practice for Documentary Credits, 2007 Revision, ICC Publicatio
Inkassi unterliegen den Einheitlichen Richtlinien für Inkassi, Revision 2007 ICC Publikation Nr. 522. /
Collections are subject to Uniform Rules for Collections, 2007 Revision, ICC Publication No. 522.

Deutsche Bank
Musterstadt Branch
P.O. BOX 222777
D-12345 Musterstadt

DOCUMENTARY-CREDIT ISSUANCE
PAGE 2 OF 2

Ihre Nr./Your No.	
Unsere Nr./Our No.	7770550128IA

	Währung/Currency	Betrag/Amount
+05%/-05%	EUR	45.130,00

TELEX : 888833
SWIFT : DEUTDEDE987
PHONE : 0123/456-789 MEIER

PER SWIFT ERLEDIGT
14. FEB 2003

PUSAN BANK
P.O. BOX 5555

SEOUL
KOREA, SUED

FROM ANY SOUTH KOREAN PORT
TO ANY NORTH SEA PORT SHOWING PLACE OF DELIVERY DDP 20359 HAMBURG
ON 30. APR 2003 AT THE LATEST.
THE CREDIT IS VALID UNTIL 21. MAY 2003.
PRESENTATION OF DOCUMENTS WITHIN 21 DAYS AFTER THE DATE OF SHIPMENT, BUT WITHIN THE VALIDITY OF THE CREDIT.
PARTIAL SHIPMENTS ARE NOT ALLOWED.
TRANSHIPMENT IS ALLOWED.
ADDITIONAL CONDITIONS:
A FEE OF EUR 175,00 OR EQUIVALENT WILL BE DEDUCTED FOM THE PROCEEDS FOR EACH FULL SET OF DOCUMENTS EVEN IF PRESENTED UNDER ONE REMITTANCE LETTER WHEN IT IS NECESSARY TO CONTACT THE APPLICANT VOR APPROVAL OF DISCREPANT DOCUMENTS.
FURTHERMORE WE WILL DEDUCT OUR SWIFT/TELEX CHARGES FOR EACH ADVICE OF PAYMENT.
AN ADDITIONAL FEE OF EUR 50,00 OR EQUIVALENT PER MONTH WILL BE DEDACTED FOR UNPAID DOCUMENTS IN OUR CUSTODY.
PLEASE SEND DOCUMENTS TO THE FOLLOWING ADDRESS: DEUTSCHE BANK AG, MUSTERSTADT BRANCH, FINANZPLATZ 24, 12345 MUSTERSTADT, GERMANY.
PLEASE ADVISE THIS CREDIT TO THE BENEFICIARY WITHOUT ADDING YOUR CONFIRMATION.
PLEASE ADVISE THROUGH
PUSAN BRANCH, KANG NAM BRANCH
1923-33 SEOCHO-KU, SEOCHO-DONG
SEOUL, KOREA
ACC. 012-34-56789-9
ALL CHARGES OTHER THAN OURS ARE FOR ACCOUNT OF THE BENEFICIARY.

PLEASE FORWARD THE DOCUMENTS TO US BY REGISTERED AIRMAIL. PROVIDED THE TERMS AND CONDITONS OF THIS CREDIT HAVE BEEN FULLY COMPLIED WITH AND WE HAVE RECEIVED THE DOCUMENTS; WE SHALL EFFECT PAYMENT AT MATURITY IN ACCORDANCE WITH YOUR INSTRUCTIONS.

DEUTSCHE BANK AG
MUSTERSTADT BRANCH

Dokumenten-Akkreditive unterliegen den Einheitlichen Richtlinien und Gebräuchen für Dokumenten-Akkreditive, Revision 2007, ICC Publikation Nr. 500. /
Documentary credits are subject to Uniform Customs and Practice for Documentary Credits, 2007 Revision, ICC Publication No. 500.
Inkassi unterliegen den Einheitlichen Richtlinien für Inkassi, Revision 2007, ICC Publikation Nr. 522. /
Collections are subject to Uniform Rules for Collections, 2007 Revision, ICC Publication No. 522.

Business letters

RITTER Starkstromtechnik GmbH & Co. KG,
Essener Str. 10a, 57234 Wilnsdorf, Germany [1]

RN/MB [2]
05 May 20… [3]

Silvassa Industries India Ltd [4]
Solitaire Business Centre
20th Floor
Andheri-Kula Road
MUMBAI
400 093
INDIEN

Attn. Mr Sanjeev Khurana, Sales Representative [5]

Dear Mr Khurana [6]

Offer for SCC-D-48 short circuit switches [7]

Many thanks for your enquiry dated 02 May 20.. . We offer tailor-made solutions to customers' specifications. To download more information, please visit our website at www.ritter-starkstromtechnik.de. A brochure on the SCC-D-48 short circuit switch is enclosed for your information. [8]

As regards the goods requested, we are pleased to submit the following quotation:

SCC-D-48 short circuit switch, with pneumatic drive, without cover at €…..00 each

Our price is quoted FCA Wilnsdorf (Incoterms® 2010) and our usual terms of payment for an initial order are letter of credit or cash with order. Delivery is made within approx. 3 months after receipt of order. This offer is valid until 30 June 20.. .

We hope our offer is to your liking, and look forward to doing business with you.

Yours sincerely [9]
RITTER Starkstromtechnik GmbH & Co. KG

[10]

Ralf Nordstern [11]
Export Sales Department

Enc [12]

1 **Letterhead**

2 **Reference initials:** RN = signatory's initials MB = secretary's intials

3 **Date:** Always write the month as a word to avoid confusion. Write the year with four digits.

4 **Inside address:** Write the city in capital letters and the postcode on a separate line in a letter to the UK.

5 **Attention line**

6 **Salutation:** This is linked with the complimentary close (no. 9).

7 **Subject line:** Underlined or bold

8 **Body of the letter:** Starts with a capital letter.

9 **Complimentary close:** This is linked with the salutation (no. 6).

10 **Signature**

11 **Signatory's name:** Written clearly under the signature. Signatory's initials are in no. 2.

12 **Enc** = Enclosure
Encs = Enclosures

Salutation line and complimentary close

You open a letter with	when you	and you close with
Dear Sir or Madam	don't know the person's name	Yours faithfully
Dear Mr/Mrs/Miss …	know the person	Yours sincerely
Dear Ms …	know that the person is female but are not sure whether she is Miss or Mrs	Yours sincerely

Incoterms® 2010

In international trade the eleven Incoterms® 2010 Rules (international commercial terms) are used in contracts of sale to define the rights and obligations of the buyer and seller as regards risk, transport, insurance, packing, customs duty and documentation. They are terms of delivery.

INCOTERMS 2010

RULES FOR ANY MODE OR MODES OF TRANSPORT

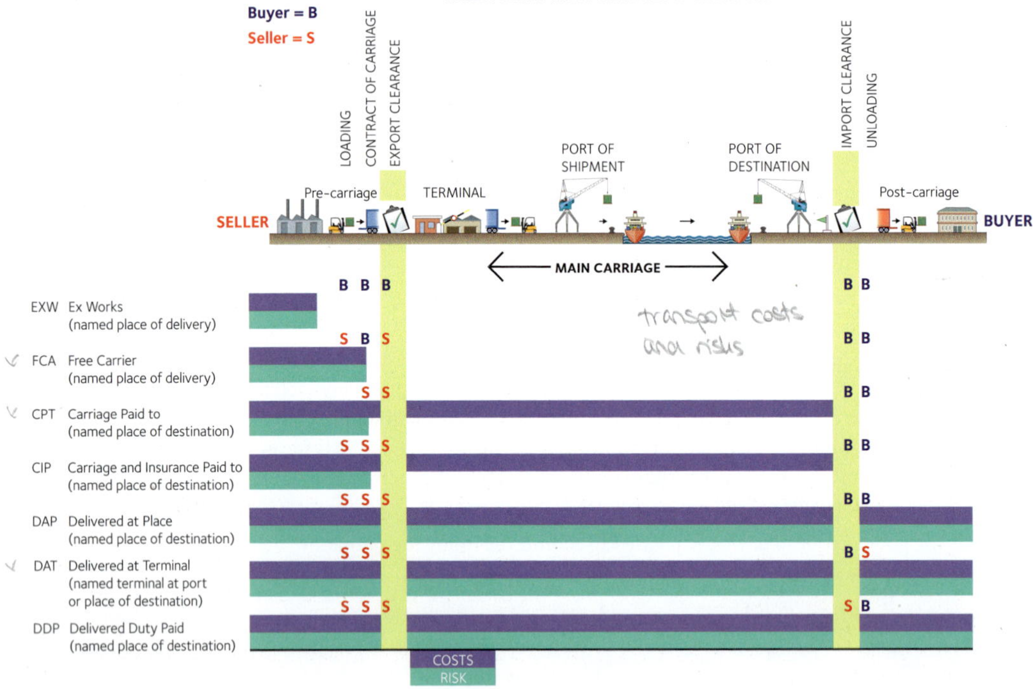

INCOTERMS 2010

RULES FOR SEA AND INLAND WATERWAY TRANSPORT

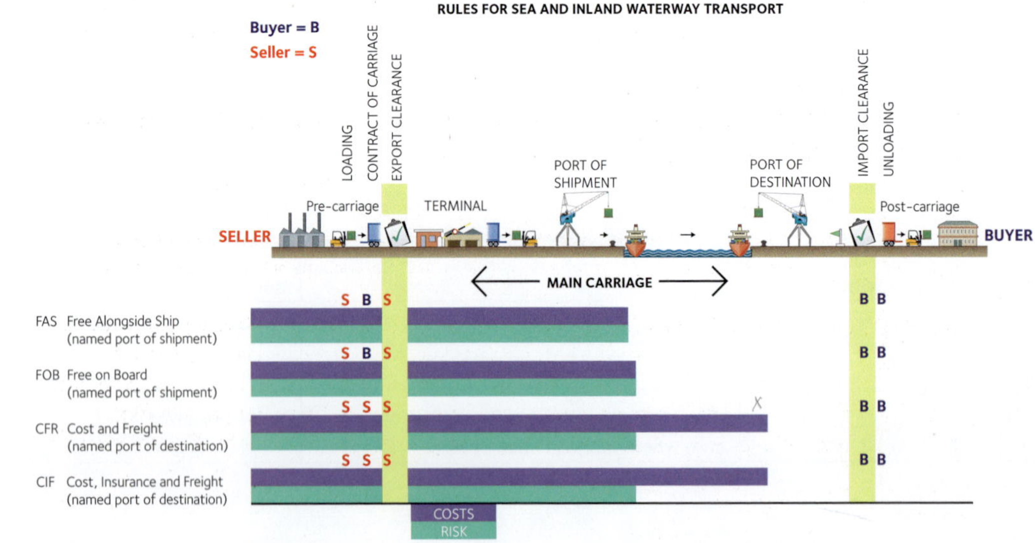

Rules for any mode or modes of transport

EXW – EX WORKS (... named place of delivery)
The seller makes the goods available at his premises in the customary packing. The seller assists the buyer in obtaining any documentation needed at the buyer's expense. The buyer is responsible for loading the goods, transporting them to their destination, customs clearance and insurance.

FCA – FREE CARRIER (... named place of delivery) Multimodal transport
The seller is not responsible for the main carriage of the goods. The seller delivers the goods at his own expense and risk, in the customary packing, cleared for export to the carrier nominated by the buyer. The seller provides the commercial invoice and, if requested, a certificate of origin at the buyer's expense. If the goods are collected at the seller's premises, the seller loads the goods. The seller bears the risks until the goods are in the custody of the first carrier. After that the buyer bears all the costs and risks of transporting the goods to their destination.

CPT – CARRIAGE PAID TO (... named place of destination) Multimodal transport
The seller pays for the main carriage of the goods. The seller delivers the goods, in [illegible] packing, cleared for export to the carrier which he nominates. The seller bears the [illegible] goods have been delivered into the custody of the first carrier. The seller pays the transp[illegible] for the goods, excluding transport insurance, up to the named destination. The buyer is responsible for insuring the goods for the main carriage and pays all import duties and taxes.

CIP – CARRIAGE AND INSURANCE PAID TO (... named place of destination) Multimodal transport
The seller pays for the main carriage of the goods. The seller delivers the goods in the customary packing, cleared for export to the carrier which he nominates. The seller bears the risk until the goods have been delivered into the custody of the first carrier. The seller pays the transport costs for the goods, including transport insurance, up to the named destination. The buyer pays all import duties and taxes.

DAP – DELIVERED AT PLACE (... named place of destination) Multimodal transport
The seller is responsible for the carriage of the goods in the customary packing, cleared for export to the named terminal at the destination by the carrier which he nominates. He bears the risk until the goods have been delivered to the named terminal. The buyer is responsible for unloading the goods at the place of destination and pays all import duties and taxes.

DAT – DELIVERED AT TERMINAL (... named terminal at port or place of destination) Multimodal transport
The seller is responsible for the carriage of the goods in the customary packing, cleared for export to the named terminal at the destination by the carrier which he nominates. He bears the risk until the goods have been delivered to the named terminal. The seller is responsible for unloading the goods at the place of destination. The buyer pays all import duties and taxes.

DDP – DELIVERED DUTY PAID (... named place of destination) Multimodal transport
The seller is responsible for the carriage of the goods in the customary packing, cleared for export to the named terminal at the destination by the carrier which he nominates. He bears the risk until the goods have been delivered to the named destination. The seller pays all import duties and taxes. The buyer is responsible for unloading the goods at the place of destination.

Rules for sea and inland waterway transport

FAS – FREE ALONGSIDE SHIP (... named port of shipment)
The seller is not responsible for the main carriage of the goods. The seller delivers the goods at his own expense and risk, in the customary packing, cleared for export, alongside the vessel selected by the buyer at the named port of shipment. Thereafter, the buyer bears all the costs and risks of transporting the goods to their destination.

FOB – FREE ON BOARD (... named port of shipment)
The seller is not responsible for the main carriage of the goods. The seller delivers the goods at his own expense and risk, in the customary packing, cleared for export, on board the vessel selected by the buyer unless otherwise agreed, at the named port of shipment. Thereafter, the buyer bears all the costs and risks of transporting the goods to their destination.

CFR – COST AND FREIGHT (... named port of destination)
The seller pays for the main carriage of the goods. The seller delivers the goods at his own expense and risk, in the customary packing, cleared for export, on board the vessel selected by the buyer, at the named port of shipment. The seller pays the transport costs for the goods, excluding transport insurance, up to the named port of destination. The buyer is responsible for insuring the goods for the main carriage and pays all import duties and taxes.

CIF – COST INSURANCE FREIGHT (... named port of destination)
The seller pays for the main carriage of the goods. The seller delivers the goods at his own expense and risk, in the customary packing, cleared for export, on board the vessel selected by the buyer, at the named port of shipment. The seller pays the transport costs for the goods, including transport insurance, up to the named port of destination. The buyer pays all import duties and taxes.

Terms of payment

payment in advance	Vorauszahlung/Vorkasse
cash with order (CWO)	Barzahlung bei Auftragserteilung
payment by irrevocable and confirmed documentary (letter of) credit	Zahlung durch unwiderrufliches und bestätigtes Dokumentenakkreditiv
documents against payment (D/P)/ cash against documents (CAD)	Kasse gegen Dokumente
cash on delivery (COD)	gegen Nachnahme
1/3 with order, 1/3 on delivery, 1/3 within 30 days after delivery	1/3 bei Auftragserteilung, 1/3 bei Lieferung, 1/3 innerhalb von 30 Tagen nach Lieferung
payment within 60 days from date of invoice	Zahlung innerhalb von 60 Tagen nach Rechnungsdatum
10 days 2%, 30 days net	Zahlung innerhalb 10 Tagen abzüglich 2 % Skonto oder innerhalb 30 Tagen netto
payment on receipt of goods	Zahlung bei Erhalt der Waren
payment on receipt of invoice	Zahlung bei Rechnungserhalt
documents against (three months') acceptance (D/A)	Dokumente gegen (Dreimonats)akzept
open account terms with monthly/quarterly settlement	offenes Zahlungsziel mit monatlicher/vierteljährlicher Abrechnung

KMK mock exam (Stufe II)

Schriftliche Prüfung

Zeit:	**90 Minuten**
Hilfsmittel:	**allgemeines zweisprachiges Wörterbuch**
Maximale Punktzahl:	**100 Punkte**

Im Rahmen der schriftlichen Prüfung werden die Aufgabenanteile für die drei Kompetenzbereiche wie folgt gewichtet:

- **Rezeption 40 %**
- **Produktion 30 %**
- **Mediation 30 %.**

Im Folgenden werden vier Aufgaben vorgelegt, die Sie bearbeiten sollen. Die erste und die zweite Aufgabe beziehen sich auf Ihre Fähigkeit, englische Texte (gesprochene und geschriebene) zu verstehen = **Rezeption**. In der dritten Aufgabe sollen Sie ein Schriftstück erstellen = **Produktion** eines englischen Textes. Bei der vierten Aufgabe wird von Ihnen erwartet, dass Sie Texte von der deutschen oder englischen in die jeweils andere Sprache übertragen = **Mediation**.

Die Prüfung beginnt mit der Hörverständnisaufgabe. Alle weiteren Aufgaben können in beliebiger Reihenfolge bearbeitet werden.

Rezeption I: Hörverstehen — 20 Punkte

22

Situation: Sie hören Ihren Anrufbeantworter ab, auf dem eine Nachricht eines Anrufers hinterlassen wurde.

Aufgabe:

- Schreiben Sie die persönlichen Daten des Anrufers auf (siehe Telefonnotiz).
- Nutzen Sie dann die Notiz um den Inhalt des Gesprächs in Stichworten auf Deutsch aufzuschreiben.
- Sie hören die Nachricht zwei Mal.

Telefonnotiz	
Für:	...
Name des Anrufers:	...
Firma:	...
Betreff:	...
Kontaktdaten:	...

Rezeption II: Leseverstehen 20 Punkte

Situation: Sie arbeiten bei einem Batteriehersteller als Auszubildende/r. Ihr Vorgesetzter bittet Sie folgenden Text einer englischen Website zu analysieren und zu prüfen inwiefern Brennstoffzellen eine Konkurrenz darstellen könnten.

Aufgabe: Lesen Sie dazu den Text und schreiben Sie sich Notizen zu den folgenden Punkten auf Deutsch auf.

1 Vorteile von Brennstoffzellen	...
2 Nachteile von Brennstoffzellen	...
3 Zukunftsfähigkeit von Brennstoffzellen	...
4 Einsatzmöglichkeiten der Brennstoffzellen	...
5 Funktionsweise der Technik	...

Fuel Cells on Their Way to Success

Small electronic devices provide a new market for commercial fuel cell solutions

Consumers might be on the verge of switching to lower weight and extended operating lifetime of battery-powered devices. This comes as new developments in fuel cell technology have been made public. This technology offers an alternative energy source in an unbelievable variety of applications. Advantages of the cells include close to no emissions, mostly renewable fuels, and a much higher energy capacity compared to present-day batteries. Environmentalists have waited for years – at least since fuel-cell-powered devices were used in the NASA programmes of the 1960s and 70s. The main competitors of fuel-cells are the improved versions of highly effective lithium-batteries for hand-held devices. The commercialization of the new technology has advanced more slowly than expected. This a shame because their costs are rather low. On the other hand, fuel cell technology must provide new security solutions, because consumers will have no peace of mind as long as there is methanol on-board commercial aircraft to power devices such as notebook PCs.

Fuel cells are expected to take over from established energy sources soon. Possible applications for consumer products range from 3 to 20W. This applies to mobile phones, laptops or cameras. A fuel-cell power pack in the size of a drinking can can make a laptop run for about 20 hours – a great plus. By about 2015, it is thought, the fuel cell will come into the mass market offering consumer-oriented solutions concerning safety and size. The technology works by producing electrical power in a chemical reaction between a fuel containing hydrogen (e.g. methanol) and an oxidant. The resulting exchange of ions is used to create an electrical current. Energy is released without burning, which means no poisonous fumes are produced by the reaction. The dominant by-product is water, which gives the fuel cell its appeal as an environmentally friendly energy source. Solid fuels may be able to appease airlines' safety and security concerns surrounding methanol-based fuel cells, and also provide extra opportunities to control energy conversion, and manage the lifetime of the fuel cell.

The first portable power solutions for consumer electronic products, now being prepared for launch, will almost certainly be battery-charging devices, but the final goal for fuel cells has to be the direct replacement of the battery itself.

Produktion (Schriftstücke erstellen) 30 Punkte

Situation: Sie sind Auszubildende/r bei der Süddeutsche Industrie GmbH in Neustadt. Diese Unternehmung stellt Seile und Zubehörteile zur Absicherung von Personen und Gegenständen her. Ihre Vorgesetzte und Abteilungsleiterin des Einkaufs, Frau Gertrud Maßmann, erteilt Ihnen die Aufgabe, bei einem potentiell neuen Zulieferer eine Anfrage zu stellen.

Aufgabe: Ihre Aufgabe besteht darin, einen unterschriftsreifen Brief als Anfrage zu erstellen. Formulieren Sie den gesamten Brieftext einschließlich Anrede und Betreff. Formulieren Sie einen Schlusssatz und gehen Sie von einem Anhang in Form einer Unternehmensbroschüre aus.

- *Brief Anfrage erstellen bei Buckles Europe, ul. Grybowska 30, 00-805 Warsawa, Polen, bereit zur Unterschrift durch mich*
- *Ansprechpartner: Herr Jeszniak, Verkauf*
- *Anfrage über 6500 Schnallen (buckles), BBE 451*349*
- *Haben Schnallen das TÜV-Prüfzeichen?*
- *Rabatte möglich? Garantieleistungen?*
- *Geschäftsbedingungen?, Zahlungsbedingungen?*
- *Teilnahme an Messe in Rom?*

Mediation (Übertragen eines Textes) 30 Punkte

Situation: Sie sollen für eine internationale Projektwoche in Ihrem Betrieb einen Vortrag auf Englisch darüber erstellen, welche Vor- und welche Nachteile Messen mit sich bringen. Der Ihnen vorliegende Eintrag aus einem Online-Lexikon hilft Ihnen bei der Erstellung.

Aufgabe: Geben Sie für Ihre Mitazubis aus unterschiedlichen Ländern in Stichworten auf Englisch nur die Informationen weiter, die von Bedeutung sind. Schließen Sie Wiederholungen aus.

Verkaufsmessen [Bearbeiten]

Messen sind Ausstellungen, die es Unternehmen erlauben ihre Produkte und Dienstleistungen anzubieten, neue Kunden zu erreichen und so neue Umsätze zu generieren. Den Besuchern wird die Möglichkeit gegeben, die Produkte vor Ort zu testen, sie zu betrachten und mit anderen Waren anderer Hersteller zu vergleichen.

Messen ermöglichen es der Industrie neue Kontakte zu finden und alte zu pflegen.

Wenn Messeauftritte gut geplant sind, dann können sie sogar in der Werbestrategie von Unternehmen eine wichtige Rolle spielen.
Eine ergänzende Möglichkeit, Messen zu nutzen, besteht darin, dass potentielle Kunden die Produkte vor Ort ausprobieren oder sich schwer zu verstehende Abläufe demonstrieren lassen. Auf der Messe kann sich auch ein Gespräch mit zukünftigen Kunden ergeben, die an einem Messestand dem Unternehmen Anregungen zur Planung neuer Verfahren oder zur Produktion bis dahin noch unbekannter Produkte gibt. Die Messe ist die seit langem praktizierte Version des schon seit Jahrtausenden bekannten Marktes: viele Anbieter treffen auf viele Nachfrager. Die Messe kann so auch einen Marktpreis von bestimmten Gütern bilden und finden.

Die Vorteile überwiegen zwar, aber man sollte die Nachteile nicht ausblenden: Messeauftritte und die dafür nötigen Reisen, Hotelunterkünfte, Messestände und dergleichen sind vor allem teuer. Ein Unternehmen sollte sich auch vor der Messe darüber im Klaren sein, dass es genau weiß, was es auf der Messe erreichen will. Es ist nicht hilfreich, wenn man nach der Messe zwar keine neuen Verträge in der Tasche hat, aber 5000 Bonbons und 3500 Kugelschreiber weniger, die auf den Messeständen ausgelegt waren. Nach Messen ist eine Evaluation der Ergebnisse nötig.

Mündliche Prüfung

Die Prüfung ist eine Gruppenprüfung, bei der Sie Gespräche persönlichen und fachlichen Inhalts in der Fremdsprache führen sollen. Es wird von Ihnen erwartet, dass Sie der vorgegebenen Situation entsprechend sprachlich agieren und reagieren. Es kommt dabei vor allem darauf an, dass Sie sich spontan äußern, dass Sie versuchen, sich verständlich zu machen, und dass Sie gut zuhören.

Die Prüfung besteht aus zwei Teilen und dauert insgesamt ca. 20 Minuten. Zur Vorbereitung haben Sie 20 Minuten Zeit.
Im **ersten Teil** der mündlichen Prüfung werden Sie gebeten, sich zu persönlichen oder beruflichen Themen zu äußern.
Im **zweiten Teil** sollen Sie zusammen mit einem anderen Kandidaten ein Rollenspiel durchführen. Dazu erhalten Sie vom Prüfer Rollenkarten, auf denen eine Situation beschrieben ist, die Sie vorspielen sollen.

Hilfsmittel: allgemeines zweisprachiges Wörterbuch.

Mündliche Prüfung Teil II — 15 Punkte

Kandidat/in A

Situation: Ihr Name ist Marc/ia Jones. Sie arbeiten im Verkauf der britischen Aktiengesellschaft Plymouth Controls. Ein/e Anrufer/in aus Deutschland kontaktiert Sie um sich nach dem Verbleib einer Warensendung zu erkundigen.

Aufgabe:
- Melden Sie sich am Telefon mit Ihrem Namen und der Abteilung.
- Führen Sie mit dem/r Anrufer/in Small-Talk.
- Überprüfen Sie die Bestellung der Schaltereinheiten am PC und finden Sie heraus, dass es bei der Nachlieferung der Teile aus Spanien Probleme wegen der Überflutung des dortigen Werkes gibt.
- Entschuldigen Sie sich und bieten die Lösung an, dass aus einer polnischen Tochtergesellschaft ähnliche Teile geliefert werden könnten. Die Maße unterscheiden sich nur geringfügig. Die deutsche Produktionsabteilung soll vergleichen, ob die Teile PSXJ 78/3B/ (auf Katalogseite 75) ebenfalls passen.
- Sie bieten einen Rückruf in einer Stunde an.
- Entschuldigen Sie sich erneut und verabschieden sich bis später.

Kandidat/in B

Situation: Sie haben von Ihrer Ausbilderin, Frau Margret Seilmann, die Aufgabe erhalten, einen Zulieferer in Großbritannien zu kontaktieren und sich nach dem Verbleib einer Sendung zu erkundigen. Ihr/e Gesprächspartner/in ist Marc/Marcia Jones von Plymouth Controls, mit der/m Sie schon häufig telefoniert haben.

Aufgabe: Rufen Sie bei Plymouth Controls an.
- Stellen Sie sich vor und freuen Sie sich, wieder einmal mit Marc/ia zu sprechen.
- Führen Sie Small-Talk mit Marc/ia.
- Erkundigen Sie sich nach dem Verbleib der bestellten 250 Schaltereinheiten SXJ 78/3B, die bei Ihnen dringend benötigt werden.
- Drücken Sie Ihr Bedauern über die Überflutung aus, aber weisen Sie darauf hin, dass Sie spätestens bis Ende nächster Woche über die Teile verfügen müssten.
- Notieren Sie sich die angebotene Lösung und versichern Sie, dass Sie diese von der Produktionsabteilung überprüfen lassen werden.
- Akzeptieren Sie das Angebot des Rückrufs und sagen Sie, dass Sie in einer Stunde unter der Nummer (…) erreichbar sein werden.
- Danken Sie für die angebotene Lösung und verabschieden sich bis später.

Useful phrases

Introducing yourself

Unit 1

Greeting people you do not know	Menschen, die man nicht kennt, begrüßen
▪ Good morning/afternoon/evening. I'm …	▪ *Guten Morgen/Tag/Abend. Ich bin …*
▪ How do you do? My name is …	▪ *Wie geht's? Mein Name ist …*
▪ Nice/Pleased to meet you.	▪ *Es freut mich, Sie kennen zu lernen.*
▪ Nice to meet you, too.	▪ *Ganz meinerseits.*
▪ Excuse me. Are you …?	▪ *Entschuldigung. Sind Sie …?*
▪ Yes, I am. / No, I'm not. I'm …	▪ *Ja, das bin ich. / Nein, das bin ich nicht. Ich heiße …*
▪ Welcome to …	▪ *Herzlich willkommen bei …*
▪ Thank you. It's nice to be here.	▪ *Dankeschön. Es ist schön, hier zu sein.*
▪ Hi, I don't think we've met. I'm …	▪ *Hi. Ich glaube nicht, dass wir uns kennen gelernt haben. Ich bin …*

Introducing someone else	Jemanden vorstellen
▪ This is … These are my colleagues, John and Mary.	▪ *Das ist … Das sind meine Kollegen, John und Mary.*
▪ Let me introduce you to …, from the … department.	▪ *Darf ich Ihnen vorstellen, das ist … aus der …-abteilung.*
▪ Have you met …?	▪ *Haben Sie … schon kennen gelernt?*

Giving a presentation

Welcoming the audience	Das Publikum begrüßen
▪ Good morning, ladies and gentlemen and welcome to …	▪ *Sehr geehrte Damen und Herren, ich begrüße Sie zu …*
▪ Hello, everyone. Thank you for coming today. It's good to see you all here.	▪ *Hallo zusammen. Vielen Dank für Ihr heutiges Erscheinen. Schön, dass Sie alle da sind.*
▪ Ladies and gentlemen, I would like to welcome you to this presentation.	▪ *Sehr geehrte Damen und Herren, ich möchte Sie zu diesem Vortrag willkommen heißen.*

Introducing your topic	Ihr Thema vorstellen
▪ The purpose of my presentation is to …	▪ *Das Ziel meiner Präsentation ist …*
▪ Today I'm going to talk about …	▪ *Heute werde ich über … sprechen.*
▪ I'd like to begin by giving you a presentation about …	▪ *Ich möchte mit einem Vortrag über … anfangen.*

Structuring the presentation	Die Präsentation strukturieren
▪ I have divided my talk into three main parts. Part one deals with …, part two …, part three …	▪ *Ich habe meinen Vortrag in drei Hauptteile unterteilt. Der erste Teil behandelt …, der zweite Teil …, der dritte Teil …*
▪ My presentation consists of three parts. I'll begin with …, then move on to … and after that I'll tell you …	▪ *Mein Vortrag setzt sich aus drei Teilen zusammen. Ich fange mit … an, gehe dann über zu … und danach erzähle ich …*

Moving on to the next point	Zum nächsten Punkt überleiten
▪ Now, let's move on to our next point …	▪ *Nun komme ich zum nächsten Punkt …*
▪ Let's now take a look at …	▪ *Schauen wir uns nun einmal … an.*
▪ Now let's turn to …	▪ *Wenden wir uns nun … zu.*

Describing visuals	Illustrationen beschreiben
▪ As you can see from this slide/chart/diagram/table …	▪ *Wie Sie an dieser Folie / dieser Grafik / diesem Diagramm / dieser Tabelle sehen können …*
▪ This pie chart shows … . You can see that the biggest segment indicates the …	▪ *Dieses Kuchendiagramm zeigt … . Sie können sehen, dass das größte Segment/Kuchenstück … angibt.*
▪ These illustrations show …	▪ *Diese Abbildungen zeigen …*
▪ I'd like to draw your attention to this organizational chart.	▪ *Ich möchte Ihre Aufmerksamkeit nun auf dieses Organigramm lenken.*

Dealing with questions	Mit Fragen umgehen
▪ If you have any questions, please feel free to interrupt.	▪ *Wenn Sie irgendwelche Fragen haben, unterbrechen Sie mich einfach.*
▪ I'd prefer to answer any questions after finishing my presentation.	▪ *Ich möchte Fragen lieber nach dem Vortrag beantworten.*
▪ Now if you'd like to ask any questions, I'd be delighted to answer them.	▪ *Wenn Sie noch Fragen haben, würde ich sie gerne jetzt beantworten.*
Conclusion	**Schluss**
▪ To sum up …	▪ *Zusammenfassend …*
▪ I'd like to finish my presentation with …	▪ *Ich würde meinen Vortrag gerne mit … schließen.*
▪ And finally, …	▪ *Und schließlich …*
▪ In conclusion …	▪ *Abschließend …*

Asking for and giving directions — Unit 2

Asking for directions	Nach dem Weg fragen
▪ Excuse me, I'm looking for …	▪ *Entschuldigung, ich suche …*
▪ Can you tell me where I can find …, please?	▪ *Können Sie mir sagen, wo ich … finde, bitte?*
▪ Could you tell me the way to …, please?	▪ *Können Sie mir den Weg nach … beschreiben?*
▪ Do you happen to know …?	▪ *Wissen Sie vielleicht …?*
Giving directions	**Den Weg beschreiben**
▪ Please take one of the lifts/elevators to the first floor.	▪ *Bitte nehmen Sie einen der Aufzüge in den ersten Stock.*
▪ When you come out of the lift, turn left/right.	▪ *Wenn Sie aus dem Aufzug kommen, gehen Sie nach links/rechts.*
▪ Continue to the end of the corridor.	▪ *Gehen Sie weiter bis zum Ende des Flurs.*
▪ Go straight ahead/on.	▪ *Gehen Sie geradeaus.*
▪ It's the first door on the right, just after …	▪ *Es ist die erste Tür auf der rechten Seite, gleich hinter …*
▪ to the right/left of …	▪ *nach rechts/links von …*
▪ You'll find it between the … and the …	▪ *Sie sehen es zwischen … und …*
▪ It's just next to …	▪ *Es ist genau neben …*
▪ Go upstairs/downstairs.	▪ *Gehen Sie die Treppe hoch/runter.*

Making a telephone call — Unit 3

Making a call	Telefonieren
▪ Good morning. My name is …	▪ *Guten Morgen. Ich heiße …*
▪ Good afternoon. This is … from (company).	▪ *Guten Tag. Hier spricht … von (Unternehmen).*
▪ I'd like to speak to Mr/Mrs/Ms/Miss …	▪ *Ich hätte gern Herrn/Frau … gesprochen.*
▪ Could you put me through to the … department, please?	▪ *Könnten Sie mich zur …-abteilung durchstellen, bitte?*
▪ Is your Managing Director available at the moment?	▪ *Ist Ihr Geschäftsführer gerade zu sprechen?*
Making small talk	**Smalltalk halten**
▪ How are you?	▪ *Wie geht es Ihnen?*
▪ How's the weather today?	▪ *Wie ist das Wetter bei Ihnen heute?*
▪ Did you have a nice holiday?	▪ *Haben Sie einen schönen Urlaub gehabt?*
Saying what the call is about	**Sagen Sie, worum es bei dem Anruf geht**
▪ I'm interested in …	▪ *Ich interessiere mich für …*
▪ I was wondering if you could help me.	▪ *Ich wollte fragen, ob Sie mir weiterhelfen könnten.*
▪ I'm enquiring about …	▪ *Ich wollte mich nach … erkundigen.*
▪ I'd like some information on …	▪ *Ich möchte Informationen zu … erhalten.*
▪ The reason I'm calling is …	▪ *Der Grund, warum ich anrufe, ist …*

Useful phrases

Answering the phone	Ans Telefon gehen
Good morning, Fynton Industries Ltd. How can I help you?	*Guten Morgen, Fynton Industries GmbH. Wie kann ich Ihnen weiterhelfen?*
Hello, … speaking.	*Hallo, hier ist … .*
Asking the caller for more information	**Den Anrufer nach mehr Informationen fragen**
Could you tell me what it's about, please?	*Könnten Sie mir bitte sagen, worum es geht?*
May I ask why you're calling?	*Darf ich fragen, warum Sie anrufen?*
Transferring the call	**Den Anruf weiterleiten**
I'll put you through to …	*Ich leite Sie an … weiter.*
I'll connect you with …	*Ich verbinde Sie mit …*
Can you hold the line for a moment, please?	*Könnten Sie bitte kurz in der Leitung bleiben?*
Explaining that someone is busy	**Erklären, dass jemand gerade keine Zeit hat**
I'm afraid that … is in a meeting at the moment.	*Es tut mir leid, … ist gerade in einer Besprechung.*
I'm sorry, but … isn't available at the moment.	*Es tut mir leid, aber … ist gerade nicht erreichbar.*
I'm afraid his/her line is engaged.	*Es tut mir leid, sein/ihr Anschluss ist besetzt.*
Can I get him/her to call you back?	*Kann ich ihm/ihr ausrichten, dass er/sie Sie zurückrufen soll?*
Can I take a message?	*Kann ich etwas ausrichten?*
Would you like to leave a message?	*Würden Sie gerne eine Nachricht hinterlassen?*
What number can he/she reach you on?	*Unter welcher Nummer kann er/sie Sie erreichen?*
Saying what you want to do	**Sagen, was Sie tun wollen**
Can I leave a message?	*Kann ich eine Nachricht hinterlassen?*
I'll call again later.	*Ich rufe später noch mal an.*
There's a very urgent matter that I need to discuss with you.	*Ich muss mit Ihnen über eine ganz dringende Angelegenheit sprechen.*
Asking the caller to repeat something	**Den Anrufer bitten, etwas zu wiederholen**
Sorry, I didn't catch that.	*Es tut mir leid, das habe ich nicht verstanden.*
Could you say that again, please?	*Könnten Sie das bitte noch einmal sagen?*
Could you spell that for me, please?	*Könnten Sie mir das bitte buchstabieren?*
Ending the call	**Das Telefongespräch beenden**
Is there anything else I can do for you?	*Kann ich noch etwas für Sie tun?*
Thanks for your help/assistance.	*Vielen Dank für Ihre Hilfe/Unterstützung.*
You're welcome. Goodbye.	*Kein Problem / Keine Ursache. Auf Wiederhören.*
Have a nice day/evening.	*Schönen Tag/Abend noch.*

Making travel arrangements — Unit 4

Asking for help making travel reservations	Nach Hilfe zum Buchen einer Reise fragen
Could you take care of our travel and hotel reservations?	*Könnten Sie sich um unsere Reise- und Hotelbuchungen kümmern?*
Can you look after the car rental for me, please?	*Können Sie sich um den Mietwagen kümmern?*
Could you book me a flight to …, please?	*Könnten Sie mir einen Flug nach … buchen?*
Could you possibly look after the arrangements of our trip?	*Könnten Sie unsere Reise-Arrangements überprüfen?*
Asking for details about travel arrangements	**Nach Details zu Reise-Arrangements fragen**
What are the dates of your trip?	*Was sind die Daten Ihrer Reise?*
When are you planning to travel?	*Wann wollen Sie verreisen?*
When will you be returning?	*Wann kommen Sie zurück?*
What time would you like to depart?	*Um wie viel Uhr möchten Sie gerne fliegen?*
Is there anything special I need to know?	*Gibt es irgendetwas Besonderes, das ich wissen sollte?*

Giving details about when you want to travel	Angaben darüber machen, wann man reisen möchte
▪ We'd like to travel early on …	▪ *Wir würden gerne früh am … abreisen.*
▪ I'm going to stay until …	▪ *Ich werde bis … bleiben.*
▪ I'd like to catch a flight early/late in the evening.	▪ *Ich würde gerne einen Flug früh/spät am Abend nehmen.*
▪ Ideally, I'd like to fly out in the early afternoon.	▪ *Im Idealfall würde ich am frühen Nachmittag fliegen.*

Writing an email

Unit 5

Salutation	Begrüßungsformel
▪ Dear Mr/Mrs/Ms/Miss …	▪ *Sehr geehrte(r) …*
▪ Dear Sirs / Dear Sir or Madam	▪ *Sehr geehrte Damen und Herren*
▪ Dear Paul	▪ *Lieber Paul*
Opening sentence	**Einleitungssatz**
▪ How are things?	▪ *Wie geht's dir/Ihnen?*
▪ I hope you're well.	▪ *Ich hoffe, es geht dir/Ihnen gut.*
▪ I am writing to …	▪ *Ich schreibe dir/Ihnen, um zu …*
▪ Just a quick note/message to say …	▪ *Nur eine ganz kurze Bemerkung/Nachricht, um zu sagen, dass …*
Answering or forwarding an email	**Eine E-Mail beantworten oder weiterleiten**
▪ I was delighted to receive your email.	▪ *Ich habe mich sehr über Ihre E-Mail gefreut.*
▪ Thanks for your emails about …	▪ *Vielen Dank für Ihre E-Mails zu …*
▪ I've just received the email below from …	▪ *Ich habe gerade untenstehende E-Mail von … bekommen.*
Giving information	**Auskunft geben**
▪ Please refer to the attachment for …	▪ *Bitte schauen Sie sich den Anhang an, um …*
▪ Click on the link for more details.	▪ *Klicken Sie auf den folgenden Link, um nähere Informationen zu erhalten.*
Closing sentence	**Schlusssatz**
▪ Many thanks for your assistance/help.	▪ *Vielen Dank für Ihre Hilfe.*
▪ Looking forward to …	▪ *Ich freue mich auf …*
▪ I look forward to meeting you.	▪ *Ich freue mich darauf, Sie bald zu treffen.*
Complimentary close	**Grußformel (am Briefende)**
▪ Regards / Best wishes / (*fml*) Yours sincerely	▪ *Mit freundlichen Grüßen*
▪ Yours faithfully	▪ *Hochachtungsvoll*
▪ All the best / Best regards	▪ *Liebe / Schöne Grüße*

Describing trends

▪ to rise/grow negligibly from … to …	▪ *geringfügig von … auf … ansteigen/wachsen*
▪ to go up / increase slightly by …%	▪ *leicht um … % (an)steigen*
▪ to keep stable / remain constant at …	▪ *gleich / konstant bei … bleiben*
▪ to even out at …	▪ *sich bei … ausgleichen*
▪ to fall/drop significantly from … to …	▪ *deutlich von … auf … fallen / zurückgehen*
▪ to go down / decrease considerably by …%	▪ *erheblich um … % sinken / abnehmen*

Useful phrases

Writing a press release — Unit 6

Saying what the company does and where it is based	Sagen, was das Unternehmen macht und wo es seinen Sitz hat
▪ Brinson Operations Ltd, the … company based in …	▪ *Brinson Operations GmbH, das … Unternehmen mit seinem Sitz in …*
▪ Obtrax Plc, the manufacturer of … which has its headquarters in …	▪ *Obtrax Plc, der Hersteller von …, das seinen Hauptsitz in … hat*
Quoting someone important from the company	**Eine wichtige Person aus dem Unternehmen zitieren**
▪ "The last year has been a highly successful time for the company," commented Managing Director …	▪ *„Das letzte Jahr war eine höchst erfolgreiche Zeit für unser Unternehmen," kommentierte Hauptgeschäftsführer/in …*
▪ "We're looking forward to another busy but profitable year," said … Chief Operations Officer with the company.	▪ *„Wir freuen auf ein weiteres arbeitsreiches aber profitables Jahr," sagte der/die Haupteinsatzleiter/in.*
▪ According to …, the company's Production Director, "…"	▪ *Laut …, dem/der Produktionsleiter/in des Unternehmens, „…".*
Giving details of the company's history	**Nähere Informationen zur Geschichte des Unternehmens geben**
▪ Tristop Corp., which started life as … before …	▪ *Tristorp Corp., das vor … als … angefangen hat …*
▪ Noximon, which was founded in … as a manufacturer of … before …	▪ *Noximon, das in … als Hersteller von … gegründet wurde, bevor …*
Explaining what the company specializes in	**Erklären, worin das Unternehmen spezialisiert ist**
▪ The company's core business is …	▪ *Das Kerngeschäft des Unternehmens ist …*
▪ The firm specializes in …	▪ *Die Firma hat sich auf … spezialisiert*
Describing the company's plans	**Die Pläne des Unternehmens beschreiben**
▪ Tristop now plans to …	▪ *Tristop plant nun …*
▪ Schaeffer AG is planning a new …	▪ *Schaeffer AG plant ein neues …*

Saying and writing numbers and figures — Unit 7

▪ 763 – seven hundred and sixty-three	▪ *763 – siebenhundertdreiundsechzig*
▪ 1,600 – one thousand six hundred	▪ *1.600 – eintausendsechshundert*
▪ 145,000 – one hundred and forty-five thousand	▪ *145.000 – einhundertfünfundvierzigtausend*
▪ 1,000,000 – one million	▪ *1.000.000 – eine Million*
▪ 1,000,000,000 – one billion	▪ *1.000.000.000 – eine Milliarde*
▪ 44.8 – forty-four point eight	▪ *44,8 – vierundvierzig Komma acht*

Talking about products

▪ This product is constructed from …	▪ *Dieses Produkt wird aus … hergestellt.*
▪ It includes …	▪ *Es beinhaltet …*
▪ Our product allows you to …	▪ *Unser Produkt ermöglicht es einem …*
▪ It comes in … and features …	▪ *Es gibt es in … und ist mit … ausgestattet.*
▪ It combines … with …	▪ *Es kombiniert … mit …*

Writing an enquiry — Unit 8

Source of address	Quelle der Anschrift
▪ We have seen your company's advertisement in the current edition of … and are most interested in your products.	▪ *Wir haben Ihre Anzeige in der aktuellen Ausgabe von … gesehen und interessieren uns sehr für Ihre Produkte.*
▪ You have been recommended to us by …, who tells us that you have a special offer for … .	▪ *Sie wurden uns von … empfohlen, der/die uns mitgeteilt hat, dass Sie derzeit ein Sonderangebot für … haben.*

Useful phrases

Description of company	Beschreibung des Unternehmens
▪ Our company is a major/well-established … with branches all over Germany.	▪ *Unser Unternehmen ist ein bedeutender/etablierter … mit Filialen überall in Deutschland.*
Reason for enquiry	**Grund für Ihre Anfrage**
▪ Our company is currently expanding …	▪ *Derzeit expandiert unser Betrieb …*
▪ … as goods of this nature are in great demand at present.	▪ *… da zur Zeit eine große Nachfrage nach Waren dieser Art besteht.*
Requirements	**Ihr Bedarf**
▪ We would therefore/also be grateful if you would let us have your latest catalogue on your entire range.	▪ *Wir wären Ihnen deshalb/auch dankbar, wenn Sie uns einen aktuellen Katalog über Ihre gesamte Produktpalette schicken würden.*
▪ … and we require … at reasonable prices.	▪ *… und wir benötigen … zu angemessenen Preisen.*
▪ … together with your current export price list.	▪ *… sowie Ihre aktuelle Exportpreisliste.*
▪ … including all discounts granted.	▪ *… einschl. aller gewährten Rabatte.*
▪ How soon can you deliver?	▪ *Wie schnell kann die Lieferung erfolgen?*
▪ Details of your terms of delivery and payment would also be appreciated.	▪ *Einzelheiten über Ihre Liefer- und Zahlungsbedingungen würden wir ebenfalls begrüßen.*
▪ Delivery would need to be made DDP to our premises.	▪ *Die Lieferung sollte DDP erfolgen.*
References	**Referenzen**
▪ References are available on request.	▪ *Referenzen sind auf Wunsch erhältlich.*
Appropriate ending	**Angemessene Verabschiedung**
▪ We look forward to hearing from you soon/in the near future.	▪ *Wir freuen uns, bald/in Kürze von Ihnen zu hören.*
▪ If you are able to offer us favourable terms and excellent quality, we will be in a position to place sizeable orders.	▪ *Wenn Ihre Konditionen günstig sind und die Qualität hervorragend ist, sind größere Aufträge möglich.*
▪ We look forward to your early reply with interest.	▪ *Wir sehen Ihrer baldigen Antwort mit Interesse entgegen.*

Writing an offer

Reference to enquiry	Bezug auf Anfrage
▪ Many thanks for the above-mentioned enquiry/your enquiry dated …	▪ *Wir danken für die oben genannte Anfrage/Ihre Anfrage vom …*
▪ We have been given your company's name by the Chamber of Commerce and Industry in …	▪ *Wir erhielten den Namen Ihres Unternehmens von der Industrie- und Handleskammer in …*
▪ … who tell us that you are interested in …	▪ *… die uns mitgeteilt hat, dass Sie sich für … interessieren.*
Description of your company/goods/services	**Beschreibung Ihrer Gesellschaft/Waren/Dienstleistungen**
▪ We are a major distributor of …	▪ *Wir sind ein bedeutender Großhändler für …*
▪ Our company manufactures a wide range of high-quality products.	▪ *Unsere Gesellschaft stellt eine breite Palette von hochwertigen Produkten her.*
▪ We have been manufacturing first-class … for the past … years	▪ *Seit den letzten … Jahren stellen wir hochwertige … her.*
▪ … with an excellent reputation in the EU and beyond.	▪ *… mit ausgezeichnetem Ruf in der EU und darüber hinaus.*
Sales material	**Verkaufsmaterial**
▪ We enclose our current catalogue and export price list for your information.	▪ *Wir fügen unseren aktuellen Katalog und die Exportpreisliste zu Ihrer Information bei.*
▪ Samples are available on request.	▪ *Muster sind auf Wunsch erhältlich.*
Price	**Preis**
▪ As regards the goods requested, we are pleased to submit the following quotation:	▪ *Was die gewünschten Waren betrifft, freuen wir uns, Ihnen folgendes Angebot zu unterbreiten:*
▪ Our prices are quoted CPT British airport.	▪ *Unsere Preise verstehen sich CPT britischer Flughafen.*

Useful phrases

Terms and discounts	Geschäftsbedingungen und Nachlässe
▪ Delivery is made CIP London Heathrow Airport.	▪ *Die Lieferung erfolgt CIP Flughafen London Heathrow.*
▪ Our terms of payment for an initial order are CWO (cash with order).	▪ *Unsere Zahlungsbedingung für einen Erstauftrag ist die Zahlung bei Auftragserteilung.*
▪ … or, with favourable references, 10 days 2%, 30 days net.	▪ *… oder bei günstigen Referenzen, 2% Skonto bei Zahlung innerhalb von 10 Tagen, netto bei Zahlung innerhalb von 30 Tagen.*
▪ Payment on receipt of goods.	▪ *Zahlung bei Erhalt der Waren.*
▪ Our terms of payment will be reviewed if you place regular orders.	▪ *Unsere Zahlungsbedingungen werden neu geprüft, wenn Sie regelmäßige Aufträge erteilen.*
Delivery	**Lieferung**
▪ Delivery is made approx. 30 days after receipt of order.	▪ *Die Lieferung erfolgt ca. 30 Tage nach Auftragseingang.*
Appropriate ending	**Angemessene Verabschiedung**
▪ We hope our offer is to your liking.	▪ *Wir hoffen, dass unser Angebot Ihnen zusagt.*
▪ We look forward to receiving your order.	▪ *Wir freuen uns, auf Ihren Auftrag.*
▪ … and look forward to doing business with you.	▪ *… und freuen uns, mit Ihnen in Geschäftsbeziehung zu treten.*
Enclosure(s)	**Anlage(n)**
▪ Catalogue / Price list	▪ *Katalog / Preisliste*

Making an appointment

Suggesting a time	Eine Zeit vorschlagen
▪ When would suit you?	▪ *Wann würde es Ihnen passen?*
▪ Would … be convenient for you?	▪ *Wäre Ihnen um … recht?*
▪ How about … on …?	▪ *Wie wäre es am … um …?*
▪ Are you free on …?	▪ *Haben Sie am … Zeit?*
Responding	**Antworten**
▪ Let me just check my diary.	▪ *Lassen Sie mich kurz in meinen Kalender schauen.*
▪ Just let me see when I'm available.	▪ *Lassen Sie mich kurz nachsehen, wann ich Zeit habe.*
▪ Yes, that's fine with me.	▪ *Ja, das passt mir.*
▪ I'm sorry, but I've already got an appointment then.	▪ *Es tut mir leid, aber da habe ich schon einen Termin.*
▪ I'm busy all day until ….	▪ *Ich habe den ganzen Tag bis … keine Zeit.*
▪ I'm afraid not. I'm tied up all day.	▪ *Leider nein. Ich bin den ganzen Tag beschäftigt.*
Suggesting an alternative	**Eine Alternative vorschlagen**
▪ Could we arrange something else?	▪ *Könnten wir wann anderes vereinbaren?*

Apologizing

Unit 9

▪ I am / We are extremely sorry to hear that …	▪ *Es tut mir/uns außerordentlich leid, zu hören, dass …*
▪ We would like to apologize for …	▪ *Wir möchten uns für … entschuldigen.*
▪ The delay was due to …	▪ *Die Verspätung war bedingt durch …*
▪ The damage resulted from …	▪ *Die Beschädigungen sind auf … zurückzuführen.*
▪ Please accept my/our sincere apologies for any inconvenience caused.	▪ *Bitte nehmen Sie meine/unsere Entschuldigungen an, für jegliche verursachte Unannehmlichkeiten.*
▪ It was due to circumstances beyond our control.	▪ *Es lag an Umständen außerhalb unserer Kontrolle.*

Writing a complaint

▪ I am writing with reference to …	▪ *Ich schreibe in Bezug auf …*
▪ I am writing to complain about …	▪ *Ich schreibe, um mich über … zu beschweren.*
▪ … to express my dissatisfaction with …	▪ *… um meine Unzufriedenheit mit … auszudrücken.*

■ There seems to have been an error/mistake made concerning …	■ *Es scheint einen Fehler/ein Missverständnis bezüglich … gegeben zu haben.*
■ We would like to remind you that the … is still within its warranty period.	■ *Wir würden Sie gerne daran erinnern, dass der/die/das … noch unter Garantie steht.*
■ This has caused us considerable inconvenience.	■ *Das hat uns erhebliche Unannehmlichkeiten verursacht.*

Writing a reminder

■ I am writing in connection with the attached unpaid invoice for work done at your premises.	■ *Ich schreibe im Zusammenhang mit der angefügten unbezahlten Rechnung für Arbeit auf Ihrem Firmengelände.*
■ I would like to draw your attention to invoice no. …	■ *Ich möchte Ihre Aufmerksamkeit auf Mahnung Nr. … lenken.*
■ Would you please settle your account by … at the latest?	■ *Bitte bezahlen Sie die Rechnung bis spätestens …*
■ We insist on payment within the next five working days.	■ *Wir bestehen auf die Zahlung innerhalb der nächsten fünf Arbeitstage.*
■ If we have not received your payment within the next seven days, we will have to instruct our solicitors to take legal action.	■ *Wenn wir Ihre Zahlung nicht innerhalb der nächsten sieben Tage erhalten, werden wir unseren Anwalt hinzuziehen, um rechtliche Schritte einzuleiten.*

Writing a cover letter

Unit 10

Showing interest and suitability	**Interesse und Eignung zeigen**
■ I was extremely interested to read your advertisement for the post of …	■ *Ich habe Ihre Anzeige für die Stelle des/der … mit großem Interesse gelesen.*
■ I wish to gain experience in …	■ *Ich möchte gerne Erfahrungen in … sammeln.*
■ I would like to make use of my foreign language skills.	■ *Ich möchte gerne meine Fremdsprachenkompetenzen einsetzen.*
■ I feel sure that your company has the post I am looking for.	■ *Ich bin sicher, dass Ihr Unternehmen die Stelle hat, die ich suche.*
■ I believe I am particularly suited for the post advertised because …	■ *Ich glaube, dass ich besonders für die annoncierte Stelle geeignet bin, weil …*
Describing your skills	**Die eigenen Fertigkeiten beschreiben**
■ As a native speaker of …	■ *Als … Muttersprachler/in …*
■ I am fluent in spoken and written …	■ *Ich beherrsche … fließend in gesprochener und geschriebener Sprache.*
■ I have a good knowledge of …	■ *Ich habe gute Kenntnisse in …*
Talking about previous experience	**Über vorherige Erfahrungen sprechen**
■ Before my traineeship, I completed a work placement at … in the … department.	■ *Vor meiner Ausbildung habe ich ein Praktikum bei … in der …-abteilung absolviert.*
■ My traineeship at … has confirmed my interest in …	■ *Meine Ausbildung bei … hat mein Interesse an … bestärkt.*
■ … has enabled me to develop my skills in …	■ *… hat mir ermöglicht, meine Fähigkeiten in … auszubauen.*
Expressing availability for an interview/the job	**Verfügbarkeit für ein Vorstellungsgespräch/die Stelle ausdrücken**
■ I am available for an interview immediately.	■ *Ich stehe ab sofort für ein Vorstellungsgespräch zur Verfügung.*
■ I would be able to start work any time after …	■ *Ich könnte jederzeit nach dem … anfangen zu arbeiten.*
■ I very much look forward to hearing from you at your earliest convenience.	■ *Ich freue mich darauf, möglichst bald von Ihnen zu hören.*

Basic word list

Diese Liste enthält ca. 700 Grundwörter, die in *Industry Matters – 2nd Edition* als bekannt vorausgesetzt werden. Nicht aufgeführt, jedoch vorausgesetzt, sind einige elementare Wörter, wie Pronomen, Zahlen, Wochentage sowie Wörter, die im Englischen und Deutschen die gleiche Bedeutung haben, wie z. B. *monitor, restaurant* und *hotel.*

A

able, to be ~ können, in der Lage sein
about über, etwa
above über, oben(stehend), oben genannt
absolutely absolut, völlig
accept annehmen, akzeptieren
across (quer) über
active aktiv(iert)
activity Tätigkeit, Aktivität
actor Schauspieler
add zusammenzählen, hinzufügen
address Adresse; adressieren
advert(isement) Werbung, Anzeige
afraid, I'm ~ leider
after nach
afternoon Nachmittag
again wieder
age Alter
agree zustimmen, vereinbaren
air Luft
airport Flughafen
all alle(s)
allow erlauben, gestatten, (zu) lassen
almost fast, beinahe
alone allein(e)
along entlang
already schon, bereits
also auch, außerdem
although obwohl
altogether insgesamt
always immer
a.m. vormittags, morgens (vor 12 Uhr)
among zwischen, unter
amount Menge, Betrag
angry wütend, verärgert
another noch eine/r/s
answer Antwort, Lösung; (be)antworten
anybody/anyone jemand, jede/r
anything etwas, alles
anyway jedenfalls, sowieso
anywhere irgendwo(hin)
apart from abgesehen von, außer
area Gebiet, Bereich
arrange arrangieren, vereinbaren
arrive ankommen
ask fragen, bitten
away weg, entfernt

B

back Rückseite, Rücken; zurück
bad schlecht, schlimm
bag Tasche, Tüte, Beutel
basic grundsätzlich, einfach
basically grundsätzlich, im Grunde
because weil
become werden
before vor(her)
begin anfangen, beginnen
beginning Anfang
behind hinter, hinten
believe glauben
belong gehören
below unter, unten(stehend)
best beste, am besten
better besser
between zwischen
big groß
biscuit Keks, Plätzchen
board Brett, Tafel
body Körper
book Buch; buchen, reservieren
boring langweilig
bored gelangweilt
born geboren
both beide
bottle Flasche
bottom Unterseite, Unterteil, Boden, Ende
box Kasten, Kästchen, Schachtel, Kiste
boy Junge
bracket Klammer
break Pause; (zer)brechen, kaputtmachen
breakfast Frühstück
bring bringen, holen
broken kaputt
brother Bruder
build bauen, aufbauen, erbauen
building Gebäude
busy beschäftigt, besetzt
buy kaufen
bye tschüs

C

call Anruf; (an)rufen, nennen
caller Anrufer/in
camera Fotoapparat, Kamera
car Auto
care, take ~ of sich kümmern um
careful(ly) vorsichtig, sorgfältig
case Fall
cash Bargeld
certain(ly) sicher(lich), gewiss, bestimmt
chair Stuhl, Sessel
change (Ver-)Änderung; (aus) wechseln, (sich) ändern
cheap billig, günstig
check überprüfen, kontrollieren
cheque Scheck
child Kind
choice Wahl, Auswahl
choose (aus)wählen
cinema Kino
city (Groß-)Stadt
class Klasse
classmate Klassenkamerad/in
clean sauber; reinigen, säubern
clear klar, deutlich
clever klug, intelligent
clock Uhr
close schließen, zumachen
close (to) nahe (bei)
clothes Kleidung, Kleider
clue Hinweis, Tip
coffee Kaffee
colour Farbe
come kommen, geliefert werden
complete vollständig; vervollständigen
completely völlig
contact Kontakt, Verbindung
control Kontrolle; kontrollieren, regeln, steuern, überwachen
copy Exemplar, Kopie; abschreiben, kopieren
corner Ecke
correct richtig, genau; korrigieren
cost Kosten; kosten
count zählen
country Land, Staat
couple Paar
create (er)schaffen, erstellen, gestalten
creative kreativ, schöpferisch
cross (an)kreuzen
culture Kultur
cup Tasse

D

damage Schaden; beschädigen
danger Gefahr
dangerous gefährlich
dark Dunkelheit; dunkel
data Daten
date Datum, Termin

date of birth Geburtsdatum
day Tag
dear liebe/r
decide entscheiden, beschließen
definite(ly) (ganz) sicher, bestimmt, eindeutig
describe beschreiben
description Beschreibung, Schilderung
desk (Schreib-)Tisch, Schalter, Arbeitsplatz
details Einzelheiten, Angaben
dialogue Gespräch, Dialog
dictionary Wörterbuch
die sterben
difference Unterschied
different unterschiedlich, verschieden
difficult schwer, schwierig
dinner (Abend-)Essen
direct direkt, gerade
dirty schmutzig
disadvantage Nachteil, Schaden
dislike nicht mögen
display Bildschirm, Anzeige
door Tür
drink Getränk; trinken
drive fahren
during während

E
each jede/r/s
early früh
east (nach) Osten, Ost-
easy, easily leicht, einfach
education Erziehung, (Aus-, Schul-)Bildung
either entweder
empty leer
end Ende, Schluss; (be)enden
ending Ende
energy Energie
enjoy genießen, gefallen, gern tun
enough ausreichend, genug
enter eintreten, betreten, eingeben
entrance Eingang, Einfahrt
especially besonders
even sogar (noch)
evening Abend
ever je(mals)
every jede/r/s
everybody jede/r
everyone jede/r/s, alle
everything alles
exactly exakt, genau
example Beispiel
excellent hervorragend, ausgezeichnet
excited aufgeregt, begeistert
exciting aufregend, spannend
excuse Ausrede, Entschuldigung; entschuldigen
exercise Übung
exercise book (Schul-)Heft
expect erwarten, annehmen
expensive teuer
experience Erfahrung; erfahren, erleben
expert Fachmann/frau
extra zusätzlich
extreme äußerst
eye Auge

F
fact Tatsache
factory Fabrik
false falsch
family Familie
far weit (entfernt)
fast schnell
feel (sich) fühlen, meinen, glauben
feeling Gefühl, Meinung, Ansicht
(a) few ein paar, wenig/e
fight Kampf; (be)kämpfen
final letzte/r/s, endgültig
finally schließlich, endlich
financial finanziell
find finden, suchen
find out herausfinden
fine nennen, benennen
finish (be)enden, abschließen, fertig werden
firm Firma
first(ly) erst; zuerst
flight Flug
floor Etage, Stockwerk; (Fuß-) Boden
fly fliegen
follow (be)folgen
(the) following der/die/das Folgende
food Essen, Nahrung
foreign ausländisch, Auslands-, fremd
forget vergessen
form Form, Formular; bilden, formen
forward nach vorne
free frei; gratis, kostenlos
friend Freund/in
friendly freund(schaft)lich
friendship Freundschaft
front Vorderseite
front, in ~ of vor
full voll
fully völlig
funny komisch, merkwürdig
further weitere/r/s
future Zukunft; (zu)künftig

G
gap Lücke
general allgemein, generell, normal
generally im Allgemeinen, normalerweise
get holen, bekommen, werden, gelangen
girl Mädchen
give geben
go gehen, fahren
go on weitermachen, fortfahren
go out ausgehen
good gut
goodbye auf Wiedersehen
great groß(artig)
greatly in hohem Maße
greet (be)grüßen
greeting Gruß(formel), Begrüßung
ground Boden, Grund
group Gruppe; gruppieren
grow wachsen, werden
guess Annahme; raten, schätzen
guest Gast

H
half Hälfte; halb
hall Diele, Saal, Halle
handle umgehen mit, bearbeiten, erledigen, fertigwerden mit
happen passieren, geschehen
happy glücklich, zufrieden
health Gesundheit
hear hören
heart Herz
heavy schwer
height Höhe, Größe
help Hilfe; helfen
helpful hilfreich, nützlich
here hier
high; highly hoch; äußerst
history Geschichte
holiday Ferien, Urlaub, Feiertag
home Zuhause, Heim; nach Hause
hope Hoffnung; hoffen
hopefully hoffentlich
horrible furchtbar, schrecklich
hot heiß, scharf
hour Stunde
house Haus
how wie
however doch, jedoch, allerdings
huge riesig
human menschlich
husband (Ehe-)Mann

I
idea Vorstellung, Idee
if wenn, falls, ob
ill krank
illness Krankheit

image Bild
important wichtig
impossible unmöglich
individual einzeln, individuell
industry Industrie, Branche
inform informieren, unterrichten
information Auskunft, Information(en), Angaben
inside innerhalb, drinnen
instead stattdessen
instead of statt
interest Interesse; interessieren
interested interessiert
interesting interessant

J
job Arbeit(sstelle), Aufgabe
join beitreten, verbinden
just einfach, nur, genau

K
keep (be)halten, weiterhin tun
key Schlüssel, Taste, Haupt-
kind freundlich; Art, Sorte
kitchen Küche
knife Messer
know kennen, wissen

L
language Sprache
large groß
last dauern; letzte/r/s
late spät
later später
latest neueste/r/s
lead führen
learn lernen, erfahren
least, at ~ wenigstens
leave lassen, verlassen, hinterlassen, ab-/wegfahren
left links; übrig
length Länge
less weniger, abzüglich
let erlauben, (zu)lassen
letter Buchstabe, Brief
level Ebene, Niveau
lie Lüge; (be)lügen
life Leben
lift Fahrstuhl, Aufzug
light Licht, Leuchte; hell, leicht
like mögen; (ähnlich) wie
line Linie, Leitung, Zeile
list Liste; auflisten, notieren
listen zuhören
little klein, wenig
live wohnen, leben
local örtlich, lokal
log in/on einloggen
log off/out ausloggen
long lang
look Blick, Aussehen; (aus)sehen, blicken
look after sich kümmern um
look for suchen nach
look forward to sth sich auf etw freuen
lose verlieren
lots of / a lot of viel, viele
love Liebe; lieben, sehr gern mögen
lovely schön, hübsch, reizend
low niedrig
lunch Mittagessen

M
machine Gerät, Maschine
magazine Zeitschrift
main Haupt-, wichtigste/r/s
make machen
manage leiten, verwalten, regeln, (es) schaffen
many viele
market Markt
match zuordnen, passen (zu)
maximum Maximum; maximal
may dürfen, können, mögen
maybe vielleicht
meal Essen, Mahlzeit
mean bedeuten, meinen, heißen
medium mittlere; Medium, Mittel
meet (zusammen)treffen, begegnen
meeting Sitzung, Besprechung, Treffen
memory Gedächtnis, Erinnerung, Speicher
message Meldung, Nachricht, Mitteilung, Botschaft
metal Metall
middle Mitte
might könnte(n) (vielleicht)
minimum Minimum; minimal
miss verpassen, vermissen
missing fehlende/r/s
mistake Fehler, Irrtum
mobile (phone) Mobiltelefon, Handy
money Geld
month Monat
more mehr
morning Morgen
most der/die/das meiste, die meisten
mountain Berg
mouse Maus
move (sich) bewegen, umziehen
movement Bewegung
much viel

N
name Name; nennen, benennen
national national, staatlich
near in der Nähe von
nearly beinahe, fast
necessary nötig, notwendig, erforderlich
need Bedarf, Bedürfnis; brauchen, benötigen
negative verneinend, negativ
neither … nor weder … noch
never nie(mals)
new neu
news Neuigkeit(en), Nachricht(en)
next nächste/r/s; danach
night Nacht
normal(ly) normal(erweise)
north (nach) Norden, Nord-
note Notiz, Anmerkung; beachten, notieren
nothing nichts
now nun, jetzt
nowadays heutzutage
number Nummer, Zahl

O
object Gegenstand
of course natürlich, selbstverständlich
offer Angebot; anbieten, bieten
office Büro
often oft, häufig
oil Öl
old alt
once einmal, einst; sobald
only nur, einzig
open öffnen, eröffnen; offen, geöffnet
opposite Gegenteil; gegensätzlich, gegenüber
option Möglichkeit, Option
or oder
order Bestellung, Reihenfolge; bestellen, ordern
organization Organisation
organize organisieren
original original, ursprünglich, Original(-)
other andere/r/s
ought to sollen
outside außerhalb (von)
own eigene/r/s; besitzen

P
page Seite
pain Schmerz
pair Paar
paper Papier, Zeitung
part Teil, Bauteil
pay Lohn, Bezahlung; zahlen, bezahlen
per cent Prozent
perfect vollkommen, perfekt
perfectly völlig
perhaps vielleicht, eventuell
period Zeit(raum)
personal persönlich

phone Telefon; anrufen
photo(graphy) Foto(grafie)
phrase Redewendung, Satz(teil)
picture Bild
piece Stück, Teil
place Stelle, Platz; setzen, stellen
plan Plan; planen
plane Flugzeug
plastic Plastik, Kunststoff
plenty viel, reichlich
p.m. nachmittags, abends (nach 12 Uhr)
point Punkt; Komma
poor arm, schlecht, mangelhaft
popular beliebt, populär
position Stellung, Lage, Position
positive positiv, bejahend
possibility Möglichkeit
possible möglich
possibly möglicherweise
power Kraft, Strom; antreiben
powerful mächtig, stark
practical praktisch
practice Praxis, Training
practise (ein)üben, trainieren
prefer vorziehen, bevorzugen, lieber mögen
prepare (sich) vorbereiten, zubereiten, erstellen
present Gegenwart; Geschenk; aktuell, gegenwärtig; vorstellen, präsentieren
press drücken
price Preis
print Druck; drucken, ausdrucken
printer Drucker/in
private privat, persönlich
probably wahrscheinlich
produce produzieren, herstellen
product Produkt, Erzeugnis
program(me) Programm, Sendung
promise Versprechen; versprechen
provide liefern, bieten, zur Verfügung stellen
public öffentlich; Öffentlichkeit
push schieben, drücken
put setzen, stellen, legen

Q

quality Eigenschaft, Qualität
(a) quarter past/to Viertel nach/vor
question Frage
quick(ly) schnell
quiet ruhig
quite ziemlich, ganz

R

rather ziemlich, lieber
reach erreichen, greifen
read lesen
reader Leser/in, Lektüre
ready bereit, fertig
real echt, wirklich
really wirklich, eigentlich, tatsächlich
reason Vernunft, Grund
receive erhalten, empfangen, bekommen
recent aktuell, neu
recently neulich, vor kurzem, in letzter Zeit
recommend empfehlen
regular(ly) regelmäßig
relative Verwandte/r; relativ
remain (ver)bleiben
remember sich erinnern, daran denken
repeat wiederholen
report Bericht; berichten
reservation Reservierung, Buchung
reserve reservieren
respect Respekt, Achtung; (be)achten, respektieren
result Resultat, Ergebnis; folgen, resultieren
return zurückkehren, zurückgeben
rich reich
right rechts, richtig
risk Risiko; riskieren
road (Land-)Straße
role play Rollenspiel
room Zimmer, Raum
round Runde; rund
rule Regel, Vorschrift
run laufen (lassen); betreiben, leiten

S

sad traurig
safe(ly) sicher
same gleiche/r/s, der-, die-, dasselbe
save retten, sichern
say sagen
school Schule
score Ergebnis, Punkt(estand)
screen Bildschirm, Leinwand
search Suche; (durch)suchen
second zweite(r/s), Sekunde
secretary Sekretär/in
see sehen, besuchen, verstehen
seem (er)scheinen
sell (sich) verkaufen
send senden, schicken
sentence Satz
serious ernst, ernsthaft
service Dienst, Dienstleistung, Service
set setzen, stellen
several etliche, einige, mehrere
shall sollen, werden
shelf Regal
shop Laden, Geschäft; einkaufen
short kurz, klein, knapp
should solle/n, sollte/n
shoulder Schulter
show zeigen
shut schließen
side Seite
sightseeing Besichtigen von Sehenswürdigkeiten
sign Zeichen, Anzeichen, Schild
simple einfach
since da, weil, seit
single einzig, einzeln
sit sitzen, sich hinsetzen
site Website
size Größe
slow langsam
small klein
smile Lächeln; lächeln
someone jemand
something etwas
sometimes manchmal
somewhere irgendwo(hin)
soon bald
sorry traurig; Verzeihung
sound Klang, Geräusch; klingen, sich anhören
south (nach) Süden, Süd-
space Raum, Platz, Abstand
speak sprechen, reden
special besondere/r/s
specially speziell, extra, besonders
speed Geschwindigkeit
spell buchstabieren, schreiben
spelling Rechtschreibung, Schreibweise
spend (Geld) ausgeben, (Zeit) verbringen
stand stehen, aushalten
start Beginn; anfangen, starten
statement Aussage, Feststellung, Erklärung
stay Aufenthalt; bleiben
step Schritt, Stufe
still still, trotzdem, (immer) noch
stop (an)halten, aufhören (mit)
street Straße
strong stark, heftig
student Student/in, Lernende/r
study lernen, studieren, untersuchen, betrachten
stuff Material, Stoff, Zeug
subject (Schul-)Fach, Thema
success Erfolg
successful erfolgreich
suggest vorschlagen, andeuten
suggestion Vorschlag
sun Sonne
sure sicher

surname Nachname, Familienname
surprise Überraschung; überraschen

T
table Tisch, Tabelle
take nehmen, bringen, dauern
take off ausziehen, abnehmen, abheben
take part teilnehmen, mitmachen
talk Gespräch, Vortrag; sprechen, reden
tall groß, hoch
task Aufgabe
teach unterrichten, lehren
teacher Lehrer/in
team Mannschaft
technology Technik, Technologie
telephone (call) Telefon(anruf)
television Fernsehen, Fernseher
tell sagen, erzählen
test untersuchen, prüfen
than als
thank danken
thank you danke
thanks Dank; danke
then dann
thin dünn
thing Sache, Ding, Gegenstand
think denken, meinen, finden, glauben
though obwohl, allerdings, aber
through durch
throw werfen
tick (off) mit einem Häkchen versehen, abhaken
ticket Karte, Fahrschein
time Zeit, Mal
tip Hinweis, Tipp
today heute
together zusammen
tomorrow morgen
tonight heute Abend/Nacht
too zu, auch
top Spitze, Gipfel; Spitzen-
topic Thema
total (Gesamt-)Summe; gesamte/r/s, Gesamt-
touch anfassen, berühren
town Stadt
traffic Verkehr
train Zug
translate übersetzen
translation Übersetzung
travel Reisen; reisen, fahren
trip Ausflug, Reise, Besuch
trouble Mühe, Umstände, Problem(e), Ärger
true wahr, richtig
try versuchen, probieren
turn (sich) drehen, wenden, werden
twice zweimal
type Art, Sorte, Typ; tippen, Schreibmaschine schreiben
typical typisch

U
unable unfähig, nicht in der Lage
under unter
understand verstehen, begreifen
university Universität
unless es sei denn, außer wenn
unlike anders als, im Gegensatz zu
until bis
use Gebrauch; gebrauchen, benutzen, verwenden
useful nützlich
user Anwender/in, Benutzer/in
usual gewöhnlich, normal, üblich
usually gewöhnlich, normalerweise, meistens

V
verb Verb
visit Besuch; besuchen, besichtigen
visitor Besucher/in, Gast

W
wait warten
wall Wand, Mauer
want wollen
wash waschen
watch Armbanduhr
water Wasser
way Weg, Methode, Art (und Weise)
weather Wetter
week Woche
weekend Wochenende
weekly wöchentlich
welcome Willkommen; willkommen heißen
well gesund, gut; also
west (nach) Westen, West-
whatever was auch immer
when wenn, als, wann
whenever immer wenn
where wo(hin)
whether ob
which welche
while während
whole ganz
why warum
wide breit, weit
wife (Ehe-)Frau
will Wille; werde(n), wollen
window Fenster
wine Wein
wish Wunsch; wünschen
with mit, bei
within innerhalb (von), in
without ohne
woman Frau
wonderful wunderbar
wood Holz
word Wort
work Arbeit; funktionieren, arbeiten
worker Arbeiter/in
world Welt
worldwide weltweit
worried besorgt, beunruhigt
worse schlechter, schlimmer
worst schlechteste/r/s, schlimmste/r/s
would würde/n
write schreiben
wrong falsch

Y
year Jahr
yesterday gestern
young jung

Chronological word list

Dieses Wörterverzeichnis enthält alle neuen Wörter aus *Industry Matters – 2nd Edition* in der Reihenfolge ihres Erscheinens (Seitenzahlen sind angegeben). Nicht angeführt sind die Wörter aus dem Grundwortschatz (vgl. *Basic word list*). Wörter aus den Hörverständnisübungen sind mit einem T *(Transkript)* und Wörter aus den *Partner files* mit einem P gekennzeichnet. Die Zahl am linken Rand gibt die Seitenzahl an.

Abkürzungen			
	AE = amerikanisches Englisch	*jdm* = jemandem	*pl* = plural noun
	BE = britisches Englisch	*jdn* = jemanden	*sb* = somebody
	etw = etwas	*jds* = jemandes	*sth* = something

Unit 1

6	**presentation** [ˌprezn'teɪʃn]	Präsentation, Vorstellung
	brochure ['brəʊʃə]	Prospekt, Werbebroschüre
	guided tour [ˌgaɪdɪd 'tʊə]	Rundgang, Führung
	booth ['bu:ð]	Messestand
	trade fair ['treɪd feə]	Handelsmesse, Fachmesse
	exhibition [ˌeksɪ'bɪʃn]	Messe, Ausstellung
	company ['kʌmpəni]	Unternehmen, Firma, Gesellschaft
	overview ['əʊvəvju:]	Überblick
	goods [gʊdz]	Ware(n)
	service ['sɜ:vɪs]	Dienstleistung
	promotional [prə'məʊʃənl]	Werbe-
	customer ['kʌstəmə]	Kunde/Kundin
	actual(ly) ['æktʃuəl]	wirklich, tatsächlich
	detailed ['di:teɪld]	genau, detailliert
	deal [di:l]	Geschäft
	method ['meθəd]	Weg, Methode, Art (und Weise)
	to **present** [prɪ'zent]	vorstellen, präsentieren
	outside world [ˌaʊtsaɪd 'wɜ:ld]	Außenwelt
	sales representative ['seɪlz reprɪzentətɪv]	Vertreter/in, Handelsvertreter/in
7	**head** [hed]	Leiter/in, Chef/in
	sales [seɪlz]	Vertrieb, Verkauf
	employee [ɪm'plɔɪi:]	Angestellte/r, Beschäftigte/r
	worldwide ['wɜ:ldwaɪd]	weltweit
	approximately [ə'prɒksɪmətli]	ungefähr, zirka
	turnover ['tɜ:nəʊvə]	Umsatz
	headquarters [ˌhed'kwɔ:təz]	Zentrale, Firmensitz
	production [prə'dʌkʃn]	Produktion, Herstellung, Fertigung
	body-shaping ['bɒdi ʃeɪpɪŋ]	Dosenformung, Zargenformung
	necking ['nekɪŋ]	Verengen
	beading ['bi:dɪŋ]	Sicken
	flanging ['fleɪndʒɪŋ]	Bördeln
	sealing ['si:lɪŋ]	Abdichten, Versiegeln
	stamping press ['stæmpɪŋ pres]	Stanzmaschine
	curling press ['kɜ:lɪŋ pres]	Bördelpresse
	rotary cap liner [ˌrəʊtəri 'kæp laɪnə]	Dichtungssmaschine für Schraubverschlüsse
	production line [prə'dʌkʃn laɪn]	Fertigungsstraße
	welding machine ['weldɪŋ məʃi:n]	Schweißmaschine
	slitter ['slɪtə]	Längsschneidemaschine, Streifenschneider
	seam covering ['si:m kʌvərɪŋ]	Falzabdeckung
	curing oven ['kjuːrɪŋ ʌvn]	Aushärteofen
	core competence [ˌkɔ: 'kɒmpɪtəns]	Kernkompetenz
	high-performance [ˌhaɪ pə'fɔ:məns]	Hochleistungs-
	three-part ['θri: pɑ:t]	dreiteilig
	lid [lɪd]	Deckel
	to **supply** [sə'plaɪ]	liefern
	entire [ɪn'taɪə]	ganze/r/s, vollständig
	manufacturing unit [ˌmænju'fæktʃərɪŋ ju:nɪt]	Produktionseinheit
	process ['prəʊses]	Verfahren
	percentage [pə'sentɪdʒ]	Anteil, Prozentsatz
	market share [ˌmɑ:kɪt 'ʃeə]	Marktanteil
T	**ladies and gentlemen** ['leɪdiz ən 'dʒentlmən]	Meine Damen und Herren
	agenda [ə'dʒendə]	Tagesordnung, Programm
	folder ['fəʊldə]	Mappe
	background ['bækgraʊnd]	Hintergrund
	statistics *(pl)* [stə'tɪstɪks]	Statistik(en)
	to **move on** [ˌmu:v 'ɒn]	weitergehen, übergehen (zu)
	high-tech [ˌhaɪ 'tek]	Hochtechnologie-

	to **manufacture** [ˌmænjuˈfæktʃə]	herstellen, fertigen
	high-end [ˌhaɪˈend]	der Spitzenklasse
	can [kæn]	Dose
	workforce [ˈwɜːkfɔːs]	Belegschaft
	to **range** [reɪndʒ]	sich erstrecken, reichen
	engineer [ˌendʒɪˈnɪə]	Ingenieur/in
	technician [tekˈnɪʃn]	Techniker/in
	trainee [treɪˈniː]	Auszubildende/r
	annual [ˈænjuəl]	jährlich, Jahres-
	global [ˈgləʊbl]	weltweit, Welt-
	to **belong to sb/sth** [bɪˈlɒŋ tə]	zu jdm/etw gehören
	parent company [ˌpeərənt ˈkʌmpəni]	Muttergesellschaft
	to **be located in …** [bi ləʊˈkeɪtɪd ɪn]	in … ansässig sein, seinen/ihren Sitz in … haben
	subsidiary [səbˈsɪdiəri]	Niederlassung
	specialty [ˈspeʃəlti]	Spezialität, Spezialgebiet
	to **provide sb sth** [prəˈvaɪd]	jdm etw liefern, bieten, zur Verfügung stellen
	turnkey system [ˌtɜːnkiː ˈsɪstəm]	Komplettsystem
	speed [spiːd]	Geschwindigkeit
	range [reɪndʒ]	Auswahl, Palette, Sortiment
	to **guarantee** [ˌgærənˈtiː]	garantieren
	customer service [ˌkʌstəmə ˈsɜːvɪs]	Kundendienst, Kundenbetreuung
	illustration [ˌɪləˈstreɪʃn]	Grafik, Illustration
	to **turn out** [ˌtɜːn ˈaʊt]	produzieren
	can body [ˈkæn bɒdi]	Zarge, Body
	can end [ˈkæn end]	Boden, Deckel (einer Dose)
	state-of-the-art [ˌsteɪt əv ði ˈɑːt]	auf dem neuesten Stand der Technik
	to **consist of sth** [kənˈsɪst əv]	aus etw bestehen
	metal [ˈmetl]	Metall
	cutter [ˈkʌtə]	Schneidegerät
	conveyor belt [kənˈveɪə belt]	Förderband
	oven [ˈʌvn]	Ofen
	component [kəmˈpəʊnənt]	Bauteil, Teil, Komponente
	to **assemble** [əˈsembl]	montieren
	on site [ɒn ˈsaɪt]	vor Ort
	to **design** [dɪˈzaɪn]	gestalten, entwerfen
	brief [briːf]	knapp, kurz
	to **be delighted to do sth** [bi dɪˈlaɪtɪd tə]	etw gern tun
8	to **be based in …** [bi ˈbeɪst ɪn]	in … ansässig sein, seinen/ihren Sitz in … haben
	head office [ˌhed ˈɒfɪs]	Zentrale, Firmensitz
	to **bake** [beɪk]	backen, erhitzen
9	**appropriate** [əˈprəʊpriət]	passend, angemessen
	to **highlight** [ˈhaɪlaɪt]	hervorheben
	audience [ˈɔːdiəns]	Publikum, Zuhörer(schaft), Zuschauer
	to **introduce** [ˌɪntrəˈdjuːs]	vorstellen, einführen
	to **structure** [ˈstrʌktʃə]	strukturieren
	visuals [ˈvɪʒuəlz]	visuelle Hilfsmittel
	conclusion [kənˈkluːʒn]	Schluss
	expression [ɪkˈspreʃn]	Ausdruck
	to **include** [ɪnˈkluːd]	einschließen, beinhalten
	session [ˈseʃn]	Sitzung
	visual aids [ˈvɪʒuəl eɪdz]	visuelle Hilfsmittel
	transparency [trænsˈpærənsi]	Overhead-Folie
	poster [ˈpəʊstə]	Plakat
	prompt card [ˈprɒmpt kɑːd]	Moderationskarte
	to **face sb** [feɪs]	sich jdm zuwenden, jdn ansehen
	to **turn your back to sb** [ˌtɜːn jɔː ˈbæk tə]	jdm den Rücken zudrehen
	to **point to sth** [ˈpɔɪnt tə]	auf etw zeigen
	eye contact [ˈaɪ kɒntækt]	Blickkontakt
	to **take sth into account** [ˌteɪk ɪntu əˈkaʊnt]	etw berücksichtigen
	gesture [ˈdʒestʃə]	Geste
	in public [ɪn ˈpʌblɪk]	öffentlich, in der Öffentlichkeit
	to **make sure** [ˌmeɪk ˈʃʊə]	sicherstellen, gewährleisten, sich vergewissern
	to **hand over** [ˌhænd ˈəʊvə]	übergeben
10	**enterprise** [ˈentəpraɪz]	Unternehmen
	profile [ˈprəʊfaɪl]	Porträt, Profil
	to **start out** [ˌstɑːt ˈaʊt]	(zunächst) beginnen
	packing [ˈpækɪŋ]	Verpackung
	unit [ˈjuːnɪt]	Bau, Gebäude, Halle
	industrial estate [ɪnˌdʌstriəl ɪˈsteɪt]	Industriegebiet
	demand [dɪˈmɑːnd]	Nachfrage, Bedarf
	rapid(ly) [ˈræpɪdli]	rasch, schnell
	to **double** [ˈdʌbl]	sich verdoppeln
	to **retire** [rɪˈtaɪə]	sich zur Ruhe setzen, sich (aus dem Berufsleben) zurückziehen

	to **diversify** [daɪ'vɜ:sɪfaɪ]	breiter fächern, diversifizieren
	portfolio [pɔ:t'fəʊliəʊ]	Sortiment, Angebot
	organic [ɔ:'gænɪk]	biologisch, Bio-
	variety [və'raɪəti]	Sorte
	to **rent** [rent]	mieten
	to **incorporate a company** [ɪn,kɔ:pəreɪt ə 'kʌmpəni]	eine AG/GmbH gründen
	managing director [,mænɪdʒɪŋ də'rektə]	Geschäftsführer/in, geschäftsführende/r Gesellschafter/in
	member ['membə]	Mietglied
	board [bɔ:d]	Geschäftsführung, Vorstand
	accountant [ə'kaʊntənt]	Buchhalter/in
	solicitor [sə'lɪsɪtə]	Anwalt/Anwältin *(für Zivilrecht)*
	to **be incorporated** [bi ɪn'kɔ:pəreɪtɪd]	eine AG/GmbH sein
	healthy ['helθi]	gesund
	conventional [kən'venʃənl]	herkömmlich, konventionell
	reputation [,repju'teɪʃn]	Ruf, Ansehen
	to **spread** [spred]	sich verbreiten
	increasing [ɪn'kri:sɪŋ]	zunehmend, steigend
	overseas [,əʊvə'si:z]	aus/nach Übersee, aus dem/ins Ausland
	to **keep up with sth** [,ki:p 'ʌp wɪð]	mit etw Schritt halten, mit etw mitkommen
	volume ['vɒlju:m]	Umfang, Volumen
	common ['kɒmən]	üblich, verbreitet
	sole trader [,səʊl 'treɪdə]	Einzelunternehmer
	decision [dɪ'sɪʒn]	Entscheidung
	to **take a decision** [,teɪk ə dɪ'sɪʒn]	eine Entscheidung fällen
	profit ['prɒfɪt]	Gewinn
	Private limited company (Ltd) *(BE)* [,praɪvət ,lɪmɪtɪd 'kʌmpəni]	Gesellschaft mit beschränkter Haftung (GmbH)
	Limited liability company (LLC) *(AE)* [,lɪmɪtɪd ,laɪə'bɪləti kʌmpəni]	Gesellschaft mit beschränkter Haftung (GmbH)
	Proprietory Limited company (Pty Ltd) *(AusE)* [prə,praɪətri ,lɪmɪtɪd 'kʌmpəni]	Gesellschaft mit beschränkter Haftung (GmbH)
	to **share sth** [ʃeə]	sich etw teilen
	to **invest** [ɪn'vest]	investieren
	Public limited company (plc) *(BE)* [,pʌblɪk ,lɪmɪtɪd 'kʌmpəni]	Aktiengesellschaft (AG)
	Corporation (Corp./Inc.) *(AE)* [,kɔ:pə'reɪʃn]	Aktiengesellschaft (AG)
	shareholder ['ʃeəhəʊldə]	Aktionär/in, Anteilseigner/in
	the public [ðə 'pʌblɪk]	die Öffentlichkeit
	director [də'rektə]	Vorstand
	share [ʃeə]	Aktie, Anteil
11	to **operate sth** ['ɒpəreɪt]	etw bedienen, betreiben
	canning machinery ['kænɪŋ məʃi:nəri]	Maschinen zur Dosenherstellung
	to **purchase** ['pɜ:tʃəs]	kaufen
	department [dɪ'pɑ:tmənt]	Abteilung
	comfortable ['kʌmftəbl]	bequem, angenehm, komfortabel
T	**human resources (HR)** [,hju:mən rɪ'sɔ:sɪz]	Personalabteilung
	Pleased to meet you. [,pli:zd tə 'mi:t ju]	Nett, Sie kennen zu lernen.
	translator [træns'leɪtə]	Übersetzer/in
	lift [lɪft]	Aufzug
	upstairs [,ʌp'steəz]	(nach) oben
	meeting room ['mi:tɪŋ ru:m]	Besprechungsraum
	seat [si:t]	Platz, Sitz
	production manager [prə'dʌkʃn mænɪdʒə]	Produktionsleiter/in
	senior ['si:niə]	leitende/r
	close to ['kləʊs tə]	nahe bei, in der Nähe von
	copy ['kɒpi]	Exemplar
	programme ['prəʊgræm]	Programm
	to **go for a meal** [,gəʊ fər ə 'mi:l]	essen gehen
	Chief Executive Officer (CEO) [,tʃi:f ɪg'zekjətɪv ɒfɪsə]	Vorstandsvorsitzende/r, Geschätsführer/in
	commercial director [kə,mɜ:ʃl də'rektə]	kaufmännische/r Leiter/in
	case [keɪs]	Fall
	pleasant ['pleznt]	angenehm
	formal ['fɔ:ml]	förmlich, formell
	informal [ɪn'fɔ:ml]	informell, zwanglos, locker
	to **introduce sb to sb** [,ɪntrə'dju:s]	jdn mit jdm bekannt machen, jdn jdm vorstellen
12	**introduction** [,ɪntrə'dʌkʃn]	Bekanntmachen, Vorstellen
	business card ['bɪznəs kɑ:d]	Visitenkarte
13	**contract** ['kɒntrækt]	Vertrag
	to **pass sth on** [,pɑ:s 'ɒn]	etw weiterreichen, -geben, -leiten
	instruction [ɪn'strʌkʃn]	Anleitung, Anweisung
	downstairs [,daʊn'steəz]	(nach) unten
	conversation [,kɒnvə'seɪʃn]	Gespräch

	to **get in touch with sb** [get ɪn 'tʌtʃ wɪð]	mit jdm in Kontakt treten
	order ['ɔ:də]	Auftrag, Bestellung
	to **reduce** [rɪ'dju:s]	reduzieren, senken
	significant(ly) [sɪg'nɪfɪkənt]	erheblich, bedeutend
	terms [tɜ:mz]	Konditionen, Bedingungen
	supplier [sə'plaɪə]	Lieferant/in, Zulieferer
14	**career** [kə'rɪə]	Karriere, Beruf, Laufbahn
	location [ləʊ'keɪʃn]	Standort
15	**the basics** [ðə 'beɪsɪks]	die grundsätzlichen Dinge
	professional [prə'feʃənl]	berufsmäßig, beruflich, Berufs-, professionell
	beginner [bɪ'gɪnə]	Anfänger/in
	guide [gaɪd]	Handbuch, Führer
	to **set sth up** [ˌset 'ʌp]	etw einrichten, aufbauen
	finish ['fɪnɪʃ]	Ende
	in total [ɪn 'təʊtl]	insgesamt
	to **sign up** [ˌsaɪn 'ʌp]	sich anmelden
	advice [əd'vaɪs]	Rat, Ratschlag, Tipp
	memorable ['memərəbl]	leicht zu merken
	to **stuff** [stʌf]	stopfen
	recommendation [ˌrekəmen'deɪʃn]	Empfehlung
	to **promote sb/sth** [prə'məʊt]	für jdn/etw Werbung machen
	to **investigate sb/sth** [ɪn'vestɪgeɪt]	Erkundigungen über jdn/etw einholen, Nachforschungen über jdn/etw anstellen
	major ['meɪdʒə]	größte/r/s, Haupt-, bedeutendste/r/s
	research [rɪ'sɜ:tʃ]	Recherche
	support [sə'pɔ:t]	Unterstützung, Kundendienst
	to **outsource** ['aʊtsɔ:s]	auslagern
	ethical ['eθɪkl]	moralisch, ethisch
	design [dɪ'zaɪn]	Gestaltung
	to **manage sth** ['mænɪdʒ]	etw verwalten
	popular ['pɒpjələ]	beliebt
	previous ['pri:viəs]	vorherige/r/s, Vor-, frühere/r/s
	knowledge ['nɒlɪdʒ]	Wissen, Kenntniss(e)
	extra ['ekstrə]	zusätzlich, Zusatz-
	profitable ['prɒfɪtəbl]	gewinnbringend, profitabel
	to **advertise sth** ['ædvətaɪz]	für etw Werbung machen
	to **charge** [tʃɑ:dʒ]	Gebühren verlangen
	to **claim** [kleɪm]	behaupten
	expense [ɪk'spens]	Kosten
	to **work sth out** [ˌwɜ:k 'aʊt]	etw ausrechnen, etw herausfinden
	operator ['ɒpəreɪtə]	Betreiber/in
	to **disagree** [ˌdɪsə'gri:]	nicht zustimmen, anderer Meinung sein
	constructive [kən'strʌktɪv]	konstruktiv

Unit 2

16	**role** [rəʊl]	Rolle
	responsibility [rɪˌspɒnsə'bɪləti]	Verantwortlichkeit, Aufgabenbereich, Zuständigkeit
	company car ['kʌmpəni kɑ:]	Firmenwagen
	independence [ˌɪndɪ'pendəns]	Unabhängigkeit
	outdoor ['aʊtdɔ:]	draußen, im Freien
	promotion prospects [prə'məʊʃn prɒspekts]	Beförderungsaussichten, Aufstiegschancen
	salary ['sæləri]	Lohn, Gehalt
	self-employed [ˌself ɪm'plɔɪd]	selbstständig
	medium-sized ['mi:diəmsaɪzd]	mittel, mittelständisch
	traineeship [treɪ'ni:ʃɪp]	Ausbildung, Lehre
	in the long term [ɪn ðə lɒŋ 'tɜ:m]	langfristig
	in the short term [ɪn ðə ˌʃɔ:t 'tɜ:m]	kurzfristig
	for the time being [fə ðə ˌtaɪm 'bi:ɪŋ]	einstweilen, vorerst
	to **set up a business** [set ˌʌp ə 'bɪznəs]	ein Unternehmen gründen
17	**in-house** [ˌɪn 'haʊs]	intern
	reception [rɪ'sepʃn]	Empfang
T	**packaging** ['pækɪdʒɪŋ]	Verpackung
	to **turn right/left** [tɜ:n 'raɪt/'left]	rechts/links abbiegen
	straight ahead [ˌstreɪt ə'hed]	geradeaus
	past sth [pɑ:st]	an etw vorbei
	corridor ['kɒrɪdɔ:]	Flur, Korridor
	logistics *(pl)* [lə'dʒɪstɪks]	Logistik
	men's room ['menz ru:m]	Herrentoilette
	restroom *(AE)* ['restru:m]	Toilette
	plant [plɑ:nt]	Werk, Fabrik
	engineering [ˌendʒɪ'nɪərɪŋ]	Maschinenbau
	to **invite** [ɪn'vaɪt]	einladen
	event [ɪ'vent]	Veranstaltung
	financial controlling [faɪˌnænʃl kən'trəʊlɪŋ]	Rechnungswesen

17	**directions** [də'rekʃnz]	Wegbeschreibung
	floor [flɔː]	Etage
	design [dɪ'zaɪn]	Konstruktion
	press [pres]	Presse
	works council [ˌwɜːks 'kaʊnsl]	Betriebsrat
	purchasing ['pɜːtʃəsɪŋ]	Einkauf
	photocopier ['fəʊtəʊkɒpiə]	Fotokopierer
	pricing ['praɪsɪŋ]	Kalkulation
	quality management ['kwɒləti mænɪdʒmənt]	Qualitätssicherung, -management
	spare part [ˌspeə 'pɑːt]	Ersatzteil
	accounts [ə'kaʊnts]	Buchhaltung
	entrance ['entrəns]	Eingang
	stairs [steəz]	Treppe
18	to **give sb directions** [gɪv də'rekʃnz]	jdm den Weg erklären
	to **ask for directions** [ɑːsk fə də'rekʃnz]	nach dem Weg fragen
	to **happen to do sth** ['hæpən]	etw zufällig tun
	elevator *(AE)* ['elɪveɪtə]	Aufzug
	to **continue** [kən'tɪnjuː]	weitergehen
	pleasure ['pleʒə]	Vergnügen
	My pleasure. [maɪ 'pleʒə]	Gern geschehen.
	opposite ['ɒpəzɪt]	gegenüber von
	ground floor [ˌgraʊnd 'flɔː]	Erdgeschoss
	escalator ['eskəleɪtə]	Rolltreppe
19	**departmental** [ˌdiːpɑːt'mentl]	Abteilungs-
	training ['treɪnɪŋ]	Schulung, Ausbildung
	to **sit in on sth** [ˌsɪt 'ɪn ɒn]	bei etw dabei/ anwesend sein
	to **mention** ['menʃn]	erwähnen
	to **get started** [get 'stɑːtɪd]	loslegen, anfangen
	pleased [pliːzd]	erfreut, froh
	enquiry [ɪn'kwaɪəri]	Anfrage
	corn [kɔːn]	Mais
	to **be aware of sth** [bi ə'weə əv]	sich einer Sache bewusst sein, etw wissen
	to **process** ['prəʊses]	bearbeiten, abwickeln, verarbeiten
	as I go along [əz aɪ ˌgəʊ ə'lɒŋ]	zwischendurch
	capacity [kə'pæsəti]	Kapazität
	step [step]	Schritt
	requirement [rɪ'kwaɪəmənt]	Anforderung, Wunsch
	once [wʌns]	sobald
	firm offer [ˌfɜːm 'ɒfə]	verbindliches Angebot
	down payment ['daʊn peɪmənt]	Anzahlung
	completion [kəm'pliːʃn]	(Aufrags-)Erfüllung
	invoice ['ɪnvɔɪs]	Rechnung
	as soon as [əz 'suːn əz]	sobald
	to **co-ordinate** [kəʊ'ɔːdɪneɪt]	koordinieren
	manpower ['mænpaʊə]	Arbeitskraft, Personal
	to **draw sth up** [ˌdrɔː 'ʌp]	etw erstellen
	schedule ['ʃedjuːl]	Plan, Zeitplan
	assembly [ə'sembli]	Montage
	to **arrange** [ə'reɪndʒ]	planen, arrangieren, ausmachen
	to **ship** [ʃɪp]	verschicken, versenden, verschiffen
20	**organization chart** [ˌɔːgənaɪ'zeɪʃn tʃɑːt]	Organigramm
	research and development (R&D) [rɪˌsɜːtʃ ən dɪ'veləpmənt]	Forschung(s-) und Entwicklung(sabteilung)
	to **monitor** ['mɒnɪtə]	überwachen
	to **improve** [ɪm'pruːv]	verbessern
	existing [ɪg'zɪstɪŋ]	bestehend, vorhanden
	responsible [rɪ'spɒnsəbl]	verantwortlich, zuständig
	to **employ sb** [ɪm'plɔɪ]	jdn einstellen, beschäftigen
	to **train sb** [treɪn]	jdn ausbilden
21	**in charge of** [ɪn 'tʃɑːdʒ əv]	zuständig für, verantwortlich für
	equipment [ɪ'kwɪpmənt]	Geräte, Maschinen, Ausrüstung
	to **deal with sth** ['diːl wɪð]	etw bearbeiten, erledigen, sich um etw kümmern
	to **convince** [kən'vɪns]	überzeugen
	position [pə'zɪʃn]	Stellung, Position
	issue ['ɪʃuː]	Ausgabe
	smooth [smuːð]	glatt, problemlos, einwandfrei
	running ['rʌnɪŋ]	Betrieb
	overall [ˌəʊvər'ɔːl]	Gesamt-
	responsibility [rɪˌspɒnsə'bɪləti]	Verantwortung
	to **attend sth** [ə'tend]	an etw teilnehmen, etw besuchen
	recently ['riːsntli]	neulich
	on the move [ɒn ðə 'muːv]	in Bewegung
	to **entail** [ɪn'teɪl]	mit sich bringen, beinhalten
	patience ['peɪʃns]	Geduld
	cross-cultural [ˌkrɒs'kʌltʃərəl]	kulturübergreifend, interkulturell
	competence ['kɒmpɪtəns]	Kompetenz
	understanding [ˌʌndə'stændɪŋ]	Verständnis

skill [skɪl]	Fähigkeit, Fertigkeit
relationship [rɪ'leɪʃnʃɪp]	Verhältnis, Beziehung
ceremony ['serəməni]	Zeremonie
to **involve** [ɪn'vɒlv]	beinhalten, mit sich bringen
budget ['bʌdʒɪt]	Budget, Haushalt, Etat
in advance [ɪn əd'vɑ:ns]	im Voraus
forecast ['fɔ:kɑ:st]	Voraussagen
permanently ['pɜ:mənəntli]	ständig, laufend
to **analyse** ['ænəlaɪz]	analysieren
figure ['fɪgə]	Zahl
deviation [,di:vi'eɪʃn]	Abweichung
financial report [faɪ,nænʃl rɪ'pɔ:t]	Bilanz, Finanzbericht
to **report to sb** [rɪ'pɔ:t tə]	jdm unterstehen, jdm Bericht erstatten
to **place an order** [,pleɪs ən 'ɔ:də]	einen Auftrag erteilen
to **be capable of doing sth** [bi 'keɪpəbl əv]	fähig/in der Lage sein, etw zu tun
buyer ['baɪə]	Käufer
seller ['selə]	Verkäufer
staff [stɑ:f]	Personal
to **recruit sb** [rɪ'kru:t]	jdn einstellen, anwerben
vocational college [vəʊ,keɪʃənl 'kɒlɪdʒ]	Berufsfachschule
university [,ju:nɪ'vɜ:səti]	Universität
course [kɔ:s]	Kurs, Studium
22 **summary** ['sʌməri]	Zusammenfassung
finances ['faɪnænsɪz]	Finanzen
to **exhibit** [ɪg'zɪbɪt]	ausstellen
duty ['dju:ti]	Pflicht, Aufgabe
to **keep a close eye on sth** [ki:p ə ,kləʊs 'aɪ ɒn]	etw genau im Auge behalten
spending ['spendɪŋ]	Ausgaben
conference ['kɒnfərəns]	Konferenz
frequent(ly) ['fri:kwənt]	häufig
closely ['kləʊsli]	eng
23 **delay** [dɪ'leɪ]	Verzögerung
to **progress** [prə'gres]	fortschreiten, vorankommen
timetable ['taɪmteɪbl]	Zeitplan, Stundenplan
to **be afraid of sb/sth** [bi ə'freɪd əv]	vor jdm/etw Angst haben
24 **average** ['ævərɪdʒ]	Durchschnitt, durchschnittlich
consumer [kən'sju:mə]	Verbraucher/in
eco-friendly ['i:kə frendli]	umweltfreundlich
jar [dʒɑ:]	Glas *(für Marmelade etc.)*
container [kən'teɪnə]	Behälter
steel [sti:l]	Stahl
manufacturer [,mænju'fæktʃərə]	Hersteller
canmaking ['kænmeɪkɪŋ]	Dosenherstellung
to **put the record straight** [pʊt ðə ,rekɔ:d 'streɪt]	die Dinge richtigstellen
to **consider** [kən'sɪdə]	betrachten, ansehen
apart from [ə'pɑ:t frəm]	abgesehen von
obvious ['ɒbviəs]	offensichtlich
convenience [kən'vi:niəns]	Bequemlichkeit, Praktikabilität
reusable [,ri:'ju:zəbl]	wiederverwendbar
infinitely ['ɪnfɪnətli]	unendlich oft
essential [ɪ'senʃl]	wesentlich, unerlässlich
property ['prɒpəti]	Eigenschaft
stakes [steɪks]	Rangliste
light [laɪt]	leicht
resource [rɪ'sɔ:s]	Rohstoff, Ressource
attractive [ə'træktɪv]	attraktiv
advertising campaign ['ædvətaɪzɪŋ kæmpeɪn]	Werbekampagne
initially [ɪ'nɪʃəli]	anfänglich, ursprünglich
ecological [,i:kə'lɒdʒɪkl]	ökologisch
benefit ['benɪfɪt]	Vorteil, Nutzen
in general [ɪn 'dʒenrəl]	im Allgemeinen
push [pʊʃ]	Vorstoß
downgauging ['daʊngeɪdʒɪŋ]	Reduzierung der Materialdicke
to **cut sth** [kʌt]	etw senken
raw material [,rɔ: mə'tɪəriəl]	Rohstoff, Rohmaterial
carbon ['kɑ:bən]	Kohlenstoff, Kohlendioxid
footprint ['fʊtprɪnt]	Fußabdruck
responsible [rɪ'spɒnsəbl]	verantwortungsbewusst
environmental [ɪn,vaɪrən'mentl]	Umwelt-
to **be designed for sth** [bi dɪ'zaɪnd fə]	für etw gedacht sein, etw beabsichtigen
to **make sb aware of sth** [,meɪk ə'weər əv]	jdm über etw informieren, jdm etw ins Bewusstsein rufen
largely ['lɑ:dʒli]	weitgehend
unspoken [,ʌn'spəʊkən]	unausgesprochen
unperceived [,ʌnpə'si:vd]	nicht wahrgenommen
ultimately ['ʌltɪmətli]	letzendlich, letztlich
perception [pə'sepʃn]	Wahrnehmung
rate [reɪt]	Anteil, Rate
to **achieve** [ə'tʃi:v]	erreichen, erzielen
objective [əb'dʒektɪv]	Ziel

25	to **take over** [ˌteɪk 'əʊvə]	(die Führung) übernehmen
	net [net]	netto, Netto-
	loss [lɒs]	Verlust
	sales [seɪlz]	Verkäufe, Absatz
	stock level ['stɒk levl]	Lagerbestand
	wasted ['weɪstɪd]	nicht genutzt, brachliegend
	rival ['raɪvl]	Konkurrent, konkurrierend
	carmaker ['kɑːmeɪkə]	Autobauer
	to **fine-tune** [ˌfaɪn 'tjuːn]	fein abstimmen
	delivery [dɪ'lɪvəri]	Lieferung
	philosophy [fɪ'lɒsəfi]	Philosophie
	to **base on sth** ['beɪs ɒn]	auf etw basieren
	principle ['prɪnsəpl]	Prinzip
	at the expense of [ət ði ɪk'spens əv]	auf Kosten von
	goal [gəʊl]	Ziel
	continuous [kən'tɪnjuəs]	fortlaufend, kontinuierlich
	flow [fləʊ]	Fluß, Ablauf
	surface ['sɜːfɪs]	Oberfläche
	to **avoid** [ə'vɔɪd]	vermeiden, verhindern
	overproduction [ˌəʊvəprə'dʌkʃn]	Überproduktion
	to **level out** [ˌlevl 'aʊt]	nivellieren, ausgleichen
	workload ['wɜːkləʊd]	Arbeitspensum
	to **fix** [fɪks]	*(Problem)* beheben
	in order to [ɪn 'ɔːdə tə]	um … zu
	standardized ['stændədaɪzd]	standardisiert
	foundation [faʊn'deɪʃn]	Grundlage, Basis, Fundament
	improvement [ɪm'pruːvmənt]	Verbesserung
	employee empowerment [ɪmˌplɔɪiː ɪm'paʊəmənt]	Übertragung von Verantwortung und Kompetenz auf Untergebene
	visual ['vɪʒuəl]	visuell, Sicht-
	to **hide** [haɪd]	verbergen, verstecken
	reliable [rɪ'laɪəbl]	zuverlässig
	thoroughly ['θʌrəli]	gründlich
	to **serve** [sɜːv]	dienen
	to **grow sb** [grəʊ]	jdn aufbauen, heranziehen
	leader ['liːdə]	Führungspersönlichkeit
	to **develop** [dɪ'veləp]	entwickeln
	exceptional(ly) [ɪk'sepʃənl]	außergewöhnlich
	extended [ɪk'stendɪd]	ausgedehnt
	network ['netwɜːk]	Netzwerk
	to **challenge sb** ['tʃælɪndʒ]	jdn herausfordern, jdm schwierige Aufgaben stellen
	to **improve** [ɪm'pruːv]	besser werden, sich verbessern
	consensus [kən'sensəs]	Konsens
	by consensus [baɪ kən'sensəs]	auf Konsensbasis
	to **consider sth** [kən'sɪdə]	berücksichtigen, in Betracht ziehen
	to **implement sth** ['ɪmplɪmənt]	etw umsetzen
	relentless [rɪ'lentləs]	unnachgiebig
	reflection [rɪ'flekʃn]	Reflexion, Nachdenken, Überdenken
	inefficiency [ˌɪnɪ'fɪʃnsi]	Ineffizienz
	to **correspond to sth** [ˌkɒrɪ'spɒnd tə]	einer Sache entsprechen
	to **encourage** [ɪn'kʌrɪdʒ]	ermutigen, motivieren
	immediately [ɪ'miːdiətli]	unverzüglich, sofort
	to **motivate** ['məʊtɪveɪt]	motivieren
	efficient [ɪ'fɪʃnt]	effizient
	period ['pɪəriəd]	Zeitabschnitt, Zeit
	to **take the trouble** [ˌteɪk ðə 'trʌbl]	sich die Mühe machen

Unit 3

26	**piece of advice** [piːs əv əd'vaɪs]	Ratschlag, Tipp
	breath [breθ]	Atem
	to **take a deep breath** [teɪk ə ˌdiːp 'breθ]	tief einatmen, durchatmen
27	**clothing** ['kləʊðɪŋ]	Bekleidung, Kleidung
	chain [tʃeɪn]	Kette
	wear [weə]	Bekleidung, Kleidung
	to **stock sth** [stɒk]	etw *(Ware)* führen, ins Sortiment nehmen
	to **put sb through** [ˌpʊt 'θruː]	*(Telefon:)* jdn durchstellen, verbinden
	to **hold (the line)** [həʊld]	*(Telefon:)* am Apparat bleiben
	to **take a message** [ˌteɪk ə 'mesɪdʒ]	*(Telefon:)* etw ausrichten
	to **dial** ['daɪəl]	*(Telefon:)* wählen
	extension [ɪk'stenʃn]	Durchwahl
	to **catch sth** [kætʃ]	etw verstehen
	to **reach sb** [riːtʃ]	jdn erreichen
	engaged [ɪn'geɪdʒd]	*(Telefon:)* besetzt
	to **return sb's call** [rɪˌtɜːn sʌmbədiz 'kɔːl]	jdn zurückrufen
	urgent ['ɜːdʒənt]	dringend
	to **put sb on hold** [pʊt ɒn 'həʊld]	*(Telefon:)* jdn in die Warteschleife stellen/legen

	Hold on. [ˌhəʊld 'ɒn]	Einen Moment.
	to **step** [step]	treten, gehen
28	**secretary** ['sekrətri]	Sekretär/in
	boss [bɒs]	Chef/in
	to **summarize** ['sʌməraɪz]	zusammenfassen
	to **address sb** [ə'dres]	jdn anreden, ansprechen
	first name ['fɜːst neɪm]	Vorname
	to **appear** [ə'pɪə]	scheinen, erscheinen, auftreten
	to **invite sb to do sth** [ɪn'vaɪt]	jdn dazu auffordern, etw zu tun
	business contact ['bɪznəs kɒntækt]	Geschäftspartner
	approach [ə'prəʊtʃ]	Vorgehen(sweise), Ansatz, Herangehensweise
	old-fashioned [ˌəʊld'fæʃənd]	veraltet, altmodisch
	acceptable [ək'septəbl]	akzeptabel
	similar ['sɪmələ]	ähnlich
	meaning ['miːnɪŋ]	Bedeutung
	to **get back to sb** [ˌget 'bæk ət]	jdn zurückrufen, sich bei jdm melden
	connection [kə'nekʃn]	Verbindung
	to **connect** [kə'nekt]	verbinden
	busy ['bɪzi]	*(Telefon:)* besetzt
29	**digit** ['dɪdʒɪt]	Ziffer
	separate(ly) ['seprət]	einzeln
	except for [ɪk'sept fə]	außer
	country code ['kʌntri kəʊd]	Ländervorwahl
	landline ['lændlaɪn]	Festnetz
	to **act out** [ˌækt 'aʊt]	spielen, vor-/durchspielen
30	to **transfer** ['trænsfɜː]	weiterleiten, weitergeben
	to **apologize** [ə'pɒlədʒaɪz]	sich entschuldigen, um Entschuldigung bitten
	to **be available** [bi ə'veɪləbl]	*(Telefon:)* zu sprechen sein
	to **spell** [spel]	buchstabieren
	to **express** [ɪk'spres]	ausdrücken, zum Ausdruck bringen
T	**Never mind.** [ˌnevə 'maɪnd]	Das macht nichts.
	publicity [pʌb'lɪsəti]	Werbung, Werbe-
	straight [streɪt]	sofort, gleich
	first thing ['fɜːst θɪŋ]	gleich, als erstes
31	to **note down** [ˌnəʊt 'daʊn]	notieren, aufschreiben
	dot [dɒt]	Punkt
	hyphen ['haɪfn]	Bindestrich
	forward slash ['fɔːwəd slæʃ]	Schrägstrich
	underscore [ˌʌndə'skɔː]	Unterstrich
	answerphone ['ɑːnsəfəʊn]	Anrufbeantworter
	to **leave a message** [liːv ə 'mesɪdʒ]	eine Nachricht hinterlassen
T	**unfortunately** [ʌn'fɔːtʃənətli]	leider, unglücklicherweise
	to **bother sb** ['bɒðə]	jdm Umstände bereiten, jdn belästigen
	to **confirm** [kən'fɜːm]	bestätigen
32	**brand** [brænd]	Marke
	to **take place** [teɪk 'pleɪs]	stattfinden
	alternatively [ɔːl'tɜːnətɪvli]	alternativ, oder, auch
	cheers [tʃɪəz]	danke
	tone [təʊn]	Ton
	to **record** ['rekɔːd]	aufnehmen, aufzeichnen
	politeness [pə'laɪtnəs]	Höflichkeit
	polite [pə'laɪt]	höflich
	helpful ['helpfl]	hilfsbereit
	impression [ɪm'preʃn]	Eindruck
	rude [ruːd]	unhöflich, unverschämt
	to **mind** [maɪnd]	etw dagegen haben
	Would you mind … [ˌwʊd juː 'maɪnd]	Könnten Sie bitte …
	to **soften** ['sɒfn]	abmildern
33	to **slow down** [ˌsləʊ 'daʊn]	langsamer werden/sprechen
	unclear(ly) [ˌʌn'klɪə]	undeutlich, unklar
	clear(ly) ['klɪəli]	deutlich, klar
	to **speak up** [ˌspiːk 'ʌp]	lauter sprechen
	to **put sth into action** [ˌpʊt ɪntu 'ækʃn]	etw in die Tat umsetzen
	to **rephrase** [ˌriː'freɪz]	neu formulieren, umformulieren
34	**cap** [kæp]	Mütze, Kappe
	series ['sɪəriːz]	Reihe, Serie
P	**reference** ['refərəns]	Bezug, Referenz
	availability [əˌveɪlə'bɪləti]	Verfügbarkeit, Lieferbarkeit
	quantity ['kwɒntəti]	Menge
	to **specify** ['spesɪfaɪ]	(genau) angeben, bestimmen
	to **compromise** ['kɒmprəmaɪz]	sich einigen, einen Kompromiss eingehen
	consignment [kən'saɪnmənt]	Sendung, Lieferung
	despite [dɪ'spaɪt]	trotz
	on time [ɒn 'taɪm]	pünktlich
	traffic jam ['træfɪk dʒæm]	Stau
	lunchtime ['lʌntʃtaɪm]	Mittag(szeit)
35	**greeting** ['griːtɪŋ]	Begrüßung, Grußformel
	complicated ['kɒmplɪkeɪtɪd]	kompliziert

	power ['paʊə]	Macht, Stärke, Kraft
	honest ['ɒnɪst]	ehrlich
	listener ['lɪsnə]	Zuhörer/in
	to **tend to do sth** ['tend tə]	dazu neigen, etw zu tun
	to **mirror** ['mɪrə]	spiegeln, widerspiegeln
	state [steɪt]	Zustand
	to **respond** [rɪ'spɒnd]	reagieren
	chances are [ˌtʃɑ:nsɪz 'ɑ:]	es ist wahrscheinlich, dass
	edge [edʒ]	Kante
	sincerity [sɪn'serəti]	Aufrichtigkeit
	sincere [sɪn'sɪə]	aufrichtig
	glad [glæd]	froh
	sentiment ['sentɪmənt]	Gefühl, Sentimentalität
	brevity ['brevəti]	Kürze
	to **fear** [fɪə]	befürchten
	to **run out of sth** [ˌrʌn 'aʊt əv]	ausgehen, wegbleiben
	excessive(ly) [ɪk'sesɪv]	übertrieben, übermäßig
	to **execute** ['eksɪkju:t]	ausführen
	to **waste** [weɪst]	verschwenden, vergeuden
	fortunately ['fɔ:tʃənətli]	glücklicherweise
	guideline ['gaɪdlaɪn]	Richtlinie
	to **assure** [ə'ʃʊə]	sicherstellen
36	**brick** [brɪk]	Backstein, Ziegel
	to **weigh** [weɪ]	wiegen
	to **recharge** [ˌri:'tʃɑ:dʒ]	*(Akku)* aufladen
	battery ['bætəri]	Akku
	power ['paʊə]	Strom
	at a time [ət ə 'taɪm]	auf einmal, jeweils
	neat(ly) [ni:t]	schlank, formschön, elegant
	computing power [kəm'pju:tɪŋ paʊə]	Rechenleistung
	moon [mu:n]	Mond
	to **access sth** ['ækses]	auf etw zugreifen
	database ['deɪtəbeɪs]	Datenbank
	demonstration [ˌdemən'streɪʃn]	Vorführung
	incredible [ɪn'kredəbl]	unglaublich
	device [dɪ'vaɪs]	Gerät
	to **argue** ['ɑ:gju:]	argumentieren
	tool [tu:l]	Werkeug
	obsolete ['ɒbsəli:t]	veraltet, überholt
	globalized ['gləʊbəlaɪzd]	globalisiert
	increasingly [ɪn'kri:sɪŋli]	in zunehmendem Maße
	context ['kɒntekst]	Zusammenhang
	solution [sə'lu:ʃn]	Lösung
	to **give up on sth** [ˌgɪv 'ʌp ɒn]	etw aufgeben, auf etw verzichen
	pain [peɪn]	Schmerz(en)
	shoulder ['ʃəʊldə]	Schulter
	to **fit** [fɪt]	passen
	jacket ['dʒækɪt]	Jacke, Sakko
	pocket ['pɒkɪt]	Tasche
	frustrating [frʌ'streɪtɪŋ]	frustrierend
	compared to [kəm'peəd tə]	im Vergleich zu
	saving ['seɪvɪŋ]	Einsparung, Ersparnis
	to **switch to** ['swɪtʃ tə]	wechseln zu
	current(ly) ['kʌrəntli]	aktuell, momentan
	reality [ri'æləti]	Wirklichkeit
	to **equip** [ɪ'kwɪp]	ausstatten, ausrüsten
	infrastructure ['ɪnfrəstrʌktʃə]	Infrastruktur
	impressive [ɪm'presɪv]	beeindruckend
	functionality [ˌfʌŋkʃə'næləti]	Funktionalität
	headline ['hedlaɪn]	Überschrift
	to **replace** [rɪ'pleɪs]	ersetzen
	to **outsmart** [ˌaʊt'smɑ:t]	überlisten
	to **make sense** [meɪk 'sens]	sinnvoll sein

Unit 4

37	**item** ['aɪtəm]	Gegenstand, Artikel, Sache
	credit card ['kredɪt kɑ:d]	Kreditkarte
	passport ['pɑ:spɔ:t]	Reisepass
	boarding card ['bɔ:dɪŋ kɑ:d]	Bordkarte
38	**connector** [kə'nektə]	Stecker, Steckverbinder
	terminal ['tɜ:mɪnl]	Anschluss, Anschlussleiste
	business development ['bɪznəs dɪveləpmənt]	Geschäftsentwicklung
	colleague ['kɒli:g]	Kollege/-in
	to **return** [rɪ'tɜ:n]	zurückfahren, -fliegen, -kommen, -kehren
	rental car [ˌrentl 'kɑ:]	Mietwagen
	to **depart** [dɪ'pɑ:t]	abfahren, -fliegen, -reisen
	to **catch sth** [kætʃ]	etw bekommen, erreichen, erwischen
	accommodation [əˌkɒmə'deɪʃn]	Unterkunft
	exhibition and conference centre [eksɪˌbɪʃn ənd 'kɒnfərəns sentə]	Ausstellungs- und Konferenzzentrum
	smoker ['sməʊkə]	Raucher/in
	to **smoke** [sməʊk]	rauchen
	pretty ['prɪti]	ziemlich
	to **keep sth in mind** [ˌki:p ɪn 'maɪnd]	an etw denken

	gym [dʒɪm]	Fitnessstudio
	to **pick sb/sth up** [ˌpɪk ˈʌp]	jdn/etw abholen
	possibly [ˈpɒsəbli]	eventuell, möglicherweise, vielleicht
	return journey [rɪˌtɜːn ˈdʒɜːni]	Rückfahrt, -flug, -reise
39	**ideally** [aɪˈdiːəli]	im Idealfall
40	to **require** [rɪˈkwaɪə]	benötigen, wünschen
P	**destination** [ˌdestɪˈneɪʃn]	Reiseziel, Zielort
	departure [dɪˈpɑːtʃə]	Abreise, Abfahrt, Abflug
	arrival [əˈraɪvl]	Ankunft
	to **note sth** [nəʊt]	etw beachten
	confusion [kənˈfjuːʒn]	Verwirrung, Verwechslung
	worth [wɜːθ]	wert
41	to **search** [sɜːtʃ]	suchen
	surname [ˈsɜːneɪm]	Nachname
	baggage [ˈbægɪdʒ]	Gepäck
	charge [tʃɑːdʒ]	Gebühr
	excess baggage [ˌekses ˈbægɪdʒ]	Übergepäck
	to **insure** [ɪnˈʃʊə]	versichern
	to **accept** [əkˈsept]	akzeptieren
	payment [ˈpeɪmənt]	Zahlung
	to **cancel** [ˈkænsl]	stornieren
	terms and conditions [ˌtɜːmz ənd kənˈdɪʃnz]	Konditionen, (Allgemeine) Geschäftsbedingungen
	to **be in a hurry** [bi ɪn ə ˈhʌri]	in Eile sein, es eilig haben
	speedy [ˈspiːdi]	schnell
	boarding [ˈbɔːdɪŋ]	An-Bord-Gehen
	frequent [ˈfriːkwənt]	häufig
	expiry [ɪkˈspaɪəri]	Ablauf
	customer loyalty [ˌkʌstəmə ˈlɔɪəlti]	Kundentreue, Kundenbindung
	scheme [skiːm]	Programm
	insurance [ɪnˈʃʊərəns]	Versicherung
	luggage [ˈlʌgɪdʒ]	Gepäck
	to **check in** [ˌtʃek ˈɪn]	einchecken
	to **enter sth** [ˈentə]	etw *(Text etc.)* eingeben
42	to **do business** [du ˈbɪznəs]	Geschäfte machen
	car park [ˈkɑː pɑːk]	Parkplatz, Parkhaus, Tiefgarage
	facilities [fəˈsɪlətiz]	Einrichtungen
	to **stroll** [strəʊl]	schlendern, gehen
	to **make use of sth** [meɪk ˈjuːs əv]	etw nutzen, benutzen
	bus service [ˈbʌs sɜːvɪs]	Busverbindung
	splendid [ˈsplendɪd]	prachtvoll, herrlich, großartig

country house [ˈkʌntri haʊs]	Landsitz
acre [ˈeɪkə]	*Flächenmaß, entspricht 0,405 Hektar*
lush [lʌʃ]	üppig, satt
parkland [ˈpɑːklænd]	Parklandschaft, Grünland
to **comprise** [kəmˈpraɪz]	umfassen, bestehen aus
suite [swiːt]	Suite
single room [ˌsɪŋgl ˈruːm]	Einzelzimmer
double room [ˌdʌbl ˈruːm]	Doppelzimmer
fully-equipped [ˌfʊli ɪˈkwɪpt]	voll ausgestattet
en-suite bathroom [ɒ ˌswiːt ˈbɑːθruːm]	eigenes Badezimmer
to **accommodate** [əˈkɒmədeɪt]	unterbringen, Platz bieten für
participant [pɑːˈtɪsɪpənt]	Teilnehmer/in
latest [ˈleɪtɪst]	neueste/r/s
digital projector [ˌdɪdʒɪtl prəˈdʒektə]	Beamer
cordless [ˈkɔːdləs]	schnurlos
microphone [ˈmaɪkrəfəʊn]	Mikrofon
to **complement** [ˈkɒmplɪmənt]	ergänzen
to **photocopy** [ˈfəʊtəʊkɒpi]	fotokopieren
secure [sɪˈkjʊə]	sicher
access [ˈækses]	Zugang, Zugriff
wireless [ˈwaɪələs]	drahtlos
available [əˈveɪləbl]	verfügbar, erhältlich
from … onwards [ˌfrəm ˈɒnwədz]	ab …
in the event of [ɪn ði ɪˈvent əv]	für den Fall, dass
to **check out** [ˌtʃek ˈaʊt]	auschecken
arrangement [əˈreɪndʒmənt]	Vereinbarung, Abmachung
by prior arrangement [baɪ ˌpraɪə əˈreɪndʒmənt]	nach vorheriger Vereinbarung
leisure [ˈleʒə]	Freizeit
to **unwind** [ˌʌnˈwaɪnd]	sich entspannen, abschalten
court [kɔːt]	(Tennis-, Squash-)Platz
to **dine** [daɪn]	speisen
to **be spoilt for choice** [bi ˌspɔɪlt fə ˈtʃɔɪs]	die Qual der Wahl haben
eatery [ˈiːtəri]	Restaurant, Speiselokal
star [stɑː]	Stern
rating [ˈreɪtɪŋ]	Bewertung
restaurant guide [ˈrestrɒnt gaɪd]	Restaurantführer

	blend [blend]	Mixtur, Mischung
	cuisine [kwɪ'zi:n]	(Landes-)Küche
	cabin ['kæbɪn]	Hütte
	to **prove** [pru:v]	beweisen, nachweisen, den Nachweis erbringen
	cake [keɪk]	Kuchen
	pastry ['peɪstri]	(Süß-)Gebäck
	to die for [tə 'daɪ fə]	umwerfend
	delicious [dɪ'lɪʃəs]	köstlich
	to **combine** [kəm'baɪn]	kombinieren
	romantic [rəʊ'mæntɪk]	romantisch
	view [vju:]	Aussicht, Ausblick
	to **entertain sb** [ˌentə'teɪn]	jdn bewirten
	to **impress** [ɪm'pres]	beeindrucken
	peace and quiet [ˌpi:s ənd 'kwaɪət]	Ruhe und Frieden
	to **be pleased to do sth** [bi 'pli:zd tə]	etw gern tun
	comfort ['kʌmfət]	Komfort, Annehmlichkeit
	to **operate sth** ['ɒpəreɪt]	*hier:* vertreten, umsetzen
	policy ['pɒləsi]	Politik, Vorgehensweise, Linie
	premises ['premɪsɪz]	Räumlichkeiten, Gelände
43	**feature** ['fi:tʃə]	Merkmal, Punkt, Besonderheit
	to **refer to sb/sth** [rɪ'fɜ: tə]	sich auf jdn/etw beziehen, auf jdn/etw verweisen, jdn/etw bezeichnen
	secretarial [ˌsekrə'teəriəl]	Sekretariats-
	smoking area ['sməʊkɪŋ eəriə]	Raucherbereich
	to **differ** ['dɪfə]	sich unterscheiden
T	**within walking distance** [wɪðɪn 'wɔ:kɪŋ dɪstəns]	in Laufweite
	in addition [ɪn ə'dɪʃn]	zusätzlich
	snack [snæk]	Imbiss
	limited ['lɪmɪtɪd]	begrenzt, beschränkt
	conservatory [kən'sɜ:vətri]	Wintergarten, Gewächshaus
	worried ['wʌrid]	besorgt
	to **depend on/upon sth** [dɪ'pend ɒn/əpɒn]	von etw abhängen, auf etw ankommen
	to **vacate** [və'keɪt]	räumen
	to **drop sth off** [ˌdrɒp 'ɒf]	etw abgeben, dalassen
	receptionist [rɪ'sepʃənɪst]	Empfangsmitarbeiter/in
	logical ['lɒdʒɪkl]	logisch
44	**twin room** [ˌtwɪn 'ru:m]	Zweibettzimmer

P	**closed** [kləʊzd]	geschlossen
	to **exceed** [ɪk'si:d]	überschreiten, übertreffen
	mileage allowance [ˌmaɪlɪdʒ ə'laʊəns]	Freikilometer *(bzw.* -meilen*)*
	rental ['rentl]	Miete
	rental period [ˌrentl 'pɪəriəd]	Mietzeitraum
	tank [tæŋk]	Tank
	fuel ['fju:əl]	Treibstoff, Benzin
	vehicle ['vi:əkl]	Fahrzeug
	confirmation [ˌkɒnfə'meɪʃn]	Bestätigung
	delighted [dɪ'laɪtɪd]	erfreut
	to **bill sb sth** [bɪl]	jdm etw in Rechnung stellen
	mile [maɪl]	Meile
	additionally [ə'dɪʃənəli]	außerdem
	return [rɪ'tɜ:n]	Rückgabe
	to **charge sb sth** [tʃɑ:dʒ]	jdm etw in Rechnung stellen
	to **refill** [ˌri:'fɪl]	auffüllen
	Best regards [best rɪ'gɑ:dz]	Mit freundlichen Grüßen
	to **quote** [kwəʊt]	*(Preis)* angeben, nennen
	VAT (value added tax) [ˌvælju: 'ædɪd tæks]	Mehrwertsteuer
45	**bags** [bægz]	Gepäck, Koffer
46	**client** ['klaɪənt]	Kunde/-in
	refreshment [rɪ'freʃmənt]	Erfrischung
	broken ['brəʊkən]	kaputt
	to **cause** [kɔ:z]	verursachen
47	to **put the brakes on sth** [ˌpʊt ðə 'breɪks ɒn]	etw herunterfahren, einer Sache einen Riegel vorschieben
	rising ['raɪzɪŋ]	steigend
	unlike [ˌʌn'laɪk]	anders als
	strategy ['strætədʒi]	Strategie
	advisor [əd'vaɪzə]	Berater/in
	corporate ['kɔ:pərət]	Unternehmens-, Geschäfts-
	wasteful ['weɪstfl]	verschwenderisch
	according to [ə'kɔ:dɪŋ tə]	laut, nach, gemäß
	survey ['sɜ:veɪ]	Umfrage, Studie
	mid-sized [ˌmɪd'saɪzd]	mittelgroß, mittelständisch
	to **enforce** [ɪn'fɔ:s]	durchsetzen, umsetzen
	pattern ['pætn]	Muster
	to **negotiate** [nɪ'gəʊʃieɪt]	verhandeln, aushandeln
	price cut ['praɪs kʌt]	Preisnachlass
	preferred [prɪ'fɜ:d]	bevorzugt
	wise [waɪz]	klug

	to look closely at sth [ˌlʊk ˈkləʊsli ət]	sich etw genau ansehen, einen genauen Blick auf etw werfen
	travel expenses [ˈtrævl ɪkspensɪz]	Reisespesen
	to carry out [ˌkæri ˈaʊt]	durchführen
	to take action [teɪk ˈækʃn]	Maßnahmen ergreifen
	abuse [əˈbjuːs]	Missbrauch
	to audit [ˈɔːdɪt]	prüfen
	claim [kleɪm]	Forderung, Anspruch
	to advise [ədˈvaɪz]	raten
	to lower [ˈləʊə]	senken
	in the first place [ɪn ðə ˈfɜːst pleɪs]	überhaupt
	to minimize [ˈmɪnɪmaɪz]	minimieren
	to demonstrate [ˈdemənstreɪt]	vorführen, zeigen
	section [ˈsekʃn]	Abschnitt
	provider [prəˈvaɪdə]	Anbieter

Unit 5

48	**to label** [ˈleɪbl]	etikettieren, beschriften, benennen
	conference call [ˈkɒnfərəns kɔːl]	Konferenzschaltung
	face-to-face [ˌfeɪs tə ˈfeɪs]	persönlich
	suitable [ˈsuːtəbl]	geeignet
	extreme [ɪkˈstriːm]	extrem
	condition [kənˈdɪʃn]	Bedingung
	to fire sb [ˈfaɪə]	jdn entlassen
	job interview [ˈdʒɒb ɪntəvjuː]	Vorstellungsgespräch
	North Sea [ˌnɔːθ ˈsiː]	Nordsee
	weekly [ˈwiːkli]	wöchentlich
	to draw [drɔː]	zeichnen
	to rank [ræŋk]	einstufen
	importance [ɪmˈpɔːtns]	Wichtigkeit, Bedeutung
49	**circle** [ˈsɜːkl]	Kreis
	branch [brɑːntʃ]	Ast
	to radiate [ˈreɪdieɪt]	sternförmig ausgehen
	thin [θɪn]	dünn
	screen [skrin]	Bildschirm
	brewery [ˈbruːəri]	Brauerei
	to brew [bruː]	brauen
	draft [drɑːft]	Entwurf
	doubt [daʊt]	Zweifel
	no doubt [ˌnəʊ ˈdaʊt]	zweifellos, bestimmt
	to postpone [pəˈspəʊn]	verschieben
	to consult sb [kənˈsʌlt]	jdn fragen, sich mit jdm beraten
	to schedule [ˈʃedjuːl]	*(Besprechung etc.)* ansetzen
	to install [ɪnˈstɔːl]	installieren
	any other business (AOB) [ˌeni ˌʌðə ˈbɪznəs]	Sonstiges
	suggestion [səˈdʒestʃən]	Vorschlag
	as regards [əz rɪˈgɑːdz]	bezüglich, was … anbelangt
	to circulate sth [ˈsɜːkjəleɪt]	etw verteilen, verschicken
	minutes [ˈmɪnɪts]	Protokoll
50	**record** [ˈrekɔːd]	Aufzeichnung, Unterlage
	to finalize [ˈfaɪnəlaɪz]	festlegen, beschließen
	to reply [rɪˈplaɪ]	antworten
	to suggest [səˈdʒest]	vorschlagen
	issue [ˈɪʃuː]	Frage, Thema, Problem
	complaint [kəmˈpleɪnt]	Reklamation, Beschwerde
	punctual [ˈpʌŋktʃuəl]	pünktlich
	second-hand [ˌsekəndˈhænd]	gebraucht
	after-sales service [ˈɑːftəseɪlz sɜːvɪs]	Kundendienst
	wholesale [ˈhəʊlseɪl]	Großhandel
	repair [rɪˈpeə]	Reparatur
	to be in agreement with sth [bi ɪn əˈgriːmənt wɪð]	einer Sache zustimmen
	Yours sincerely [jɔːz sɪnˈsɪəli]	Hochachtungsvoll, Mit freundlichen Grüßen
51	**recipient** [rɪˈsɪpiənt]	Empfänger/in
	to sign off [ˌsaɪn ˈɒf]	einen Brief beenden, unterschreiben
	otherwise [ˈʌðəwaɪz]	ansonsten, sonst, auch
	capital letter [ˈkæpɪtl letə]	Großbuchstabe
	to split [splɪt]	teilen, aufteilen
	paragraph [ˈpærəgrɑːf]	*(Text:)* Absatz
	to separate [ˈsepəreɪt]	trennen
	free line [ˌfriː ˈlaɪn]	Leerzeile
	attachment [əˈtætʃmənt]	*(E-Mail:)* Anhang
	convention [kənˈvenʃn]	Versammlung
	theme [θiːm]	Motto, Thema
	passionate(ly) [ˈpæʃənət]	leidenschaftlich
	to support [səˈpɔːt]	unterstützen
	fee [fiː]	Honorar
52	**to forward sth** [ˈfɔːwəd]	etw weiterleiten
	to get to the point [get tə ðə ˈpɔɪnt]	zum Thema kommen
	request [rɪˈkwest]	Bitte, Wunsch
	closing sentence [ˈkləʊzɪŋ sentəns]	Schlussatz
	assistance [əˈsɪstəns]	Hilfe, Unterstützung
	to come on board [ˌkʌm ɒn ˈbɔːd]	an Bord kommen, dabei sein
	to act [ækt]	handeln, fungieren

	agent ['eɪdʒənt]	Agent/in
	on **behalf** of sb [ɒn bɪ'hɑ:f əv]	für jdn
	to **go ahead** [ˌɡəʊ ə'hed]	anfangen
	upward ['ʌpwəd]	nach oben
	to **conclude** [kən'klu:d]	abschließend
	to **be well received** [bi ˌwel rɪ'si:vd]	gut *(beim Publikum etc.)* ankommen
	to **comment** ['kɒment]	sich äußern, etw dazu sagen
53	**graph** [ɡrɑ:f]	Diagramm
	thoroughly ['θʌrəli]	völlig
	to **cover sth** ['kʌvə]	*(Thema)* behandeln
	to **wrap sth up** [ˌræp 'ʌp]	etw abschließen
54	to **interrupt** [ˌɪntə'rʌpt]	unterbrechen
	to **rise** [raɪz]	steigen
	to **grow** [ɡrəʊ]	zunehmen, wachsen
	to **increase** ['ɪŋkri:s]	zunehmen, steigen
	stable ['steɪbl]	stabil
	to **remain** [rɪ'meɪn]	bleiben
	to **even out** [ˌi:vn 'aʊt]	sich einpendeln
	downward ['daʊnwəd]	nach unten
	to **drop** [drɒp]	fallen, sinken
	to **decrease** ['di:kri:s]	abnehmen, sinken
	to **indicate** ['ɪndɪkeɪt]	anzeigen
	degree [dɪ'ɡri:]	Ausmaß, Grad
	negligibly ['neɡlɪdʒəbli]	vernachlässigbar
	slightly ['slaɪtli]	geringfügig
	considerably [kən'sɪdərəbli]	erheblich
	sharply ['ʃɑ:pli]	drastisch, rapide
	dramatically [drə'mætɪkli]	dramatisch
	chart [tʃɑ:t]	Diagramm
	hectolitre [ˌhektə'li:tə]	Hektoliter
55	**press officer** ['pres ɒfɪsə]	Pressereferent/in
	industrial business management assistant [ɪnˌdʌstriəl ˌbɪznəs 'mænɪdʒmənt əsɪstənt]	Industriekaufmann/-frau
	training officer ['treɪnɪŋ ɒfɪsə]	Ausbildungsleiter/in
T	**(suit)case** ['su:tkeɪs]	Koffer
	to **suppose** [sə'pəʊz]	annehmen, glauben
	inquisitive [ɪn'kwɪzətɪv]	neugierig
	sight [saɪt]	Sehenswürdigkeit
	aeroplane ['eərəpleɪn]	Flugzeug
	meat [mi:t]	Fleisch
	dish [dɪʃ]	Gericht, Speise
	cow [kaʊ]	Kuh
	beef [bi:f]	Rindfleisch
	sausage ['sɒsɪdʒ]	Wurst, Würstchen

	celebrity [sə'lebrəti]	Prominente/r
	fashion ['fæʃn]	Mode
56	**native speaker** [ˌneɪtɪv 'spi:kə]	Muttersprachler/in
	to **be considered sth** [bi kən'sɪdəd]	als etw gelten
	atmosphere ['ætməsfɪə]	Atmosphäre
	politics *(pl)* ['pɒlətɪks]	Politik
	heat [hi:t]	Hitze
	to **shadow sb** ['ʃædəʊ]	bei jdm hospitieren
	return visit [rɪ'tɜ:n vɪsɪt]	Gegenbesuch
P	**homestay accommodation** ['həʊmsteɪ əkɒmədeɪʃn]	Unterbringung bei Gastfamilien
	exam [ɪɡ'zæm]	Prüfung
	flat [flæt]	Wohnung
	workmate ['wɜ:kmeɪt]	Arbeitskollege/-in
	Easter ['i:stə]	Ostern
	to **take the minutes** [ˌteɪk ðə 'mɪnɪts]	Protokoll führen
	to **receive** [rɪ'si:v]	erhalten, bekommen
57	to **review sth** [rɪ'vju:]	etw Revue passieren lassen
T	**review** [rɪ'vju:]	Rückschau
	especially [ɪ'speʃəli]	besonders, insbesondere
	to **enrol for sth** [ɪn'rəʊl fə]	sich für etw anmelden
	time difference ['taɪm dɪfrəns]	Zeitverschiebung
	a good cause [ə ˌɡʊd 'kɔ:z]	ein guter Zweck, eine gute Sache
	disability [ˌdɪsə'bɪləti]	Behinderung
	Count me in. [ˌkaʊnt mi: 'ɪn]	Ich bin dabei.
	helper ['helpə]	Helfer/in
	freedom ['fri:dəm]	Freiheit
	I suppose so. [aɪ sə'pəʊz səʊ]	Mag sein. Kann schon sein.
	internal(ly) [ɪn'tɜ:nəli]	intern
	charity ['tʃærəti]	Wohltätigkeit, guter Zweck
	to **sum up** [ˌsʌm 'ʌp]	zusammenfassen
	attendee [əˌten'di:]	Anwesende/r
	charitable ['tʃærətəbl]	Wohltätigkeits-
	community [kə'mju:nəti]	Gemeinde, Gemeinschaft
58	**beer** [bɪə]	Bier
	to **greet sb** [ɡri:t]	jdn begrüßen
	chat [tʃæt]	Unterhaltung, Schwätzchen
	to **invent** [ɪn'vent]	erfinden
	opening hours ['əʊpənɪŋ aʊəz]	Öffnungszeiten
	gallery ['ɡæləri]	Galerie
59	to **stink** [stɪŋk]	stinken

extract ['ekstrækt]	Auszug
tense [tens]	angespannt
sociology [ˌsəusi'ɒlədʒi]	Soziologie
to **sense** [sens]	spüren, erspüren
to **seek** [si:k]	suchen
goggles ['gɒglz]	(Schutz-)Brille
to **glow** [gləu]	leuchten
human ['hju:mən]	Mensch
vibes [vaɪbz]	Schwingungen, Atmosphäre
particularly [pə'tɪkjələli]	insbesondere, ganz besonders
averse [ə'vɜ:s]	abgeneigt
to **assert** [ə'sɜ:t]	behaupten
explanation [ˌeksplə'neɪʃn]	Erklärung, Erläuterung
definite(ly) ['defɪnətli]	bestimmt
to **ignore** [ɪg'nɔ:]	ignorieren, nicht beachten
crazy ['kreɪzi]	verrückt
to **roll eyeballs** [ˌrəul 'aɪbɔ:lz]	mit den Augen rollen
blank stare [ˌblæŋk 'steə]	starrer Gesichtsausdruck
silence ['saɪləns]	Schweigen
to **laugh at sb** ['lɑ:f ət]	jdn auslachen
to **slouch** [slautʃ]	sich lümmeln
to **entertain** [ˌentə'teɪn]	unterhalten
to **get along** [ˌget ə'lɒŋ]	gut miteinander auskommen, sich gut verstehen
decent ['di:snt]	anständig
joke [dʒəuk]	Witz, Scherz
gossip ['gɒsɪp]	Klatsch, Tratsch
educational [ˌedʒu'keɪʃənl]	lehrreich
seriously ['sɪəriəsli]	im Ernst
to **get into full swing** [get ɪntə ˌful 'swɪŋ]	richtig ins Rollen kommen
to **degenerate** [dɪ'dʒenəreɪt]	ausarten
particular [pə'tɪkjələ]	bestimmt
agency ['eɪdʒənsi]	Agentur
dozen ['dʌzn]	Dutzend
government ['gʌvənmənt]	Regierung, öffentliche Verwaltung
to **whip sth out** [ˌwɪp 'aut]	etw zücken
leather portfolio [ˌleðə pɔ:t'fəuliəu]	lederne Aktenmappe
group dynamics [ˌgru:p daɪ'næmɪks]	Gruppendynamik
to **go into motion** [ˌgəu ɪntə 'məuʃn]	in Bewegung geraten
behaviour [bɪ'heɪvjə]	Verhalten, Benehmen
boring ['bɔ:rɪŋ]	langweilig

Unit 6

60	**stage** [steɪdʒ]	Phase, Abschnitt, Stadium
	various ['veəriəs]	verschieden
	to **package** ['pækɪdʒ]	verpacken
	distributor [dɪ'strɪbjətə]	Vertrieb, Händler
	feature ['fi:tʃə]	Eigenschaft
	market research [ˌmɑ:kɪt rɪ'sɜ:tʃ]	Marktforschung
61	**innovative** ['ɪnəveɪtɪv]	innovativ
	to **specialize in sth** ['speʃəlaɪz ɪn]	sich auf etw spezialisieren
	manufacture [ˌmænju'fæktʃə]	Herstellung, Fertigung
	front panel [ˌfrʌnt 'pænl]	Frontplatte, Geräte-/ Gehäusefront
	housing unit ['hauzɪŋ ju:nɪt]	Gehäuse
	electrical device [ɪˌlektrɪkl dɪ'vaɪs]	Elektrogerät
	partnership ['pɑ:tnəʃɪp]	Zusammenarbeit, Partnerschaft
	Fire away. [ˌfaɪər ə'weɪ]	Schieß los.
	lean manufacturing [ˌli:n mænju'fæktʃərɪŋ]	schlanke Produktion
	to **cut down** [ˌkʌt 'daun]	reduzieren, senken
	waste [weɪst]	Verschwendung, Vergeudung
	inventory ['ɪnvəntri]	Lagerbestand, Warenbestand
	scrap [skræp]	Schrott
	extent [ɪk'stent]	Maß, Ausmaß
	short production run [ˌʃɔ:t prə'dʌkʃn rʌn]	Kleinserie
	prototype ['prəutətaɪp]	Prototyp
	to **gear out** [ˌgɪər 'aut]	ausrichten
	to **link** [lɪŋk]	verbinden
	to **over-produce** ['əuvəprə'dju:s]	zu viel produzieren
	batch production ['bætʃ prədʌkʃn]	Kleinserienfertigung
	costly ['kɒstli]	kostspielig
	to **input** ['ɪnput]	eingeben, einspeisen
	numerical [nju:'merɪkl]	digital
	CNC (milling) machine [si: en ˌsi: 'mɪlɪŋ məʃi:n]	CNC-Fräse
	monitoring ['mɒnɪtərɪŋ]	Kontrolle, Überwachung
	job [dʒɒb]	Auftrag
	feasability [ˌfi:sə'bɪləti]	Machbarkeit, Durchführbarkeit
	automated ['ɔ:təmeɪtɪd]	automatisch, automatisiert
	order system ['ɔ:də sɪstəm]	Auftragssystem, Bestellsystem
	to **feed** [fi:d]	einspeisen
	plant [plɑ:nt]	Maschinen

Chronological word list

	automation [ˌɔːtəˈmeɪʃn]	Automatisierung
	to **ensure** [ɪnˈʃʊə]	sicherstellen, gewährleisten
	for instance [fəˈrɪnstəns]	zum Beispiel
	to **automate** [ˈɔːtəmeɪt]	automatisieren
	to **streamline** [ˈstriːmlaɪn]	rationalisieren
	kind of [ˈkaɪnd əv]	irgendwie, ziemlich
62	**electronics** [ˌɪlekˈtrɒnɪks]	Elektronik
	electronic [ˌɪlekˈtrɒnɪk]	elektronisch
	to **aim** [eɪm]	anstreben
	robot [ˈrəʊbɒt]	Roboter
	titanium [tɪˈteɪniəm]	Titan
	to **meet standards** [miːt ˈstændədz]	Anforderungen einhalten
	to **cut costs** [kʌt ˈkɒsts]	Kosten senken
	to **store** [stɔː]	lagern
63	**sourcing** [ˈsɔːsɪŋ]	Beschaffung
	mass production [ˌmæs prəˈdʌkʃn]	Massenproduktion
	job production [ˈdʒɒb prədʌkʃn]	Einzelfertigung
	outsourcing [ˈaʊtsɔːsɪŋ]	Auslagern
	multiple sourcing [ˌmʌltɪpl ˈsɔːsɪŋ]	Beschaffung durch mehrere Bezugsquellen
	domestic sourcing [dəˌmestɪk ˈsɔːsɪŋ]	Beschaffung durch inländische Bezugsquellen
	unit [ˈjuːnɪt]	Einheit
	specification [ˌspesɪfɪˈkeɪʃn]	Spezifikation, Vorgabe
	to **assess** [əˈses]	einschätzen
	inventory [ˈɪnvəntri]	Bestandsliste
	shop floor [ˌʃɒp ˈflɔː]	Fertigungs-, Produktionsbereich
	to **replenish** [rɪˈplenɪʃ]	auffüllen
	surplus [ˈsɜːpləs]	überschüssig
	paint [peɪnt]	Farbe
	bubble wrap [ˈbʌbl ræp]	Luftpolsterfolie
	turn-around time [ˈtɜːnəraʊnd taɪm]	Durchlaufzeit, Bearbeitungszeitraum
64	to **mount** [maʊnt]	montieren
	mounting area [ˈmaʊntɪŋ eəriə]	Montagebereich, Montagefläche
	warehouse [ˈweəhaʊs]	Lager, Lagerhalle
	finishing shop [ˈfɪnɪʃɪŋ ʃɒp]	Endmontage
T	**in stock** [ɪn ˈstɒk]	auf Lager
	supply [səˈplaɪ]	Lieferung, Versorgung
	aim [eɪm]	Ziel
	increase [ˈɪŋkriːs]	Steigerung
	security [sɪˈkjʊərəti]	Sicherheit
	to **note** [nəʊt]	bemerken
	to **generate** [ˈdʒenəreɪt]	erzeugen, generieren

	quality control [ˈkwɒləti kəntrəʊl]	Qualitätskontrolle
	to **drive** [draɪv]	antreiben, steuern
	magic [ˈmædʒɪk]	Zauberei
	to **cut out** [ˌkʌt ˈaʊt]	ausschneiden
	to **drill** [drɪl]	bohren
	hole [həʊl]	Loch
	to **engrave** [ɪnˈɡreɪv]	gravieren
	flaw [flɔː]	Mangel
	to **fit** [fɪt]	anbringen, ausstatten, einpassen
	threaded bolt [ˌθredɪd ˈbəʊlt]	Gewindebolzen, Gewindestange
	threaded bush [ˌθredɪd ˈbʊʃ]	Gewindebuchse
	application [ˌæplɪˈkeɪʃn]	Auftragen *(von Farbe)*
	to **examine** [ɪɡˈzæmɪn]	untersuchen
	to **apply** [əˈplaɪ]	*(Farbe)* auftragen
	appropriate [əˈprəʊpriət]	entsprechend
	to **dry** [draɪ]	trocknen
	skilled [skɪld]	geschult
	to **lay out** [ˌleɪ ˈaʊt]	auslegen
	shipping [ˈʃɪpɪŋ]	Versand
	carton [ˈkɑːtn]	Karton
	to **address** [əˈdres]	adressieren
	shipping agent [ˈʃɪpɪŋ eɪdʒənt]	Spediteur
	worth [wɜːθ]	Wert
	to **keep track** [ˌkiːp ˈtræk]	nachverfolgen
	fresh [freʃ]	neu, frisch
	supplies [səˈplaɪz]	Vorräte, Ware
65	**acronym** [ˈækrənɪm]	Akronym, Abkürzung
	press release [ˈpres rɪliːs]	Pressemitteilung
	to **issue** [ˈɪʃuː]	veröffentlichen
	to **publicize sth** [ˈpʌblɪsaɪz]	auf etw aufmerksam machen, für etw Werbung machen
	publication [ˌpʌblɪˈkeɪʃn]	Publikation, Veröffentlichung
	to **aim sth at sb/sth** [ˈeɪm ət]	etw an jdn/etw richten
	customized [ˌkʌstəmaɪzd]	individuell gefertigt, auf Kundenwünsche zugeschnitten
	operations [ˌɒpəˈreɪʃnz]	Betrieb, Geschäftstätigkeit
	solid [ˈsɒlɪd]	solide, tüchtig, beachtlich
	board member [ˈbɔːd membə]	Vorstandmitglied
	founder [ˈfaʊndə]	Gründer/in
	customer base [ˈkʌstəmə beɪs]	Kundenstamm
	to **anticipate** [ænˈtɪsɪpeɪt]	erwarten

	amusement [ə'mju:zmənt]	Unterhaltung
	scientific measuring instrument [saɪən,tɪfɪk 'meʒərɪŋ ɪnstrəmənt]	wissenschaftliches Messinstrument
	to **adopt** [ə'dɒpt]	annehmen, übernehmen
	to **realize sth** ['rɪəlaɪz]	etw erkennen, etw bemerken
	market potential [,mɑ:kɪt pə'tenʃl]	Marktpotenzial
	to **transfer** ['trænsfɜ:]	übertragen
	to **launch** [lɔ:ntʃ]	einführen
	intention [ɪn'tenʃn]	Absicht
	to **fulfil** [fʊl'fɪl]	erfüllen
	user interface [,ju:zər 'ɪntəfeɪs]	Benutzeroberfläche
	to **enable** [ɪ'neɪbl]	befähigen, (es) ermöglichen
	sheeting ['ʃi:tɪŋ]	Blech, Platte
	thickness ['θɪknəs]	Dicke, Stärke
	latter ['lætə]	letztgenannt
	to **accommodate** [ə'kɒmədeɪt]	berücksichtigen, beinhalten
	introduction [,ɪntrə'dʌkʃn]	Einführung
	to **construct** [kən'strʌkt]	konstruieren, bauen
	core business ['kɔ: bɪznəs]	Kerngeschäft
	dedicated to sth ['dedɪkeɪtɪd tə]	(eigens) für etw bestimmt
	purpose ['pɜ:pəs]	Zweck
	to **expand** [ɪk'spænd]	erweitern
	sign [saɪn]	Schild, Verkehrszeichen
	to **identify** [aɪ'dentɪfaɪ]	feststellen, herausfinden
	opportunity [,ɒpə'tju:nəti]	Chance, Gelegenheit
66	to **concentrate on sth** ['kɒnsntreɪt ɒn]	sich auf etw konzentrieren
	sub-heading ['sʌbhedɪŋ]	Zwischenüberschrift
	made-to-order [,meɪd tu 'ɔ:də]	in Auftragsfertigung, auf Bestellung gefertigt
	to **stipulate** ['stɪpjuleɪt]	fordern, festlegen
67	to **shut down** [,ʃʌt 'daʊn]	schließen
	to **found** [faʊnd]	gründen
	technique [tek'ni:k]	Methode, Technik
	quarter ['kwɔ:tə]	Quartal
68	**versus** ['vɜ:səs]	gegenüber
	quality assurance ['kwɒləti əʃʊərəns]	Qualitätssicherung
	to **operate** ['ɒpəreɪt]	(geschäftlich) tätig sein, operieren

	to **compete with sb/sth** [kəm'pi:t wɪð]	mit jdm/etw konkurrieren
	to **win** [wɪn]	gewinnen
	to **satisfy** ['sætɪsfaɪ]	zufriedenstellen
	to **focus on sth** ['fəʊkəs ɒn]	sich auf etw konzentrieren
	buzzword ['bʌzwɜ:d]	Schlagwort, Modewort
	to **secure** [sɪ'kjuə]	sichern
	to **be in place** [bi ɪn 'pleɪs]	bereit stehen, in Kraft sein, angewendet werden
	to **roll off** [,rəʊl 'ɒf]	verlassen, vom Band laufen
	to **be up to standard** [bi ,ʌp tə 'stændəd]	den Vorgaben entsprechen
	inspection [ɪn'spekʃn]	Kontrolle, Überprüfung
	sample ['sɑ:mpl]	Muster, Stichprobe, Probe
	to **exclude** [ɪk'sklu:d]	ausschließen
69	**contractor** [kən'træktə]	externer Dienstleister, Zulieferer
	realistic [,ri:ə'lɪstɪk]	realistisch
	base [beɪs]	Basis, Sitz
	to **sub-contract** [,sʌbkən'trækt]	(als Zulieferer) unter Vertrag nehmen
	promising ['prɒmɪsɪŋ]	vielversprechend
	to **arise** [ə'raɪz]	auftreten, entstehen
	to **look into sth** [,lʊk 'ɪntə]	einer Sache nachgehen
	to **cut corners** [,kʌt 'kɔ:nəz]	es nicht so genau nehmen
	to **sort sth out** [,sɔ:t 'aʊt]	etw in Ordnung bringen, sich um etw kümmern
	sub-contractor [,sʌbkən'træktə]	Zulieferer, Subunternehmer
	to **admit** [əd'mɪt]	zugeben, gestehen, eingestehen
	disaster [dɪ'zɑ:stə]	Katastrophe
	to **burn** [bɜ:n]	verbrennen
	to **solve** [sɒlv]	lösen
	to **complain** [kəm'pleɪn]	sich beschweren

Unit 7

70	to **market** ['mɑ:kɪt]	vermarkten
	potential [pə'tenʃl]	potenziell
	to **represent** [,reprɪ'zent]	vertreten, repräsentieren
	media ['mi:diə]	Medien
	to **involve sb in sth** [ɪn'vɒlv ɪn]	jdn an etw beteiligen, jdn in etw einbeziehen
71	**carrying case** ['kæriɪŋ keɪs]	Tasche, Etui, Gehäuse
	protective [prə'tektɪv]	Schutz-
	work experience ['wɜ:k ɪkspɪəriəns]	Praktikum
	unsure [,ʌn'ʃʊə]	unsicher

	to retail at ... ['ri:teɪl ət]	einen Ladenpreis von ... haben
	to sort sth out [ˌsɔ:t 'aʊt]	klären, lösen
	launch [lɔ:ntʃ]	Markteinführung
	competitive [kəm'petətɪv]	Wettbewerbs-, Konkurrenz-
	ongoing ['ɒngəʊɪŋ]	kontinuierlich, laufend, ständig
	to update [ˌʌp'deɪt]	aktualisieren, auf den neusten Stand bringen
	impact ['ɪmpækt]	Einfluss, Auswirkungen
	resource [rɪ'sɔ:s]	Mittel
	extensive [ɪk'stensɪv]	ausgedehnt, umfassend
	uptake ['ʌpteɪk]	Aufnahme
	to emerge [ɪ'mɜ:dʒ]	zum Vorschein kommen, sich herausstellen
	specific [spə'sɪfɪk]	bestimmt, speziell
	target group ['tɑ:gɪt gru:p]	Zielgruppe
	questionnaire [ˌkwestʃə'neə]	Fragebogen
72	**to collect** [kə'lekt]	sammeln, zusammentragen
	to gather ['gæðə]	sammeln, zusammentragen
	examination [ɪgˌzæmɪ'neɪʃn]	Untersuchung
	marketplace ['mɑ:kɪtpleɪs]	Marktplatz
	set [set]	Gruppe, Menge
	to obtain [əb'teɪn]	erhalten, bekommen
	word spider ['wɜ:d spaɪdə]	Wortnetz
73	**to spot** [spɒt]	entdecken, erkennen
	valuable ['væljuəbl]	wertvoll
	to enrich [ɪn'rɪtʃ]	bereichern
	word power ['wɜ:d paʊə]	*etwa:* Wortschatz, Sprachkenntnis
	to come across sth [ˌkʌm ə'krɒs]	etw finden
	combination [ˌkɒmbɪ'neɪʃn]	Kombination
	set [set]	fest
	instance ['ɪnstəns]	Fall, Beispiel
	to influence ['ɪnfluəns]	beeinflussen
	purchasing decision ['pɜ:tʃəsɪŋ dɪsɪʒn]	Kaufentschluss
	pastime ['pɑ:staɪm]	Freizeitbeschäftigung
74	**interim report** [ˌɪntərɪm rɪ'pɔ:t]	Zwischenbericht
	related to [rɪ'leɪtɪd tə]	bezüglich
	to discover [dɪ'skʌvə]	entdecken, erfahren
	response [rɪ'spɒns]	Antwort, Reaktion
	rate [reɪt]	Quote
	indication [ˌɪndɪ'keɪʃn]	Anzeichen
	enthusiasm [ɪn'θju:ziæzəm]	Begeisterung, Enthusiasmus
	statistical breakdown [stəˌtɪstɪkl 'breɪkdaʊn]	statistische Aufschlüsselung
	respondent [rɪ'spɒndənt]	Befragte/r
	massive ['mæsɪv]	gewaltig, überwältigend
	to engage in sth [ɪn'geɪdʒ ɪn]	sich mit etw beschäftigen
	to sail [seɪl]	segeln
	rock climbing ['rɒk klaɪmɪŋ]	(Fels-)Klettern
	per annum [pər 'ænəm]	pro Jahr
	conclusion [kən'klu:ʒn]	Schlussfolgerung
	segment ['segmənt]	Teil, Segment
	to pursue sth [pə'sju:]	etw *(Tätigkeit etc.)* nachgehen
	reasonable ['ri:znəbl]	vernünftig
	to conclude [kən'klu:d]	schließen, den Schluß ziehen
	to attract [ə'trækt]	anziehen
	due to ['dju: tə]	aufgrund
	protection [prə'tekʃn]	Schutz
	moreover [mɔ:r'əʊvə]	außerdem
	since [sɪns]	da
	bulk [bʌlk]	Großteil, Löwenanteil
	spend [spend]	Ausgaben
	to target sb ['tɑ:gɪt]	jdn (als Zielgruppe) ansprechen, jdn als Zielgruppe haben
	sailor ['seɪlə]	Segler/in
	effort ['efət]	Anstrengungen
	editorial [ˌedɪ'tɔ:riəl]	redaktionell
	coverage ['kʌvərɪdʒ]	Berichterstattung
	to target sth at sb/sth ['tɑ:gɪt ət]	etw an jdn/etw richten
	walker ['wɔ:kə]	Wanderer
75	**to enclose** [ɪn'kləʊz]	beifügen, einlegen
76	**to rewrite** [ˌri:'raɪt]	umformulieren, umschreiben
	to navigate ['nævɪgeɪt]	navigieren
	to state [steɪt]	sagen, erklären
T	**to be up to sth** [bi 'ʌp tə]	etw vorhaben, etw anstellen
	to break sth down [ˌbreɪk 'daʊn]	etw aufschlüsseln, etw aufteilen
	category ['kætəgəri]	Kategorie
	specific [spə'sɪfɪk]	speziell
	characteristic [ˌkærəktə'rɪstɪk]	Merkmal, Eigenschaft
	to characterize ['kærəktəraɪz]	charakterisieren
	smart [smɑ:t]	schick, elegant
	to feature sth ['fi:tʃə]	etw (als Merkmal) haben
	strap [stræp]	Gurt, Schlaufe

	sleeve [sli:v]	Hülle
	weird [wɪəd]	seltsam, verrückt, bizarr
	considering [kən'sɪdərɪŋ]	angesichts (der Tatsache, dass)
	limitation [,lɪmɪ'teɪʃn]	Einschränkung, Beschränkung
	competition [,kɒmpə'tɪʃn]	Konkurrenz
	to **come (in/with)** [kʌm]	*(Produkt:)* erhältlich sein
	unusual [ʌn'ju:ʒʊəl]	ungewöhnlich
	typical ['tɪpɪkl]	typisch
	defining [di'faɪnɪŋ]	entscheidend
	tartan check [,tɑ:tn 'tʃek]	Schottenkaro
	untypical [ʌn'tɪpɪkl]	untypisch
	waterproof ['wɔ:təpru:f]	wasserdicht
	given that ['gɪvn ðət]	angesichts der Tatsache, dass
	cloth [klɒθ]	Stoff, Wolltuch
	unlikely [ʌn'laɪkli]	unwahrscheinlich
	fairly ['feəli]	ziemlich
	sleek [sli:k]	elegant, schnittig
	sporty ['spɔ:ti]	sportlich
	waterproofed ['wɔ:təpru:ft]	wasserdicht imprägniert
	presumably [prɪ'zju:məbli]	vermutlich
	exception [ɪk'sepʃn]	Ausnahme
	in particular [ɪn pə'tɪkjələ]	insbesondere, speziell
	blurb [blɜ:b]	Werbetext
	water-resistant ['wɔ:tə rɪzɪstənt]	wasserabweisend
77	**watertight** ['wɔ:tətaɪt]	wasserdicht
	impact proof ['ɪmpækt pru:f]	stoßsicher
	unbeatable [ʌn'bi:təbl]	unschlagbar
	What's the point …? [,wɒts ðə 'pɔɪnt]	Was hat es für einen Sinn …?
	wet [wet]	nass
	tough [tʌf]	solide, widerstandsfähig
	knock [nɒk]	Schlag, Stoß
	drop [drɒp]	Fallenlassen, Hinfallen
	removable [rɪ'mu:vəbl]	abnehmbar
	cover ['kʌvə]	Abdeckung, Hülle, Deckel
	retail price [,ri:teɪl 'praɪs]	Ladenpreis
	specialist magazine [,speʃəlɪst ,mægə'zi:n]	Fachzeitschrift
78	to **stir up** [,stɜ:r 'ʌp]	aufwirbeln
	marketeer [,mɑ:kɪ'tɪə]	Vermarkter/in, *(im Plural:)* Marketingleute

	to **appeal to sb** [ə'pi:l tə]	jdn ansprechen, jdm gefallen
	unproductive [,ʌnprə'dʌktɪv]	unproduktiv
	to **distribute** [dɪ'strɪbju:t]	vertreiben
	inappropriate [,ɪnə'prəʊpriət]	unangemessen
	distribution channel [,dɪstrɪ'bju:ʃn tʃænl]	Vertriebskanal
	crucial ['kru:ʃl]	entscheidend
	to **return** [rɪ'tɜ:n]	*(Gewinn)* erzielen, abwerfen
	to **establish** [ɪ'stæblɪʃ]	feststellen
	to **be likely to do sth** [bi 'laɪkli tə]	etw wahrscheinlich tun (werden)
	unique selling point [ju,ni:k 'selɪŋ pɔɪnt]	Alleinstellungsmerkmal
	to **differentiate sth from sth** [,dɪfə'renʃieɪt frəm]	etw von etw unterscheiden
	to **pitch** [pɪtʃ]	anbieten
	to **consider sth sth** [kən'sɪdə]	etw für etw halten
	retail ['ri:teɪl]	Einzelhandel
	door-to-door [,dɔ: tə 'dɔ:]	an der Haustür, von Tür zu Tür
	by means of [baɪ 'mi:nz əv]	mittels
	satisfactory [,sætɪs'fæktəri]	zufriedenstellend, befriedigend
	promotion [prə'məʊʃn]	Werbung
79	to **head for** ['hed fə]	hinführen zu, zulaufen auf
	straightforward [,streɪt'fɔ:wəd]	einfach, unkompliziert
	to **hire sb** ['haɪə]	jdn beauftragen
	media buying agency ['mi:diə baɪɪŋ eɪdʒənsi]	Agentur für Medienplanung/-einkauf
	to **place** [pleɪs]	platzieren
	to **sit back** [,sɪt 'bæk]	sich zurücklehnen
	to **communicate** [kə'mju:nɪkeɪt]	kommunizieren
	to **get up to speed** [get ,ʌp tə 'spi:d]	sich auf den neuesten Stand bringen
	arrival [ə'raɪvl]	Einführung
	willingness ['wɪlɪŋnəs]	Bereitschaft
	value ['vælju:]	Wert
	nevertheless [,nevəðə'les]	trotzdem, dennoch, nichtsdestotrotz
	buzz [bʌz]	Aufmerksamkeit (durch Mundpropaganda)
	crude(ly) [kru:d]	primitiv, simpel
	sticker ['stɪkə]	Aufkleber
	to **convey** [kən'veɪ]	vermitteln

	unconventional [ˌʌnkən'venʃənl]	unkonventionell
	concrete ['kɒŋkriːt]	konkret

Unit 8

80	**procurement** [prə'kjʊəmənt]	Beschaffung
	mail shot ['meɪlʃɒt]	Werbesendung (per Briefpost)
	chamber of commerce [ˌtʃeɪmbər əv 'kɒmɜːs]	Handelskammer
	tender ['tendə]	Angebot, Ausschreibung
	to **issue** ['ɪʃuː]	*(Dokument)* ausstellen
	delivery note [dɪ'lɪvəri nəʊt]	Versandanzeige
	order acknowledgement [ˌɔːdər ək'nɒlɪdʒmənt]	Auftragsbestätigung
	quotation [kwəʊ'teɪʃn]	Angebot, Preisangebot
	purchase order ['pɜːtʃəs ɔːdə]	Bestellung
81	**source** [sɔːs]	Quelle
	to **note** [nəʊt]	zur Kenntnis nehmen
	switchgear ['swɪtʃgɪə]	Schaltanlage
	mining ['maɪnɪŋ]	Bergbau
	beyond [bɪ'jɒnd]	darüber hinaus
	long-standing [ˌlɒŋ 'stændɪŋ]	langjährig, bestehend
	short circuit switch [ʃɔːt ˌsɜːkɪt 'swɪtʃ]	Kurzschlussschalter, Kurzschließer
	to **supply** [sə'plaɪ]	zur Verfügung stellen
82	**Attn. (= attention)** [ə'tenʃn]	zu Händen
	dated … ['deɪtɪd]	vom …
	tailor-made [ˌteɪlə'meɪd]	maßgeschneidert
	to **request** [rɪ'kwest]	anfordern
	to **submit** [səb'mɪt]	einreichen
	pneumatic drive [njuːˌmætɪk 'draɪv]	Druckluftantrieb
	initial order [ɪˌnɪʃl 'ɔːdə]	Erstauftrag
	letter of credit [ˌletər əv 'kredɪt]	Dokumentenakkreditiv
	cash with order [ˌkæʃ wɪð 'ɔːdə]	Vorauszahlung, Vorkasse, Zahlung bei Auftragserteilung
	to **grant sb sth** [grɑːnt]	jdm etw gewähren, einräumen
	preferential terms [prefəˌrənʃl 'tɜːmz]	Sonderkonditionen
	receipt of order [rɪˌsiːt əv 'ɔːdə]	Auftragseingang
	valid ['vælɪd]	gültig
	to **be to sb's liking** [bi tə sʌmbədɪz 'laɪkɪŋ]	jds Vorstellungen entsprechen, Gefallen finden
	enclosure [ɪn'kləʊʒə]	*(Brief:)* Anlage, Anhang
	Enc (= enclosure[s]) [ɪn'kləʊʒə]	*(Brief:)* Anlage(n), Anhang
83	**body** ['bɒdi]	*(Brief:)* Haupttext
	complimentary close [ˌkɒmplɪˌmentri 'kləʊz]	*(Brief:)* Schlußformel
	letterhead ['letəhed]	Briefkopf
	reference initials ['refərəns ɪnɪʃlz]	Zeichen, Referenz
	salutation [ˌsælju'teɪʃn]	Anrede
	signatory ['sɪgnətri]	Unterzeichner/in
	signature ['sɪgnətʃə]	Unterschrift
	subject line ['sʌbdʒɪkt laɪn]	Betreffzeile
	high-grade [ˌhaɪ 'greɪd]	hochwertig
	cutlery ['kʌtləri]	Besteck
	to **review** [rɪ'vjuː]	neu bewerten, überprüfen
84 T	**appointment** [ə'pɔɪntmənt]	Termin
	diary ['daɪəri]	Terminkalender
	to **suit** [suːt]	passen
	preferably ['prefərəbli]	am besten, am liebsten
	copper ['kɒpə]	Kupfer
	mine [maɪn]	Mine, Bergwerk
	to **arrange** [ə'reɪndʒ]	*(Termin)* vereinbaren
P	**working breakfast** ['wɜːkɪŋ brekfəst]	Arbeitsfrühstück
	convenient [kən'viːniənt]	günstig
	to **be tied up** [bi ˌtaɪd 'ʌp]	beschäftigt sein, zu tun haben
85	**trade** [treɪd]	Handel
	contract of sale [ˌkɒntrækt əv 'seɪl]	Kaufvertrag
	obligation [ˌɒblɪ'geɪʃn]	Verpflichtung, Pflicht
	customs duties [ˌkʌstəmz 'djuːtiz]	Zollgebühren
	documentation [ˌdɒkjumen'teɪʃn]	Dokumente, Dokumentation
	FCA – Free Carrier [ˌfriː 'kæriə]	frei Frachtführer
	multimodal transport [mʌltiˌməʊdl 'trænspɔːt]	kombinierte Beförderung, multimodaler Transport
	carriage ['kærɪdʒ]	Beförderung
	customary ['kʌstəməri]	handelsüblich
	to **clear for export** [ˌklɪə fər 'ekspɔːt]	Ausfuhrformalitäten erledigen
	cleared for export [ˌklɪəd fər 'ekspɔːt]	zur Ausfuhr freigemacht/verzollt
	carrier ['kæriə]	Frachtführer
	to **select** [sɪ'lekt]	auswählen
	commercial invoice [kəˌmɜːʃl 'ɪnvɔɪs]	Warenrechnung, Handelsrechnung
	certificate of origin [səˌtɪfɪkət əv 'ɒrɪdʒɪn]	Ursprungszeugnis

	to **load** [ləʊd]	verladen
	to **bear** [beə]	tragen
	custody ['kʌstədi]	Obhut
	destination [ˌdestɪ'neɪʃn]	Bestimmungsort, Zielort
	to **nominate** ['nɒmɪneɪt]	benennen
	import duty ['ɪmpɔːt djuːti]	Einfuhrzoll
	tax [tæks]	Steuer
	terminal ['tɜːmɪnl]	Entladestation, -stelle, Terminal
	to **unload** [ˌʌn'ləʊd]	entladen
	willing ['wɪlɪŋ]	bereit, willens
	prepared [prɪ'peəd]	bereit
	lorry ['lɒri]	Lastwagen
	freight forwarder ['freɪt fɔːwədə]	Spediteur, Spedition
	formality [fɔː'mæləti]	Formalität
86	**import clearance** ['ɪmpɔːt klɪərəns]	Einfuhrverzollung, -abfertigung
	documents against payment [ˌdɒkjumənts əgenst 'peɪmənt]	Dokumente gegen Zahlung, Kasse gegen Dokumente
	to **deal with sb** ['diːl wɪð]	mit jdm zu tun haben, mit jdm Geschäfte machen
	electrical engineering [ɪˌlektrɪkl ˌendʒɪ'nɪərɪŋ]	Elektrotechnik
87	to **enter** ['entə]	hineingelangen, hineinkommen
	permission [pə'mɪʃn]	Genehmigung, Erlaubnis
88	**spring** [sprɪŋ]	Frühling, Frühjahr
	to **break down** [ˌbreɪk 'daʊn]	kaputtgehen
	order form ['ɔːdə fɔːm]	Auftragsformular, Bestellformular
	to **rectify** ['rektɪfaɪ]	berichtigen
	in line with [ɪn 'laɪn wɪð]	gemäß
	unit price [ˌjuːnɪt 'praɪs]	Einzelpreis, Preis pro Stück
	advice of dispatch [ədˌvaɪs əv dɪ'spætʃ]	Versandanzeige, Versandmitteilung
90	to **study** ['stʌdi]	studieren, prüfen
	control box [kən'trəʊl bɒks]	Steuerkasten
	total order value [təʊtl ˌɔːdə 'væljuː]	Gesamtbestellwert, Gesamtauftragswert
	approval [ə'pruːvl]	Freigabe, Genehmigung
	drawing ['drɔːɪŋ]	technische Zeichnung, Konstruktionszeichnung
	approval of drawing [əˌpruːvl əv 'drɔːɪŋ]	Freigabe (einer techn. Zeichnung)
	packing list ['pækɪŋ lɪst]	Packliste, Versandliste
	operating manual [ˌɒpəreɪtɪŋ 'mænjuəl]	Bedienungsanleitung
	technical drawing [ˌteknɪkl 'drɔːɪŋ]	technische Zeichnung
	commissioning [kə'mɪʃnɪŋ]	Auftragserteilung
	in writing [ɪn 'raɪtɪŋ]	schriftlich, in Schriftform
	party ['pɑːti]	Vertragspartei, Partei
	confidentiality [ˌkɒnfɪˌdenʃi'æləti]	Vertraulichkeit
	to **exchange** [ɪks'tʃeɪndʒ]	austauschen
	verbally ['vɜːbəli]	mündlich
	strict [strɪkt]	streng
	to **disclose** [dɪs'kləʊz]	zugänglich machen, enthüllen
	third party [ˌθɜːd 'pɑːti]	Dritte/r
	explicit(ly) [ɪk'splɪsɪt]	ausdrücklich
	arbitration [ˌɑːbɪ'treɪʃn]	Vereinbarung, Schlichtung

Unit 9

91	to **damage** ['dæmɪdʒ]	beschädigen
	transit ['trænzɪt]	Transport
	in transit [ɪn 'trænzɪt]	beim Transport
	delayed [dɪ'leɪd]	verspätet
	faulty ['fɔːlti]	mangelhaft, defekt
	incomplete [ˌɪnkəm'pliːt]	unvollständig
	purse [pɜːs]	Handtasche *(AE)*, Portemonnaie (für Damen) *(BE)*
	wallet ['wɒlɪt]	Brieftasche, Portemonnaie (für Herren)
92	to **encounter** [ɪn'kaʊntə]	begegnen, treffen (auf)
	apprentice [ə'prentɪs]	Auszubildende/r
	to **reverse** [rɪ'vɜːs]	rückwärts fahren
	fork lift ['fɔːk lɪft]	Gabelstapler
	damaged ['dæmɪdʒd]	beschädigt
	to **pass a test** [ˌpɑːs ə 'test]	eine Prüfung bestehen
	set-back ['setbæk]	Rückschlag
	to **repair** [rɪ'peə]	reparieren
	to **fix** [fɪks]	reparieren
	deadline ['dedlaɪn]	Frist, Termin
	to **let sb down** [ˌlet 'daʊn]	jdn im Stich lassen
	to **go the extra mile** [gəʊ ði ˌekstrə 'maɪl]	sich besonders anstrengen, alle Hebel in Bewegung setzen
	ferry ['feri]	Fähre
	to **appreciate** [ə'priːʃieɪt]	schätzen, zu schätzen wissen
93	to **mend** [mend]	flicken, reparieren

	to accuse sb of sth [ə'kju:z əv]	jdm etw vorwerfen
	packet ['pækɪt]	Packung, Päckchen
	to work overtime [ˌwɜ:k 'əʊvətaɪm]	Überstunden machen
	midday [ˌmɪd'deɪ]	Mittag
94	**upcoming** ['ʌpkʌmɪŋ]	bevorstehend
	regarding [rɪ'gɑ:dɪŋ]	betreffend, bezüglich
	to resolve [rɪ'zɒlv]	lösen
	overall ['əʊvərɔ:l]	Schutzanzug
	blade [bleɪd]	Klinge, Blatt
	proper(ly) ['prɒpəli]	richtig
	to hurt [hɜ:t]	verletzen
	afterwards ['ɑ:ftəwədz]	hinterher, danach
95	**to injure** ['ɪndʒə]	verletzen
	sharp [ʃɑ:p]	scharf
	dissatisfied [dɪs'sætɪsfaɪd]	unzufrieden
	considerable [kən'sɪdərəbl]	erheblich, beträchtlich
	inconvenience [ˌɪnkən'vi:niəns]	Unannehmlichkeiten
	at your earliest convenience [ət jɔ:r ˌɜ:liɪst kən'vi:niəns]	sobald wie möglich
	upset [ˌʌp'set]	verärgert
	dissatisfaction [ˌdɪsˌsætɪs'fækʃn]	Unzufriedenheit
	replacement [rɪ'pleɪsmənt]	Ersatz, Ersatzteil(e)
	to halt [hɔ:lt]	anhalten
	unusable [ˌʌn'ju:zəbl]	unbrauchbar
	to seep in [ˌsi:p 'ɪn]	einsickern, eindringen
	door panel ['dɔ: pænl]	Türblatt, Türblech
	rusty ['rʌsti]	rostig
	to intend [ɪn'tend]	beabsichtigen
	to return [rɪ'tɜ:n]	zurücksenden, zurückschicken
	thought [θɔ:t]	Gedanke, Meinung
	matter ['mætə]	Angelegenheit, Sache
96	**leak** [li:k]	undichte Stelle, Leck
	ceiling ['si:lɪŋ]	Decke
	air-conditioning ['eə kəndɪʃnɪŋ]	Klimaanlage
	to fit [fɪt]	einbauen
	extension [ɪk'stenʃn]	Erweiterung, Anbau
	jelly ['dʒeli]	Marmelade, Gelee
	to leak through [ˌli:k 'θru:]	durchdringen, durchsickern
	maintenance ['meɪntənəns]	Wartung, Instand-haltung
	to concern [kən'sɜ:n]	betreffen
97	**damage** ['dæmɪdʒ]	Schaden
	to result from sth [rɪ'zʌlt frəm]	sich aus etw ergeben, aus etw resultieren
	circumstances ['sɜ:kəmstənsɪz]	Umstände
	beyond [bɪ'jɒnd]	jenseits, außerhalb
	apology [ə'pɒlədʒi]	Entschuldigung
	concerning [kən'sɜ:nɪŋ]	betreffend
	due [dju:]	fällig
	bill [bɪl]	Rechnung
	prompt [prɒmpt]	prompt, unverzüglich
	prompt payment [ˌprɒmpt 'peɪmənt]	unverzügliche Zahlung
98	**to remind sb** [rɪ'maɪnd]	jdn daran erinnern
	correspondence [ˌkɒrɪ'spɒndəns]	Korrespondenz
	accounts manager [ə'kaʊnts mænɪdʒə]	Leiter/in der Buchhaltung
	overdue [ˌəʊvə'dju:]	überfällig
	to attach [ə'tætʃ]	beifügen
	unpaid [ˌʌn'peɪd]	unbezahlt
	grateful ['greɪtfl]	dankbar
	concerned [kən'sɜ:nd]	besorgt, beunruhigt
	to instruct [ɪn'strʌkt]	anweisen
	account [ə'kaʊnt]	Konto
	to transfer ['trænsfɜ:]	überweisen
	somehow ['sʌmhaʊ]	irgendwie
	to overlook [ˌəʊvə'lʊk]	übersehen
99	**reminder** [rɪ'maɪndə]	Mahnung
	to fail [feɪl]	versäumen
	to notice ['nəʊtɪs]	bemerken
	immediate [ɪ'mi:diət]	unverzüglich, sofortig
	to arrange [ə'reɪndʒ]	anordnen
	to take legal action [teɪk ˌli:gl 'ækʃn]	juristische Schritte einleiten
	to settle ['setl]	begleichen, bezahlen
	outstanding [aʊt'stændɪŋ]	ausstehend
	working day ['wɜ:kɪŋ deɪ]	Werktag
	at the latest [ət ðə 'leɪtɪst]	spätestens
	further to ['fɜ:ðə tu]	bezüglich
	to draw sb's attention to sth [ˌdrɔ: sʌmbədiz ə'tenʃn tə]	jds Aufmerksamkeit auf etw lenken
101	**to deal with sth** ['di:l wɪð]	etw erledigen
	to limit ['lɪmɪt]	begrenzen
	damage limitation ['dæmɪdʒ lɪmɪteɪʃn]	Schadensbegrenzung
	battle ['bætl]	Schlacht
	whilst [waɪlst]	während
	to throw [θrəʊ]	werfen
	ground [graʊnd]	Boden
	baggage handler ['bægɪdʒ hændlə]	Gepäckabfertiger/in
	padded ['pædɪd]	gepolstert
	case [keɪs]	Etui
	compensation [ˌkɒmpən'seɪʃn]	Schadenersatz, Entschädigung

	claim for compensation [,kleɪm fə kɒmpən'seɪʃn]	Antrag auf Schadenersatz
	to **expire** [ɪk'spaɪə]	*(Zeit:)* ablaufen, *(Frist:)* verstreichen
	to **correspond** [,kɒrɪ'spɒnd]	korrespondieren
	eventually [ɪ'ventʃuəli]	schließlich, am Ende
	to **be/get fed up with sb/sth** [bi/get ,fed 'ʌp wɪð]	die Nase voll von jdm/etw haben
	in the meantime [ɪn ðə 'mi:ntaɪm]	in der Zwischenzeit
	embarrassment [ɪm'bærəsmənt]	Verlegenheit, Peinlichkeit
	voucher ['vaʊtʃə]	Gutschein
	charity ['tʃærəti]	Wohltätigkeitsorganisationen
	even though ['i:vn ðəʊ]	obwohl

Unit 10

102	to **apply for a job** [ə,plaɪ fər ə 'dʒɒb]	sich um/auf eine Stelle bewerben
	abroad [ə'brɔ:d]	im/ins Ausland
	internship *(AE)* ['ɪntɜ:nʃɪp]	Praktikum
	job centre *(BE)* ['dʒɒb sentə]	Arbeitsamt
	employment center *(AE)* [ɪm'plɔɪmənt sentə]	Arbeitsamt
	recruitment agency [rɪ'kru:tmənt eɪdʒənsi]	Personalagentur, Arbeitsvermittlung
	curriculum vitae (CV) *(BE)* [kə,rɪkjələm 'vi:teɪ]	Lebenslauf
	résumé *(AE)* ['rezjumeɪ]	Lebenslauf
	certificate [sə'tɪfɪkət]	Zeugnis
	application [,æplɪ'keɪʃn]	Bewerbung
	applicant ['æplɪkənt]	Bewerber/in
	post [pəʊst]	Stelle, Posten
103	**job hunting** ['dʒɒb hʌntɪŋ]	Stellensuche
	stressed (out) [strest]	gestresst, fix und fertig
	to **be short-listed** [bi 'ʃɔ:tlɪstɪd]	in die engere Auswahl kommen
	short-list ['ʃɔ:tlɪst]	engere Auswahl
	careers advisor [kə'rɪəz ədvaɪzə]	Berufsberater/in, Laufbahnberater/in
	to **tailor sth to sth** ['teɪlə tə]	etw auf etw zuschneiden
	to **register with sb/sth** ['redʒɪstə wɪð]	sich bei jdm/etw anmelden
	to **bin** [bɪn]	wegwerfen
	to **prejudice** ['predʒudɪs]	beeinflussen
104	to **reassure** [,ri:ə'ʃʊə]	beruhigen
	permanent ['pɜ:mənənt]	unbefristet
	accurate ['ækjərət]	korrekt, genau
	fluent ['flu:ənt]	fließend
	confident ['kɒnfɪdənt]	selbstbewusst, selbstsicher
	calm [kɑ:m]	ruhig
	pressure ['preʃə]	Druck
	to **adapt** [ə'dæpt]	sich anpassen
	rapport [ræ'pɔ:]	gutes Verhältnis, gute Beziehung(en)
	pay [peɪ]	Bezahlung, Lohn, Gehalt
	stressful ['stresfl]	anstrengend, stressig
105	**working hours** [,wɜ:kɪŋ 'aʊəz]	Arbeitszeit(en)
	content [kən'tent]	Inhalt
	hourly rate [,aʊəli 'reɪt]	Stundenlohn
	overtime ['əʊvətaɪm]	Überstunden
	time off [,taɪm 'ɒf]	Freizeit
	generous ['dʒenərəs]	großzügig
	lunch break ['lʌntʃ breɪk]	Mittagspause
106	to **model sth on sth** ['mɒdl ɒn]	etw für etw als Muster nehmen
	qualification [,kwɒlɪfɪ'keɪʃn]	Abschluss, Qualifikation
	independent(ly) [,ɪndɪ'pendəntli]	unabhängig
	accomplishment [ə'kʌmplɪʃmənt]	Errungenschaft, Erfolg
	competition [,kɒmpə'tɪʃn]	Wettbewerb
	to **optimize** ['ɒptɪmaɪz]	optimieren
	accountancy [ə'kaʊntənsi]	Buchführung
	business studies ['bɪznəs stʌdiz]	Betriebswirtschaft(slehre)
	economics [,i:kə'nɒmɪks]	Wirtschaftswissenschaft(en)
	command [kə'mɑ:nd]	Beherrschung
	block release [,blɒk rɪli:s]	Blockunterricht
	dual system [,dju:əl 'sɪstəm]	duales Ausbildungssystem
	attendance [ə'tendəns]	Teilnahme
	grade [greɪd]	Note
	final grade [,faɪnl 'greɪd]	Abschlussnote
	merit ['merɪt]	Verdienst, *(als Schulnote:)* gut
	minor ['maɪnə]	Neben-
	history ['hɪstri]	Geschichte
	biology [baɪ'ɒlədʒi]	Biologie
	to **be awarded sth** [bi ə'wɔ:dɪd]	etw *(Preis etc.)* bekommen
	prize [praɪz]	Preis, Auszeichnung
107	**work experience** ['wɜ:k ɪkspɪəriəns]	Berufserfahrung
	to **gain** [geɪn]	gewinnen, erwerben

	insight ['ɪnsaɪt]	Einblick
	climbing ['klaɪmɪŋ]	Klettern
	skiing ['skiːɪŋ]	Skifahren
	nationality [ˌnæʃə'næləti]	Staatsangehörigkeit
	marital status [ˌmærɪtl 'steɪtəs]	Familienstand
	driving licence ['draɪvɪŋlaɪsns]	Führerschein
	to **boost** [buːst]	stärken, untermauern
	price tag ['praɪs tæg]	Preisschild
	to **sell** [sel]	sich verkaufen
	field [fiːld]	Feld
	procedure [prə'siːdʒə]	Verfahren, Ablauf
	efficiency [ɪ'fɪʃnsi]	Effizienz
	temporary ['temprəri]	befristet
	ability [ə'bɪləti]	Fähigkeit
108	**cover letter** ['kʌvə letə]	Anschreiben, Begleitschreiben
	to **be proficient in sth** [bi prə'fɪʃnt ɪn]	*(Sprache etc.)* beherrschen
	vacancy ['veɪkənsi]	offene Stelle, Stellenangebot, -ausschreibung
	recruitment manager [rɪ'kruːtmənt mænɪdʒə]	Leiter/in Personal-beschaffung
	precise(ly) [prɪ'saɪs]	genau
	vacation [və'keɪʃn]	Ferien
	hands-on [ˌhændz 'ɒn]	praxisorientiert
	working environment [ˌwɜːkɪŋ ɪn'vaɪrənmənt]	Arbeitsumfeld
	immense(ly) [ɪ'mens]	enorm
	provision [prə'vɪʒn]	Versorgung
	service provider ['sɜːvɪs prəvaɪdə]	Dienstleister
	customer-focused ['kʌstəmə fəʊkəst]	kundenorientiert
	tight [taɪt]	engere Auswahl
	time frame ['taɪm freɪm]	Zeitrahmen
	linguistic [lɪn'gwɪstɪk]	sprachlich, Sprach-
	final examination [ˌfaɪnl ɪgˌzæmɪ'neɪʃn]	Abschlussprüfung
	consideration [kənˌsɪdə'reɪʃn]	Überlegung, Erwägung
109	**suitability** [ˌsuːtə'bɪləti]	Eignung
	to **advertise** ['ædvətaɪz]	*(Stelle)* ausschreiben
	notice ['nəʊtɪs]	Bescheid, Ankündigung
	at short notice [ət ˌʃɔːt 'nəʊtɪs]	kurzfristig
	at a week's notice [ət ə ˌwiːks 'nəʊtɪs]	eine Woche im voraus
	to **accompany** [ə'kʌmpəni]	begleiten
	credit controller ['kredɪt kəntrəʊlə]	Sachbearbeiter/in Kreditcontrolling
	to **join** [dʒɔɪn]	beitreten, mitmachen
	administration [ədˌmɪnɪ'streɪʃn]	Verwaltung(stätigkeit)
	query ['kwɪəri]	Frage, Anfrage
	dispatch [dɪ'spætʃ]	Versand
	to **chase sb** [tʃeɪs]	jdn verfolgen, hinter jdm her sein
	branch [brɑːntʃ]	Abteilung
	candidate ['kændɪdət]	Kandidat/in, Bewerber/in
110	**strength** [streŋθ]	Stärke
	weakness ['wiːknəs]	Schwäche
	hard-working [ˌhɑːd 'wɜːkɪŋ]	fleißig
	lack of sth ['læk əv]	Mangel an etw
	link [lɪŋk]	Verbindung
T	**qualified** ['kwɒlɪfaɪd]	qualifiziert
	in a nutshell [ɪn ə 'nʌtʃel]	kurz gesagt
	contribution [ˌkɒntrɪ'bjuːʃn]	Beitrag
	to **make a contribution** [ˌmeɪk ə kɒntrɪ'bjuːʃn]	etw beitragen
	to **post sb** [pəʊst]	jdn versetzen
111	to **train as** ['treɪn əz]	eine Ausbildung zum/zur … machen
	point of view [ˌpɔɪnt əv 'vjuː]	Standpunkt, Gesichtspunkt
	to **justify** ['dʒʌstɪfaɪ]	rechtfertigen, begründen
112	**virtual** ['vɜːtʃuəl]	virtuell
	vacant ['veɪkənt]	frei
	close-up ['kləʊs ʌp]	Nahaufnahme
	to **transform** [træns'fɔːm]	(grundlegend) verändern
	familiar [fə'mɪliə]	vertraut, bekannt
	to **scan** [skæn]	*(Text etc.)* überfliegen, durchsuchen
	direction [də'rekʃn]	Richtung
	to **stand out** [ˌstænd 'aʊt]	herausragen
	crowded ['kraʊdɪd]	übervölkert, überfüllt
	to **resort to sth** [rɪ'zɔːt tə]	auf etw zurückgreifen
	sophisticated [sə'fɪstɪkeɪtɪd]	fortschrittlich, raffiniert
	to **throw sth up** [ˌθrəʊ 'ʌp]	etw zutage fördern
	breed [briːd]	Menschenschlag, Sorte
	job-seeker ['dʒɒbsiːkə]	Stellensuchende/r
	offering ['ɒfərɪŋ]	Darbietung, Angebot
	to **be among** [bi ə'mʌŋ]	dazu gehören
	to **bring sb to life** [ˌbrɪŋ tə 'laɪf]	jdn zum Leben erwecken, lebendig machen
	to **show sth off** [ˌʃəʊ 'ɒf]	etw zur Geltung bringen
	to **amaze** [ə'meɪz]	verblüffen, erstaunen
	to **outline** ['aʊtlaɪn]	skizzieren

Alphabetical word list

Dieses Wörterverzeichnis enthält alle neuen Wörter aus *Industry Matters – 2nd Edition* in alphabetischer Reihenfolge. Nicht angeführt sind Wörter, die zum Grundwortschatz *(Basic word list)* gehören. Die Zahl nach dem Stichwort bezieht sich auf die Seite, auf der das Wort zum ersten Mal erscheint. Wörter aus den Hörverständnisübungen sind zusätzlich mit einem T *(Transkript)* und Wörter aus den *Partner files* mit einem P gekennzeichnet.

A

ability *107* Fähigkeit
abroad *102* im/ins Ausland
abuse *47* Missbrauch
to **accept** *41* akzeptieren
acceptable *28* akzeptabel
access *42* Zugang, Zugriff
to **access sth** *36* auf etw zugreifen
to **accommodate** *42* unterbringen, Platz bieten für; *65* berücksichtigen, beinhalten
accommodation *38* Unterkunft
to **accompany** *109* begleiten
accomplishment *106* Errungenschaft, Erfolg
according to *47* laut, nach, gemäß
account *98* Konto
account, to **take sth into ~** *9* etw berücksichtigen
accountancy *106* Buchführung
accountant *10* Buchhalter/in
accounts *17* Buchhaltung
accounts manager *98* Leiter/in der Buchhaltung
accurate *104* korrekt, genau
to **accuse sb of sth** *93* jdm etw vorwerfen
to **achieve** *24* erreichen, erzielen
acre *42* *Flächenmaß, entspricht 0,405 Hektar*
acronym *65* Akronym, Abkürzung
to **act** *52* handeln, fungieren
to **act out** *29* spielen, vor-/durchspielen
action, to **put sth into ~** *33* etw in die Tat umsetzen
action, to **take ~** *47* Maßnahmen ergreifen
action, to **take legal ~** *99* juristische Schritte einleiten
actual(ly) *6* wirklich, tatsächlich
to **adapt** *104* sich anpassen
addition, in ~ *43T* zusätzlich
additionally *44* außerdem
to **address** *64T* adressieren; ~ sb *28* jdn anreden, ansprechen
administration *109* Verwaltung(stätigkeit)
to **admit** *69* zugeben, gestehen, eingestehen
to **adopt** *65* annehmen, übernehmen
advance, in ~ *21* im Voraus
to **advertise** *109* (Stelle) ausschreiben; ~ sth *15* für etw Werbung machen
advertising campaign *24* Werbekampagne
advice *15* Rat, Ratschlag, Tipp
advice of dispatch *88* Versandanzeige, Versandmitteilung
to **advise** *47* raten
advisor *47* Berater/in
aeroplane *55T* Flugzeug
afraid, to **be ~ of sb/ sth** *23* vor jdm/etw Angst haben
after-sales service *50* Kundendienst
afterwards *94* hinterher, danach
agency *59* Agentur
agenda *7T* Tagesordnung, Programm
agent *52* Agent/in
agreement, to **be in ~ with sth** *50* einer Sache zustimmen
aim *64T* Ziel
to **aim** *62* anstreben; ~ sth at sb/ sth *65* etw an jdn/etw richten
air-conditioning *96* Klimaanlage
along, as I go ~ *19* zwischendurch
along, to get ~ *59* gut miteinander auskommen, sich gut verstehen
alternatively *32* alternativ, oder, auch
to **amaze** *112* verblüffen, erstaunen
among, to **be ~** *112* dazu gehören
amusement *65* Unterhaltung
to **analyse** *21* analysieren
annual *7T* jährlich, Jahres-
annum, per ~ *74* pro Jahr
answerphone *31* Anrufbeantworter
to **anticipate** *65* erwarten
AOB (any other business) *49* Sonstiges
apart from *24* abgesehen von
to **apologize** *30* sich entschuldigen, um Entschuldigung bitten
apology *97* Entschuldigung
to **appeal to sb** *78* jdn ansprechen, jdm gefallen
to **appear** *28* scheinen, erscheinen, auftreten
applicant *102* Bewerber/in
application *64T* Auftragen (von Farbe); *102* Bewerbung
to **apply** *64T* (Farbe) auftragen; ~ for a job *102* sich um/auf eine Stelle bewerben
appointment *84* Termin
to **appreciate** *92* schätzen, zu schätzen wissen
apprentice *92* Auszubildende/r
approach *28* Vorgehen(sweise), Ansatz, Herangehensweise
appropriate *9* passend, angemessen; *64T* entsprechend
approval *90* Freigabe, Genehmigung
approval of drawing *90* Freigabe (einer techn. Zeichnung)
approximately *7* ungefähr, zirka
arbitration *90* Vereinbarung, Schlichtung
to **argue** *36* argumentieren
to **arise** *69* auftreten, entstehen
to **arrange** *19* planen, arrangieren, ausmachen; *84* (Termin) vereinbaren; *99* anordnen
arrangement *42* Vereinbarung, Abmachung
arrangement, by prior ~ *42* nach vorheriger Vereinbarung
arrival *40* Ankunft
arrival *79* Einführung
as I go along *19* zwischendurch
as regards *49* bezüglich, was … anbelangt
as soon as *19* sobald
to **ask for directions** *18* nach dem Weg fragen
to **assemble** *7T* montieren
assembly *19* Montage
to **assert** *59* behaupten
to **assess** *63* einschätzen
assistance *52* Hilfe, Unterstützung
to **assure** *35* sicherstellen
at a time *36* auf einmal, jeweils
at the latest *99* spätestens
atmosphere *56* Atmosphäre
to **attach** *98* beifügen
attachment *51* (E-Mail:) Anhang
to **attend sth** *21* an etw teilnehmen, etw besuchen
attendance *106* Teilnahme
attendee *57* Anwesende/r
attention (attn.) *82* zu Händen

attention, to **draw sb's ~ to sth** *99* jds Aufmerksamkeit auf etw lenken
to **attract** *74* anziehen
attractive *24* attraktiv
audience *9* Publikum, Zuhörer(schaft), Zuschauer
to **audit** *47* prüfen
to **automate** *61* automatisieren
automated *61* automatisch, automatisiert
automation *61* Automatisierung
availability *34P* Verfügbarkeit, Lieferbarkeit
available *42* verfügbar, erhältlich; to be ~ *30* (Telefon:) zu sprechen sein
average *24* Durchschnitt, durchschnittlich
averse *59* abgeneigt
to **avoid** *25* vermeiden, verhindern
awarded, to **be ~ sth** *106* etw (Preis etc.) bekommen
aware, to **be ~ of sth** *19* sich einer Sache bewusst sein, etw wissen
aware, to **make sb ~ of sth** *24* jdm über etw informieren, jdm etw ins Bewusstsein rufen

B

back, to **turn your ~ to sb** *9* jdm den Rücken zudrehen
background *7T* Hintergrund
baggage *41* Gepäck
baggage, excess ~ *41* Übergepäck
baggage handler *101* Gepäckabfertiger/in
bags *45* Gepäck, Koffer
to **bake** *8* backen, erhitzen
base *69* Basis, Sitz
to **base on sth** *25* auf etw basieren
based, to **be ~ in ...** *8* in ... ansässig sein, seinen/ihren Sitz in ... haben
the basics *15* die grundsätzlichen Dinge
batch production *61* Kleinserienfertigung
battery *36* Akku
battle *101* Schlacht
beading *7* Sicken
to **bear** *85* tragen
beef *55T* Rindfleisch
beer *58* Bier
beginner *15* Anfänger/in
behalf, on ~ of sb *52* für jdn
behaviour *59* Verhalten, Benehmen
to **belong to sb/sth** *7T* zu jdm/etw gehören
benefit *24* Vorteil, Nutzen
Best regards *44* Mit freundlichen Grüßen
beyond *81* darüber hinaus; *97* jenseits, außerhalb
bill *97* Rechnung
to **bill sb sth** *44* jdm etw in Rechnung stellen
to **bin** *103* wegwerfen
biology *106* Biologie
blade *94* Klinge, Blatt
blank stare *59* starrer Gesichtsausdruck
blend *42* Mixtur, Mischung
block release *106* Blockunterricht
blurb *76T* Werbetext
board *10* Geschäftsführung, Vorstand
board member *65* Vorstandmitglied
boarding *41* An-Bord-Gehen
boarding card *37* Bordkarte
body *83* (Brief:) Haupttext
body-shaping *7* Dosenformung, Zargenformung
bolt, threaded ~ *64T* Gewindebolzen, Gewindestange
to **boost** *107* stärken, untermauern
booth *6* Messestand
boring *59* langweilig
boss *28* Chef/in
to **bother sb** *31T* jdm Umstände bereiten, jdn belästigen
brake, to **put the ~s on sth** *47* etw herunterfahren, einer Sache einen Riegel vorschieben
branch *49* Ast; *109* Abteilung
brand *32* Marke
to **break down** *88* kaputtgehen; *76T* etw aufschlüsseln, etw aufteilen
breath *26* Atem
breath, to **take a deep ~** *26* tief einatmen, durchatmen
breed *112* Menschenschlag, Sorte
brevity *35* Kürze
to **brew** *49* brauen
brewery *49* Brauerei
brick *36* Backstein, Ziegel
brief *7T* knapp, kurz
to **bring sb to life** *112* jdn zum Leben erwecken, lebendig machen
brochure *6* Prospekt, Werbebroschüre
broken *46* kaputt
bubble wrap *63* Luftpolsterfolie
budget *21* Budget, Haushalt, Etat
bulk *74* Großteil, Löwenanteil
to **burn** *69* verbrennen
bus service *42* Busverbindung
bush, threaded ~ *64T* Gewindebuchse
business, to **do ~** *42* Geschäfte machen
business, to **set up a ~** *16* ein Unternehmen gründen
business card *12* Visitenkarte
business contact *28* Geschäftspartner
business development *38* Geschäftsentwicklung
business studies *106* Betriebswirtschaft(slehre)
busy *28* (Telefon:) besetzt
buyer *21* Käufer
buzz *79* Aufmerksamkeit (durch Mundpropaganda)
buzzword *68* Schlagwort, Modewort
by means of *78* mittels

C

cabin *42* Hütte
cake *42* Kuchen
calm *104* ruhig
can *7T* Dose
can body *7T* Zarge, Body (einer Dose)
can end *7T* Boden, Deckel (einer Dose)
to **cancel** *41* stornieren
candidate *109* Kandidat/in, Bewerber/in
canmaking *24* Dosenherstellung
canning machinery *11* Maschinen zur Dosenherstellung
cap *34* Mütze, Kappe
capable, to **be ~ of doing sth** *21* fähig/in der Lage sein, etw zu tun
capacity *19* Kapazität
capital letter *51* Großbuchstabe
car park *42* Parkplatz, Parkhaus, Tiefgarage
carbon *24* Kohlenstoff, Kohlendioxid
career *14* Karriere, Beruf, Laufbahn
careers advisor *103* Berufsberater/in, Laufbahnberater/in
carmaker *25* Autobauer
carriage *85* Beförderung
carrier *85* Frachtführer; Free ~ (FCA) *85* frei Frachtführer
to **carry out** *47* durchführen
carrying case *71* Tasche, Etui, Gehäuse
carton *64T* Karton
case *11T* Fall; *55T* Koffer; *101* Etui
cash with order *82* Vorauszahlung, Vorkasse, Zahlung bei Auftragserteilung

Alphabetical word list

to **catch sth** *27* etw verstehen; *38* etw bekommen, erreichen, erwischen
category *76T* Kategorie
cause, a good ~ *57T* ein guter Zweck, eine gute Sache
to **cause** *46* verursachen
ceiling *96* Decke
celebrity *55* Prominente/r
ceremony *21* Zeremonie
certificate *102* Zeugnis
certificate of origin *85* Ursprungszeugnis
chain *27* Kette
to **challenge sb** *25* jdn herausfordern, jdm schwierige Aufgaben stellen
chamber of commerce *80* Handelskammer
chances are *35* es ist wahrscheinlich, dass
characteristic *76T* Merkmal, Eigenschaft
to **characterize** *76T* charakterisieren
charge *41* Gebühr
charge, in ~ of *21* zuständig für, verantwortlich für
to **charge** *15* Gebühren verlangen; ~ sb sth *44* jdm etw in Rechnung stellen
charitable *57* Wohltätigkeits-
charity *57T* Wohltätigkeit, guter Zweck; *101* Wohltätigkeitsorganisationen
chart *54* Diagramm
to **chase sb** *109* jdn verfolgen, hinter jdm her sein
chat *58* Unterhaltung, Schwätzchen
to **check in** *41* einchecken
to **check out** *42* auschecken
cheers *32* danke
Chief Executive Officer (CEO) *11T* Vorstandsvorsitzende/r, Geschätsführer/in
circle *49* Kreis
to **circulate sth** *49* etw verteilen, verschicken
circumstances *97* Umstände
to **claim** *15* behaupten
claim *47* Forderung, Anspruch
claim for compensation *101* Antrag auf Schadenersatz
clear(ly) *33* deutlich, klar
to **clear for export** *85* Ausfuhrformalitäten erledigen
cleared for export *85* zur Ausfuhr freigemacht/verzollt
client *46* Kunde/-in
climbing *107* Klettern
close to *11T* nahe bei, in der Nähe von
close-up *112* Nahaufnahme
closed *44P* geschlossen
closely *22* eng
closing sentence *52* Schlussatz
cloth *76T* Stoff, Wolltuch
clothing *27* Bekleidung, Kleidung
CNC milling machine *61* CNC-Fräse
to **collect** *72* sammeln, zusammentragen
colleague *38* Kollege/-in
combination *73* Kombination
to **combine** *42* kombinieren
to **come (in/with)** *76T* (Produkt:) erhältlich sein
to **come across sth** *73* etw finden
to **come on board** *52* an Bord kommen, dabei sein
to **comment** *52* sich äußern, etw dazu sagen
comfort *42* Komfort, Annehmlichkeit
comfortable *11* bequem, angenehm, komfortabel
command *106* Beherrschung
commercial director *11T* kaufmännische/r Leiter/in
commercial invoice *85* Warenrechnung, Handelsrechnung
commissioning *90* Auftragserteilung
common *10* üblich, verbreitet
to **communicate** *79* kommunizieren
community *57* Gemeinde, Gemeinschaft
company *6* Unternehmen, Firma, Gesellschaft
company, Limited liability ~ (LLC) *(AE)* *10* Gesellschaft mit beschränkter Haftung (GmbH)
company, parent ~ *7T* Muttergesellschaft
company, Private limited ~ (Ltd) *(BE)* *10* Gesellschaft mit beschränkter Haftung (GmbH)
company, Proprietory Limited ~ (Pty Ltd) *(AusE)* *10* Gesellschaft mit beschränkter Haftung (GmbH)
company, Public limited ~ (plc) *(BE)* *10* Aktiengesellschaft (AG)
company, to **incorporate a ~** *10* eine AG/GmbH gründen
company car *16* Firmenwagen
compared to *36* im Vergleich zu
compensation *101* Schadenersatz, Entschädigung
to **compete with sb/sth** *68* mit jdm/etw konkurrieren
competence *21* Kompetenz
competition *76T* Konkurrenz; *106* Wettbewerb
competitive *71* Wettbewerbs-, Konkurrenz-
to **complain** *69* sich beschweren
complaint *50* Reklamation, Beschwerde
to **complement** *42* ergänzen
completion *19* (Aufrags-)Erfüllung
complicated *35* kompliziert
complimentary close *83* (Brief:) Schlußformel
component *7T* Bauteil, Teil, Komponente
to **comprise** *42* umfassen, bestehen aus
to **compromise** *34P* sich einigen, einen Kompromiss eingehen
computing power *36* Rechenleistung
to **concentrate on sth** *66* sich auf etw konzentrieren
to **concern** *96* betreffen
concerned *98* besorgt, beunruhigt
concerning *97* betreffend
to **conclude** *74* schließen, den Schluß ziehen
conclude, to **~** *52* abschließend
conclusion *9* Schluss
conclusion *74* Schlussfolgerung
concrete *79* konkret
condition *48* Bedingung
conference *22* Konferenz
conference call *48* Konferenzschaltung
confident *104* selbstbewusst, selbstsicher
confidentiality *90* Vertraulichkeit
to **confirm** *31T* bestätigen
confirmation *44* Bestätigung
confusion *40* Verwirrung, Verwechslung
to **connect** *28* verbinden
connection *28* Verbindung
connector *38* Stecker
consensus *25* Konsens
conservatory *43T* Wintergarten, Gewächshaus
to **consider** *24* betrachten, ansehen; ~ sth *25* berücksichtigen, in Betracht ziehen; ~ sth sth *78* etw für etw halten
considerab(ly) *54* erheblich, beträchtlich
consideration *108* Überlegung, Erwägung
considered, to **be ~ sth** *56* als etw gelten
considering *76T* angesichts (der Tatsache, dass)
consignment *34* Sendung, Lieferung

to **consist of sth** *7T* aus etw bestehen
to **construct** *65* konstruieren, bauen
constructive *15* konstruktiv
to **consult sb** *49* jdn fragen, sich mit jdm beraten
consumer *24* Verbraucher/in
container *24* Behälter
content *105* Inhalt
context *36* Zusammenhang
to **continue** *18* weitergehen
continuous *25* fortlaufend, kontinuierlich
contract *13* Vertrag
contract of sale *85* Kaufvertrag
contractor *69* externer Dienstleister, Zulieferer
contribution *110T* Beitrag
contribution, to **make a ~** *110T* etw beitragen
control box *90* Steuerkasten
convenience *24* Bequemlichkeit, Praktikabilität
convenience, at your earliest ~ *95* sobald wie möglich
convenient *84* günstig
convention *51* Versammlung
conventional *10* herkömmlich, konventionell
conversation *13* Gespräch
to **convey** *79* vermitteln
conveyor belt *7T* Förderband
to **convince** *21* überzeugen
to **co-ordinate** *19* koordinieren
copper *84* Kupfer
copy *11T* Exemplar
cordless *42* schnurlos
core business *65* Kerngeschäft
core competence *7* Kernkompetenz
corn *19* Mais
corporate *47* Unternehmens-, Geschäfts-
Corporation (Corp./Inc.) *(AE)* *10* Aktiengesellschaft (AG)
to **correspond** *101* korrespondieren; ~ to sth *25* einer Sache entsprechen
correspondence *98* Korrespondenz
corridor *17T* Flur, Korridor
costly *61* kostspielig
Count me in. *57T* Ich bin dabei.
country code *29* Ländervorwahl
country house *42* Landsitz
course *21* Kurs, Studium
court *42* (Tennis-, Squash-)Platz
to **cover sth** *53* (Thema) behandeln
cover *77* Abdeckung, Hülle, Deckel
cover letter *108* Anschreiben, Begleitschreiben
coverage *74* Berichterstattung
cow *55T* Kuh
crazy *59* verrückt
credit card *37* Kreditkarte
credit controller *109* Sachbearbeiter/in Kreditcontrolling
cross-cultural *21* kulturübergreifend, interkulturell
crowded *112* übervölkert, überfüllt
crucial *78* entscheidend
crude(ly) *79* primitiv, simpel
cuisine *42* (Landes-)Küche
curing oven *7* Aushärteofen
curling press *7* Bördelpresse
current(ly) *36* aktuell, momentan
curriculum vitae (CV) *(BE)* *102* Lebenslauf
custody *85* Obhut
customary *85* handelsüblich
customer *6* Kunde/Kundin
customer base *65* Kundenstamm
customer-focused *108* kundenorientiert
customer loyalty *41* Kundentreue, Kundenbindung
customer service *7T* Kundendienst, Kundenbetreuung
customized *65* individuell gefertigt, auf Kundenwünsche zugeschnitten
customs duties *85* Zollgebühren
to **cut sth** *24* etw senken
to **cut down** *61* reduzieren, senken
to **cut out** *64T* ausschneiden
to **cut corners** *69* es nicht so genau nehmen
to **cut costs** *62* Kosten senken
cutlery *83* Besteck
cutter *7T* Schneidegerät

D

to **damage** *91* beschädigen
damage *97* Schaden
damage limitation *101* Schadensbegrenzung
damaged *92* beschädigt
database *36* Datenbank
dated ... *82* vom ...
deadline *92* Frist, Termin
deal *6* Geschäft
to **deal with sb** *86* mit jdm zu tun haben, mit jdm Geschäfte machen
to **deal with sth** *21* etw bearbeiten, erledigen, sich um etw kümmern; *101* etw erledigen
decent *59* anständig
decision *10* Entscheidung
decision, to **take a ~** *10* eine Entscheidung fällen
dedicated to sth *65* (eigens) für etw bestimmt
to **decrease** *54* abnehmen, sinken
defining *76T* entscheidend
definite(ly) *59* bestimmt
to **degenerate** *59* ausarten
degree *54* Ausmaß, Grad
delay *23* Verzögerung
delayed *91* verspätet
delicious *42* köstlich
delighted *44* erfreut
delighted, to **be ~ to do sth** *7T* etw gern tun
delivery *25* Lieferung
delivery note *80* Versandanzeige
demand *10* Nachfrage, Bedarf
to **demonstrate** *47* vorführen, zeigen
demonstration *36* Vorführung
to **depart** *38* abfahren, -fliegen, -reisen
department *11* Abteilung
departmental *19* Abteilungs-
departure *40* Abreise, Abfahrt, Abflug
to **depend on/upon sth** *43T* von etw abhängen, auf etw ankommen
design *15* Gestaltung; *17* Konstruktion
to **design** *7T* gestalten, entwerfen
designed, to **be ~ for sth** *24* für etw gedacht sein, etw beabsichtigen
despite *34* trotz
destination *40P* Reiseziel, Zielort; *85* Bestimmungsort
detailed *6* genau, detailliert
to **develop** *25* entwickeln
deviation *21* Abweichung
device *36* Gerät
to **dial** *27* (Telefon:) wählen
diary *84* Terminkalender
die, to **~ for** *42* umwerfend
to **differ** *43* sich unterscheiden
to **differentiate sth from sth** *78* etw von etw unterscheiden
digit *29* Ziffer
digital projector *42* Beamer
to **dine** *42* speisen
direction *112* Richtung
directions *17* Wegbeschreibung
directions, to **ask for ~** *18* nach dem Weg fragen
directions, to **give sb ~** *18* jdm den Weg erklären
director *10* Vorstand
disability *57T* Behinderung

to **disagree** *15* nicht zustimmen, anderer Meinung sein
disaster *69* Katastrophe
to **disclose** *90* zugänglich machen, enthüllen
to **discover** *74* entdecken, erfahren
dish *55T* Gericht, Speise
dispatch *109* Versand
dissatisfaction *95* Unzufriedenheit
dissatisfied *95* unzufrieden
to **distribute** *78* vertreiben
distribution channel *78* Vertriebskanal
distributor *60* Vertrieb, Händler
to **diversify** *10* breiter fächern, diversifizieren
to **do business** *42* Geschäfte machen
documentation *85* Dokumente, Dokumentation
documents against payment *85* Dokumente gegen Zahlung, Kasse gegen Dokumente
domestic sourcing *63* Beschaffung durch inländische Bezugsquellen
door-to-door *78* an der Haustür, von Tür zu Tür
door panel *95* Türblatt, Türblech
dot *31* Punkt
to **double** *10* sich verdoppeln
double room *42* Doppelzimmer
doubt *49* Zweifel
doubt, no ~ *49* zweifellos, bestimmt
down payment *19* Anzahlung
downgauging *24* Reduzierung der Materialdicke
downstairs *13* (nach) unten
downward *54* nach unten
dozen *59* Dutzend
draft *49* Entwurf
dramatically *54* dramatisch
to **draw** *48* zeichnen; ~ sb's attention to sth *99* jds Aufmerksamkeit auf etw lenken
to **draw sth up** *19* etw erstellen
drawing *90* technische Zeichnung, Konstruktionszeichnung
drawing, approval of ~ *90* Freigabe (einer techn. Zeichnung)
to **drill** *64T* bohren
to **drive** *64T* antreiben, steuern
driving licence *107* Führerschein
drop *77* Fallenlassen, Hinfallen
to **drop** *54* fallen, sinken; ~ sth off *43T* etw abgeben, dalassen
to **dry** *64T* trocknen
dual system *106* duales Ausbildungssystem
due *97* fällig
due to *74* aufgrund
duty *22* Pflicht, Aufgabe
duty, customs ~ *85* Zollgebühr
duty, import ~ *85* Einfuhrzoll

E

Easter *56P* Ostern
eatery *42* Restaurant, Speiselokal
eco-friendly *24* umweltfreundlich
ecological *24* ökologisch
economics *106* Wirtschaftswissenschaft(en)
edge *35* Kante
editorial *74* redaktionell
educational *59* lehrreich
efficiency *107* Effizienz
efficient *25* effizient
effort *74* Anstrengungen
electrical device *61* Elektrogerät
electrical engineering *86* Elektrotechnik
electronic *62* elektronisch
electronics *62* Elektronik
elevator (AE) *18* Aufzug
embarrassment *101* Verlegenheit, Peinlichkeit
to **emerge** *71* zum Vorschein kommen, sich herausstellen
to **employ sb** *20* jdn einstellen, beschäftigen
employee *7* Angestellte/r, Beschäftigte/r
employee empowerment *25* Übertragung von Verantwortung und Kompetenz auf Untergebene
employment center (AE) *102* Arbeitsamt
to **enable** *65* befähigen, (es) ermöglichen
to **enclose** *75* beifügen, einlegen
enclosure (enc) *82* (Brief:) Anlage, Anhang
to **encounter** *92* begegnen, treffen (auf)
to **encourage** *25* ermutigen, motivieren
to **enforce** *47* durchsetzen, umsetzen
to **engage in sth** *74* sich mit etw beschäftigen
engaged *27* (Telefon:) besetzt
engineer *7T* Ingenieur/in
engineering *17T* Maschinenbau
to **engrave** *64T* gravieren
enquiry *19* Anfrage
to **enrich** *73* bereichern
to **enrol for sth** *57T* sich für etw anmelden
en-suite bathroom *42* eigenes Badezimmer
to **ensure** *61* sicherstellen, gewährleisten
to **entail** *21* mit sich bringen, beinhalten
to **enter** *87* hineingelangen, hineinkommen; ~ sth *41* etw (Text etc.) eingeben
enterprise *10* Unternehmen
to **entertain** *59* unterhalten; ~ sb *42* jdn bewirten
enthusiasm *74* Begeisterung, Enthusiasmus
entire *7* ganze/r/s, vollständig
entrance *17* Eingang
environmental *24* Umwelt-
to **equip** *36* ausstatten, ausrüsten
equipment *21* Geräte, Maschinen, Ausrüstung
escalator *18* Rolltreppe
especially *57T* besonders, insbesondere
essential *24* wesentlich, unerlässlich
to **establish** *78* feststellen
ethical *15* moralisch, ethisch
to **even out** *54* sich einpendeln
even though *101* obwohl
event *17T* Veranstaltung
event, in the ~ of *42* für den Fall, dass
eventually *101* schließlich, am Ende
exam *56P* Prüfung
examination *72* Untersuchung
to **examine** *64T* untersuchen
to **exceed** *44* überschreiten, übertreffen
except for *29* außer
exception *76T* Ausnahme
exceptional(ly) *25* außergewöhnlich
excess baggage *41* Übergepäck
excessive(ly) *35* übertrieben, übermäßig
to **exchange** *90* austauschen
to **exclude** *68* ausschließen
to **execute** *35* ausführen
to **exhibit** *22* ausstellen
exhibition *6* Messe, Ausstellung
exhibition and conference centre *38* Ausstellungs- und Konferenzzentrum
existing *20* bestehend, vorhanden
to **expand** *65* erweitern
expense *15* Kosten
expense, at the ~ of *25* auf Kosten von
to **expire** *101* (Zeit:) ablaufen, (Frist:) verstreichen
expiry *41* Ablauf
explanation *59* Erklärung, Erläuterung
explicit(ly) *90* ausdrücklich

to **express** 30 ausdrücken, zum Ausdruck bringen
expression 9 Ausdruck
extended 25 ausgedehnt
extension 27 Durchwahl; 96 Erweiterung, Anbau
extensive 71 ausgedehnt, umfassend
extent 61 Maß, Ausmaß
extra 15 zusätzlich, Zusatz-
extract 59 Auszug
extreme 48 extrem
eye, to **keep a close ~ on sth** 22 etw genau im Auge behalten
eye contact 9 Blickkontakt

F

to **face sb** 9 sich jdm zuwenden, jdn ansehen
face-to-face 48 persönlich
facilities 42 Einrichtungen
to **fail** 99 versäumen
fairly 76T ziemlich
familiar 112 vertraut, bekannt
fashion 55 Mode
faulty 91 mangelhaft, defekt
FCA – Free Carrier 85 frei Frachtführer
to **fear** 35 befürchten
feasability 61 Machbarkeit, Durchführbarkeit
feature 43 Merkmal, Punkt, Besonderheit; 60 Eigenschaft
to **feature sth** 76T etw (als Merkmal) haben
fed up, to **be/get ~ with sb/sth** 101 die Nase voll von jdm/etw haben
fee 51 Honorar
to **feed** 61 einspeisen
ferry 92 Fähre
field 107 Feld
figure 21 Zahl
final examination 108 Abschlussprüfung
final grade 106 Abschlussnote
to **finalize** 50 festlegen, beschließen
finances 22 Finanzen
financial controlling 17T Rechnungswesen
financial report 21 Bilanz, Finanzbericht
to **fine-tune** 25 fein abstimmen
finish 15 Ende
finishing shop 64 Endmontage
to **fire sb** 48 jdn entlassen
Fire away. 61 Schieß los.
firm offer 19 verbindliches Angebot
first name 28 Vorname
first thing 30T gleich, als erstes
first, in the ~ place 47 überhaupt
to **fit** 36 passen; 64T anbringen, ausstatten, einpassen; 96 einbauen
to **fix** 25 (Problem) beheben; 92 reparieren
flanging 7 Bördeln
flat 56P Wohnung
flaw 64T Mangel
floor 17 Etage
floor, ground ~ 18 Erdgeschoss
flow 25 Fluß, Ablauf
fluent 104 fließend
to **focus on sth** 68 sich auf etw konzentrieren
folder 7T Mappe
footprint 24 Fußabdruck
for instance 61 zum Beispiel
for the time being 16 einstweilen, vorerst
forecast 21 Voraussagen
fork lift 92 Gabelstapler
formal 11 förmlich, formell
formality 85 Formalität
fortunately 35 glücklicherweise
to **forward sth** 52 etw weiterleiten
forward slash 31 Schrägstrich
to **found** 67 gründen
foundation 25 Grundlage, Basis, Fundament
founder 65 Gründer/in
free line 51 Leerzeile
freedom 57T Freiheit
freight forwarder 85 Spediteur, Spedition
frequent 41 häufig
frequent(ly) 22 häufig
fresh 64 neu, frisch
from ... onwards 42 ab ...
front panel 61 Frontplatte, Geräte-/Gehäusefront
frustrating 36 frustrierend
fuel 44 Treibstoff, Benzin
to **fulfil** 65 erfüllen
fully-equipped 42 voll ausgestattet
functionality 36 Funktionalität
further to 99 bezüglich

G

to **gain** 107 gewinnen, erwerben
gallery 58 Galerie
to **gather** 72 sammeln, zusammentragen
to **gear out** 61 ausrichten
general, in ~ 24 im Allgemeinen
to **generate** 64T erzeugen, generieren
generous 105 großzügig
gesture 9 Geste
to **get along** 59 gut miteinander auskommen, sich gut verstehen
to **get back to sb** 28 jdn zurückrufen, sich bei jdm melden
to **get in touch with sb** 13 mit jdm in Kontakt treten
to **get into full swing** 59 richtig ins Rollen kommen
to **get started** 19 loslegen, anfangen
to **get to the point** 52 zum Thema kommen
to **get up to speed** 79 sich auf den neuesten Stand bringen
to **give sb directions** 18 jdm den Weg erklären
to **give up on sth** 36 etw aufgeben, auf etw verzichen
given that 76T angesichts der Tatsache, dass
glad 35 froh
global 7T weltweit, Welt-
globalized 36 globalisiert
to **glow** 59 leuchten
to **go ahead** 52 anfangen
go along, as I ~ 19 zwischendurch
to **go for a meal** 11T essen gehen
goal 25 Ziel
goggles 59 (Schutz-)Brille
a good cause 57T ein guter Zweck, eine gute Sache
goods 6 Ware(n)
gossip 59 Klatsch, Tratsch
government 59 Regierung, öffentliche Verwaltung
grade 106 Note
grade, final ~ 106 Abschlussnote
graph 53 Diagramm
to **grant sb sth** 82 jdm etw gewähren, einräumen
grateful 98 dankbar
to **greet sb** 58 jdn begrüßen
greeting 35 Begrüßung, Grußformel
ground 101 Boden
ground floor 18 Erdgeschoss
group dynamics 59 Gruppendynamik
to **grow** 54 zunehmen, wachsen; ~ **sb** 25 jdn aufbauen, heranziehen
to **guarantee** 7T garantieren
guide 15 Handbuch, Führer
guided tour 6 Rundgang, Führung
guideline 35 Richtlinie
gym 38 Fitnessstudio

H

to **halt** 95 anhalten
to **hand over** 9 übergeben
hands-on 108 praxisorientiert
to **happen to do sth** 18 etw zufällig tun

hard-working *110* fleißig
to **head for** *79* hinführen zu, zulaufen auf
head *7* Leiter/in, Chef/in
head office *8* Zentrale, Firmensitz
headline *36* Überschrift
headquarters *7* Zentrale, Firmensitz
healthy *10* gesund
heat *56* Hitze
hectolitre *54* Hektoliter
helper *57T* Helfer/in
helpful *32* hilfsbereit
to **hide** *25* verbergen, verstecken
high-end *7T* der Spitzenklasse
high-grade *83* hochwertig
to **highlight** *9* hervorheben
high-performance *7* Hochleistungs-
high-tech *7T* Hochtechnologie-
to **hire sb** *79* jdn beauftragen
history *106* Geschichte
hold, to **put sb on ~** *27* (Telefon:) jdn in die Warteschleife stellen/legen
to **hold (the line)** *27* (Telefon:) am Apparat bleiben
Hold on. *27* Einen Moment.
hole *64T* Loch
homestay accommodation *56P* Unterbringung bei Gastfamilien
honest *35* ehrlich
hourly rate *105* Stundenlohn
housing unit *61* Gehäuse
human *59* Mensch
Human Resources (HR) *11T* Personalabteilung
hurry, to **be in a ~** *41* in Eile sein, es eilig haben
to **hurt** *94* verletzen
hyphen *31* Bindestrich

I

ideally *39* im Idealfall
to **identify** *65* feststellen, herausfinden
to **ignore** *59* ignorieren, nicht beachten
illustration *7T* Grafik, Illustration
immediate(ly) *25* unverzüglich, sofort(ig)
immense(ly) *108* enorm
impact *71* Einfluss, Auswirkungen
impact proof *77* stoßsicher
to **implement sth** *25* etw umsetzen
import clearance *86* Einfuhrverzollung, -abfertigung
import duty *85* Einfuhrzoll
importance *48* Wichtigkeit, Bedeutung
to **impress** *42* beeindrucken
impression *32* Eindruck
impressive *36* beeindruckend
to **improve** *20* verbessern; *25* besser werden, sich verbessern
improvement *25* Verbesserung
in-house *17* intern
in order to *25* um … zu
in public *9* öffentlich, in der Öffentlichkeit
in the first place *47* überhaupt
inappropriate *78* unangemessen
to **include** *9* einschließen, beinhalten
incomplete *91* unvollständig
inconvenience *95* Unannehmlichkeiten
to **incorporate a company** *10* eine AG/GmbH gründen
incorporated, to **be ~** *10* eine AG/GmbH sein
increase *64T* Steigerung
to **increase** *54* zunehmen, steigen
increasing *10* zunehmend, steigend
increasingly *36* in zunehmendem Maße
incredible *36* unglaublich
independence *16* Unabhängigkeit
independent(ly) *106* unabhängig
to **indicate** *54* anzeigen
indication *74* Anzeichen
industrial business management assistant *55* Industriekaufmann/-frau
industrial estate *10* Industriegebiet
inefficiency *25* Ineffizienz
infinitely *24* unendlich oft
to **influence** *73* beeinflussen
informal *11* informell, zwanglos, locker
infrastructure *36* Infrastruktur
initial order *82* Erstauftrag
initially *24* anfänglich, ursprünglich
to **injure** *95* verletzen
innovative *61* innovativ
to **input** *61* eingeben, einspeisen
inquisitive *55T* neugierig
insight *107* Einblick
inspection *68* Kontrolle, Überprüfung
to **install** *49* installieren
instance *73* Fall, Beispiel
instance, for ~ *61* zum Beispiel
to **install** *49* installieren
to **instruct** *98* anweisen
instruction *13* Anleitung, Anweisung
insurance *41* Versicherung
to **insure** *41* versichern
to **intend** *95* beabsichtigen
intention *65* Absicht
interim report *74* Zwischenbericht
internal(ly) *57T* intern
internship *(AE)* *102* Praktikum
to **interrupt** *54* unterbrechen
to **introduce** *9* vorstellen, einführen; ~ sb to sb *11* jdn mit jdm bekannt machen, jdn jdm vorstellen
introduction *12* Bekanntmachen, Vorstellen; *65* Einführung
to **invent** *58* erfinden
inventory *61* Lagerbestand, Warenbestand; *63* Bestandsliste
to **invest** *10* investieren
to **investigate sb/sth** *15* Erkundigungen über jdn/etw einholen, Nachforschungen über jdn/etw anstellen
to **invite** *17T* einladen; ~ sb to do sth *28* jdn dazu auffordern, etw zu tun
invoice *19* Rechnung
invoice, commercial ~ *85* Warenrechnung, Handelsrechnung
to **involve** *21* beinhalten, mit sich bringen; ~ sb in sth *70* jdn an etw beteiligen, jdn in etw einbeziehen
issue *21* Ausgabe; *50* Frage, Thema, Problem
to **issue** *65* veröffentlichen; *80* (Dokument) ausstellen
item *37* Gegenstand, Artikel, Sache

J

jacket *36* Jacke, Sakko
jar *24* Glas (für Marmelade etc.)
jelly *96* Marmelade, Gelee
job *61* Auftrag
job centre *(BE)* *102* Arbeitsamt
job hunting *103* Stellensuche
job interview *48* Vorstellungsgespräch
job production *63* Einzelfertigung
job-seeker *112* Stellensuchende/r
to **join** *109* beitreten, mitmachen
joke *59* Witz, Scherz
to **justify** *111* rechtfertigen, begründen

K

to **keep up with sth** *10* mit etw Schritt halten, mit etw mitkommen
to **keep a close eye on sth** *22* etw genau im Auge behalten
to **keep sth in mind** *38* an etw denken
to **keep track** *64* nachverfolgen

kind of 61 irgendwie, ziemlich
knock 77 Schlag, Stoß
knowledge 15 Wissen, Kenntniss(e)

L

to **label** 48 etikettieren, beschriften, benennen
lack of sth 110 Mangel an etw
Ladies and gentlemen 7T Meine Damen und Herren
landline 29 Festnetz
largely 24 weitgehend
latest 42 neueste/r/s
latest, at the ~ 99 spätestens
latter 65 letztgenannt
to **laugh at sb** 59 jdn auslachen
launch 71 Markteinführung
to **launch** 65 einführen
to **lay out** 64T auslegen
leader 25 Führungspersönlichkeit
leak 96 undichte Stelle, Leck
to **leak through** 96 durchdringen, durchsickern
to **leave a message** 31 eine Nachricht hinterlassen
lean manufacturing 61 schlanke Produktion
leather portfolio 59 lederne Aktenmappe
legal action, to **take ~** 99 juristische Schritte einleiten
leisure 42 Freizeit
to **let sb down** 92 jdn im Stich lassen
letter of credit 82 Dokumentenakkreditiv
letterhead 83 Briefkopf
to **level out** 25 nivellieren, ausgleichen
lid 7 Deckel
life, to **bring sb to ~** 112 jdn zum Leben erwecken, lebendig machen
lift 11T Aufzug
light 24 leicht
likely, to **be ~ to do sth** 78 etw wahrscheinlich tun (werden)
liking, to **be to sb's ~** 82 jds Vorstellungen entsprechen, Gefallen finden
to **limit** 101 begrenzen
limitation 76T Einschränkung, Beschränkung
limited 43T begrenzt, beschränkt
Limited liability company (LLC) (AE) 10 Gesellschaft mit beschränkter Haftung (GmbH)
line, free ~ 51 Leerzeile
line, in ~ with 88 gemäß
linguistic 108 sprachlich, Sprach-
link 110 Verbindung
to **link** 61 verbinden

listener 35 Zuhörer/in
to **load** 85 verladen
located, to **be ~ in …** 7T in … ansässig sein, seinen/ihren Sitz in … haben
location 14 Standort
logical 43 logisch
logistics *(pl)* 17T Logistik
long-standing 81 langjährig, bestehend
to **look into sth** 69 einer Sache nachgehen
to **look closely at sth** 47 sich etw genau ansehen, einen genauen Blick auf etw werfen
lorry 85 Lastwagen
loss 25 Verlust
to **lower** 47 senken
luggage 41 Gepäck
lunch break 105 Mittagspause
lunchtime 34 Mittag(szeit)
lush 42 üppig, satt

M

made-to-order 66 in Auftragsfertigung, auf Bestellung gefertigt
magic 64T Zauberei
mail shot 80 Werbesendung (per Briefpost)
maintenance 96 Wartung, Instandhaltung
major 15 größte/r/s, Haupt-, bedeutendste/r/s
to **make sb aware of sth** 24 jdm über etw informieren, jdm etw ins Bewusstsein rufen
to **make a contribution** 110T etw beitragen
to **make sense** 36 sinnvoll sein
to **make sure** 9 sicherstellen, gewährleisten, sich vergewissern
to **make use of sth** 42 etw nutzen, benutzen
to **manage sth** 15 etw verwalten
managing director 10 Geschäftsführer/in, geschäftsführende/r Gesellschafter/in
manpower 19 Arbeitskraft, Personal
manufacture 61 Herstellung, Fertigung
to **manufacture** 7T herstellen, fertigen
manufacturer 24 Hersteller
manufacturing, lean ~ 61 schlanke Produktion
manufacturing unit 7 Produktionseinheit
marital status 107 Familienstand
to **market** 70 vermarkten
market potential 65 Marktpotenzial

market research 60 Marktforschung
market share 7 Marktanteil
marketeer 78 Vermarkter/in, (im Plural:) Marketingleute
marketplace 72 Marktplatz
mass production 63 Massenproduktion
massive 74 gewaltig, überwältigend
matter 95 Angelegenheit, Sache
meaning 28 Bedeutung
means, by ~ of 78 mittels
meantime, in the ~ 101 in der Zwischenzeit
measuring instrument 65 Messinstrument
meat 55T Fleisch
media 70 Medien
media buying agency 79 Agentur für Medienplanung/-einkauf
medium-sized 16 mittel, mittelständisch
to **meet standards** 62 Anforderungen einhalten
meet, Pleased to **~ you.** 11T Nett, Sie kennen zu lernen.
meeting room 11T Besprechungsraum
member 10 Mietglied
memorable 15 leicht zu merken
to **mend** 93 flicken, reparieren
men's room 17T Herrentoilette
to **mention** 19 erwähnen
merit 106 Verdienst, (als Schulnote:) gut
metal 7T Metall
method 6 Weg, Methode, Art (und Weise)
microphone 42 Mikrofon
mid-sized 47 mittelgroß, mittelständisch
midday 93 Mittag
mile 44 Meile
mile, to **go the extra ~** 92 sich besonders anstrengen, alle Hebel in Bewegung setzen
mileage allowance 44 Freikilometer (bzw. -meilen)
mind, to **keep sth in ~** 38 an etw denken
to **mind** 32 etw dagegen haben
mind, Never ~. 30T Das macht nichts.
mind, Would you ~ … 32 Könnten Sie bitte …
mine 84 Mine, Bergwerk
to **minimize** 47 minimieren
mining 81 Bergbau
minor 106 Neben-
minutes 49 Protokoll
minutes, to **take the ~** 56 Protokoll führen

to **mirror** *35* spiegeln, widerspiegeln
to **model sth on sth** *106* etw für etw als Muster nehmen
to **monitor** *20* überwachen
monitoring *61* Kontrolle, Überwachung
moon *36* Mond
moreover *74* außerdem
motion, to **go into ~** *59* in Bewegung geraten
to **motivate** *25* motivieren
to **mount** *64* montieren
mounting area *64* Montagebereich, Montagefläche
move, on the ~ *21* in Bewegung
to **move on** *7T* weitergehen, übergehen (zu)
multimodal transport *85* kombinierte Beförderung, multimodaler Transport
multiple sourcing *63* Beschaffung durch mehrere Bezugsquellen

N

nationality *107* Staatsangehörigkeit
native speaker *56* Muttersprachler/in
to **navigate** *76* navigieren
neat(ly) *36* schlank, formschön, elegant
necking *7* Verengen
negligibly *54* vernachlässigbar
to **negotiate** *47* verhandeln, aushandeln
net *25* netto, Netto-
network *25* Netzwerk
Never mind. *30T* Das macht nichts.
nevertheless *79* trotzdem, dennoch, nichtsdestotrotz
no doubt *49* zweifellos, bestimmt
to **nominate** *85* benennen
North Sea *48* Nordsee
to **note** *64T* bemerken; *81* zur Kenntnis nehmen; ~ sth *40* etw beachten
to **note down** *31* notieren, aufschreiben
to **notice** *99* bemerken
notice *109* Bescheid, Ankündigung
notice, at a week's ~ *109* eine Woche im voraus
notice, at short ~ *109* kurzfristig
numerical *61* digital
nutshell, in a ~ *110T* kurz gesagt

O

objective *24* Ziel
obligation *85* Verpflichtung, Pflicht
obsolete *36* veraltet, überholt
to **obtain** *72* erhalten, bekommen
obvious *24* offensichtlich
offer, firm ~ *19* verbindliches Angebot
offering *112* Darbietung, Angebot
on site *7T* vor Ort
on time *34* pünktlich
once *19* sobald
ongoing *71* kontinuierlich, laufend, ständig
onwards, from ... ~ *42* ab ...
opening hours *58* Öffnungszeiten
to **operate** *68* (geschäftlich) tätig sein, operieren
to **operate sth** *11* etw bedienen, betreiben; 42 vertreten, umsetzen
operating manual *90* Bedienungsanleitung
operations *(pl)* *65* Betrieb, Geschäftstätigkeit
operator *15* Betreiber/in
opportunity *65* Chance, Gelegenheit
opposite *18* gegenüber von
to **optimize** *106* optimieren
order *13* Auftrag, Bestellung
order, cash with ~ *82* Vorauszahlung, Vorkasse, Zahlung bei Auftragserteilung
order, in ~ to *25* um ... zu
order, initial ~ *82* Erstauftrag
order, made-to-~ *66* in Auftragsfertigung, auf Bestellung gefertigt
order, to **place an ~** *21* einen Auftrag erteilen
order acknowledgement *80* Auftragsbestätigung
order form *88* Auftragsformular, Bestellformular
order system *61* Auftragssystem, Bestellsystem
organic *10* biologisch, Bio-
organization chart *20* Organigramm
origin, certificate of ~ *85* Ursprungszeugnis
otherwise *51* ansonsten, sonst, auch
outdoor *16* draußen, im Freien
to **outline** *112* skizzieren
outside world *6* Außenwelt
to **outsmart** *36* überlisten
to **outsource** *15* auslagern
outsourcing *63* Auslagern
outstanding *99* ausstehend
oven *7T* Ofen
overall *21* Gesamt-; *94* Schutzanzug
overdue *98* überfällig
to **overlook** *98* übersehen
to **over-produce** *61* zu viel produzieren
overproduction *25* Überproduktion
overseas *10* aus/nach Übersee, aus dem/ins Ausland
overtime *105* Überstunden
overtime, to **work ~** *93* Überstunden machen
overview *6* Überblick

P

to **package** *60* verpacken
packaging *17T* Verpackung
packet *93* Packung, Päckchen
packing *10* Verpackung
packing list *90* Packliste, Versandliste
padded *101* gepolstert
pain *36* Schmerz(en)
paint *63* Farbe
panel, door ~ *95* Türblatt, Türblech
panel, front ~ *61* Frontplatte, Geräte-/Gehäusefront
paragraph *51* (Text:) Absatz
parent company *7T* Muttergesellschaft
parkland *42* Parklandschaft, Grünland
participant *42* Teilnehmer/in
particular *59* bestimmt
particular, in ~ *76T* insbesondere, speziell
particularly *59* insbesondere, ganz besonders
partnership *61* Zusammenarbeit, Partnerschaft
party *90* Vertragspartei, Partei
party, third ~ *90* Dritte/r
to **pass sth on** *13* etw weiterreichen, -geben, -leiten
to **pass a test** *92* eine Prüfung bestehen
passionate(ly) *51* leidenschaftlich
passport *37* Reisepass
past sth *17T* an etw vorbei
pastime *73* Freizeitbeschäftigung
pastry *42* (Süß-)Gebäck
patience *21* Geduld
pattern *47* Muster
pay *104* Bezahlung, Lohn, Gehalt
payment *41* Zahlung
payment, documents against ~ *85* Dokumente gegen Zahlung, Kasse gegen Dokumente
payment, down ~ *19* Anzahlung
peace and quiet *42* Ruhe und Frieden

per annum *74* pro Jahr
percentage *7* Anteil, Prozentsatz
perception *24* Wahrnehmung
period *25* Zeitabschnitt, Zeit
permanent *104* unbefristet
permanently *21* ständig, laufend
permission *87* Genehmigung, Erlaubnis
philosophy *25* Philosophie
photocopier *17* Fotokopierer
to **photocopy** *42* fotokopieren
to **pick sb/sth up** *38* jdn/etw abholen
piece of advice *26* Ratschlag, Tipp
to **pitch** *78* anbieten
to **place** *79* platzieren; ~ an order *21* einen Auftrag erteilen
place, in the first ~ *47* überhaupt
place, to **be in ~** *68* bereit stehen, in Kraft sein, angewendet werden
place, to **take ~** *32* stattfinden
plant *17T* Werk, Fabrik; *61* Maschinen
pleasant *11T* angenehm
pleased *19* erfreut, froh; ~ to meet you. *11T* Nett, Sie kennen zu lernen.
pleased, to **be ~ to do sth** *42* etw gern tun
pleasure *18* Vergnügen; My ~. *18* Gern geschehen.
pneumatic drive *82* Druckluftantrieb
pocket *36* Tasche
to **point to sth** *9* auf etw zeigen
point, What's the ~ ...? *77* Was hat es für einen Sinn ...?
point, to **get to the ~** *52* zum Thema kommen
point of view *111* Standpunkt, Gesichtspunkt
policy *42* Politik, Vorgehensweise, Linie
polite *32* höflich
politeness *32* Höflichkeit
politics *(pl)* *56* Politik
popular *15* beliebt
portfolio *10* Sortiment, Angebot; *59* Aktenmappe
position *21* Stellung, Position
possibly *39* eventuell, möglicherweise, vielleicht
post *102* Stelle, Posten
to **post sb** *110T* jdn versetzen
poster *9* Plakat
to **postpone** *49* verschieben
potential *70* potenziell
power *35* Macht, Stärke, Kraft; *36* Strom
precise(ly) *108* genau
preferably *84* am besten, am liebsten
preferential terms *82* Sonderkonditionen
preferred *47* bevorzugt
to **prejudice** *103* beeinflussen
premises *42* Räumlichkeiten, Gelände
prepared *85* bereit
to **present** *6* vorstellen, präsentieren
presentation *6* Präsentation, Vorstellung
press *17* Presse
press officer *55* Pressereferent/in
press release *65* Pressemitteilung
pressure *104* Druck
presumably *76T* vermutlich
pretty *38* ziemlich
previous *15* vorherige/r/s, Vor-, frühere/r/s
price cut *47* Preisnachlass
price tag *107* Preisschild
pricing *17* Kalkulation
principle *25* Prinzip
prior, by ~ arrangement *42* nach vorheriger Vereinbarung
Private limited company (Ltd) *(BE)* *10* Gesellschaft mit beschränkter Haftung (GmbH)
prize *106* Preis, Auszeichnung
procedure *107* Verfahren, Ablauf
process *7* Verfahren
to **process** *19* bearbeiten, abwickeln, verarbeiten
procurement *80* Beschaffung
production *7* Produktion, Herstellung, Fertigung
production line *7* Fertigungsstraße
production manager *11T* Produktionsleiter/in
professional *15* berufsmäßig, beruflich, Berufs-, professionell
proficient, to **be ~ in sth** *108* (Sprache etc.) beherrschen
profile *10* Porträt, Profil
profit *10* Gewinn
profitable *15* gewinnbringend, profitabel
programme *11T* Programm
to **progress** *23* fortschreiten, vorankommen
promising *69* vielversprechend
to **promote sb/sth** *15* für jdn/etw Werbung machen
promotion *78* Werbung
promotion prospects *16* Beförderungsaussichten, Aufstiegschancen
promotional *6* Werbe-
prompt *97* prompt, unverzüglich
prompt card *9* Moderationskarte
prompt payment *97* unverzügliche Zahlung
proper(ly) *94* richtig
property *24* Eigenschaft
Proprietory Limited company (Pty Ltd) *(AusE)* *10* Gesellschaft mit beschränkter Haftung (GmbH)
protection *74* Schutz
protective *71* Schutz-
prototype *61* Prototyp
to **prove** *42* beweisen, nachweisen, den Nachweis erbringen
to **provide sb sth** *7T* jdm etw liefern, bieten, zur Verfügung stellen
provider *47* Anbieter
provision *108* Versorgung
the public *10* die Öffentlichkeit
public, in ~ *9* öffentlich, in der Öffentlichkeit
Public limited company (plc) *(BE)* *10* Aktiengesellschaft (AG)
publication *65* Publikation, Veröffentlichung
publicity *30T* Werbung, Werbe-
to **publicize sth** *65* auf etw aufmerksam machen, für etw Werbung machen
punctual *50* pünktlich
to **purchase** *11* kaufen
purchase order *80* Bestellung
purchasing *17* Einkauf
purchasing decision *73* Kaufentschluss
purpose *65* Zweck
purse *91* Handtasche *(AE)*, Portemonnaie (für Damen) *(BE)*
to **pursue sth** *74* etw (Tätigkeit etc.) nachgehen
push *24* Vorstoß
to **put sb through** *27* (Telefon:) jdn durchstellen, verbinden
to **put sb on hold** *27* (Telefon:) jdn in die Warteschleife stellen/legen
to **put sth into action** *33* etw in die Tat umsetzen
to **put the brakes on sth** *47* etw herunterfahren, einer Sache einen Riegel vorschieben
to **put the record straight** *24* die Dinge richtigstellen

Q

qualification *106* Abschluss, Qualifikation
qualified *110T* qualifiziert
quality assurance *68* Qualitätssicherung
quality control *64T* Qualitätskontrolle
quality management *17* Qualitätssicherung, -management
quantity *34P* Menge

quarter *67* Quartal
query *109* Frage, Anfrage
questionnaire *71* Fragebogen
quotation *80* Angebot, Preisangebot
to **quote** *44* (Preis) angeben, nennen

R

to **radiate** *49* sternförmig ausgehen
range *7T* Auswahl, Palette, Sortiment
to **range** *7T* sich erstrecken, reichen
to **rank** *48* einstufen
rapid(ly) *10* rasch, schnell
rapport *104* gutes Verhältnis, gute Beziehung(en)
rate *24* Anteil, Rate; *74* Quote
rate, hourly ~ *105* Stundenlohn
rating *42* Bewertung
raw material *24* Rohstoff, Rohmaterial
to **reach sb** *27* jdn erreichen
realistic *69* realistisch
reality *36* Wirklichkeit
to **realize sth** *65* etw erkennen, etw bemerken
reasonable *74* vernünftig
to **reassure** *104* beruhigen
receipt of order *82* Auftragseingang
to **receive** *56* erhalten, bekommen
received, to **be well ~** *52* gut (beim Publikum etc.) ankommen
recently *21* neulich
reception *17* Empfang
receptionist *43* Empfangsmitarbeiter/in
to **recharge** *36* (Akku) aufladen
recipient *51* Empfänger/in
recommendation *15* Empfehlung
to **record** *32* aufnehmen, aufzeichnen
record *50* Aufzeichnung, Unterlage
record, to **put the ~ straight** *24* die Dinge richtigstellen
to **recruit sb** *21* jdn einstellen, anwerben
recruitment agency *102* Personalagentur, Arbeitsvermittlung
recruitment manager *108* Leiter/in Personalbeschaffung
to **rectify** *88* berichtigen
to **reduce** *13* reduzieren, senken
to **refer to sb/sth** *43* sich auf jdn/etw beziehen, auf jdn/etw verweisen, jdn/etw bezeichnen
reference *34P* Bezug, Referenz
reference initials *83* Zeichen, Referenz
to **refill** *44* auffüllen
reflection *25* Reflexion, Nachdenken, Überdenken
refreshment *46* Erfrischung
regard, as ~s *49* bezüglich, was … anbelangt
regarding *94* betreffend, bezüglich
to **register with sb/sth** *103* sich bei jdm/etw anmelden
related to *74* bezüglich
relationship *21* Verhältnis, Beziehung
relentless *25* unnachgiebig
reliable *25* zuverlässig
to **remain** *54* bleiben
to **remind sb** *98* jdn daran erinnern
reminder *99* Mahnung
removable *77* abnehmbar
to **rent** *10* mieten
rental *44* Miete
rental car *38* Mietwagen
rental period *44* Mietzeitraum
repair *50* Reparatur
to **repair** *92* reparieren
to **rephrase** *33* neu formulieren, umformulieren
to **replace** *36* ersetzen
replacement *95* Ersatz, Ersatzteil(e)
to **replenish** *63* auffüllen
to **reply** *50* antworten
to **report to sb** *21* jdm unterstehen, jdm Bericht erstatten
to **represent** *70* vertreten, repräsentieren
representative *6* Vertreter/in
reputation *10* Ruf, Ansehen
request *52* Bitte, Wunsch
to **request** *82* anfordern
to **require** *40P* benötigen, wünschen
requirement *19* Anforderung, Wunsch
research *15* Recherche
research and development (R&D) *20* Forschung(s-) und Entwicklung(sabteilung)
to **resolve** *94* lösen
to **resort to sth** *112* auf etw zurückgreifen
resource *24* Rohstoff, Ressource; *71* Mittel
to **respond** *35* reagieren
respondent *74* Befragte/r
response *74* Antwort, Reaktion
responsibility *16* Verantwortlichkeit, Aufgabenbereich, Zuständigkeit; *21* Verantwortung
responsible *20* verantwortlich, zuständig; *24* verantwortungsbewusst
restaurant guide *42* Restaurantführer
restroom *(AE) 17T* Toilette
to **result from sth** *97* sich aus etw ergeben, aus etw resultieren
résumé *(AE) 102* Lebenslauf
to **retail at …** *71* einen Ladenpreis von … haben
retail *78* Einzelhandel
retail price *77* Ladenpreis
to **retire** *10* sich zur Ruhe setzen, sich (aus dem Berufsleben) zurückziehen
to **return** *38* zurückfahren, -fliegen, -kommen, -kehren; *78* (Gewinn) erzielen, abwerfen; *95* zurücksenden, zurückschicken
to **return sb's call** *27* jdn zurückrufen
return *44* Rückgabe
return journey *39* Rückfahrt, -flug, -reise
return visit *56* Gegenbesuch
reusable *24* wiederverwendbar
to **reverse** *92* rückwärts fahren
review *57T* Rückschau
to **review** *83* neu bewerten, überprüfen; ~ sth *57* etw Revue passieren lassen
to **rewrite** *76* umformulieren, umschreiben
to **rise** *54* steigen
rising *47* steigend
rival *25* Konkurrent, konkurrierend
robot *62* Roboter
rock climbing *74* (Fels-)Klettern
role *16* Rolle
to **roll off** *68* verlassen, vom Band laufen
to **roll eyeballs** *59* mit den Augen rollen
romantic *42* romantisch
rotary cap liner *7* Dichtungsmaschine für Schraubverschlüsse
rude *32* unhöflich, unverschämt
to **run out of sth** *35* ausgehen, wegbleiben
running *21* Betrieb
rusty *95* rostig

S

to **sail** *74* segeln
sailor *74* Segler/in
salary *16* Lohn, Gehalt
sales *7* Vertrieb, Verkauf; *25* Verkäufe, Absatz
sales representative *6* Vertreter/in, Handelsvertreter/in
salutation *83* Anrede

sample *68* Muster, Stichprobe, Probe
satisfactory *78* zufriedenstellend, befriedigend
to **satisfy** *68* zufriedenstellen
sausage *55T* Wurst, Würstchen
saving *36* Einsparung, Ersparnis
to **scan** *112* (Text etc.) überfliegen, durchsuchen
schedule *19* Plan, Zeitplan
to **schedule** *49* (Besprechung etc.) ansetzen
scheme *41* Programm
scientific *65* wissenschaftlich
scrap *61* Schrott
screen *49* Bildschirm
sealing *7* Abdichten, Versiegeln
seam covering *7* Falzabdeckung
to **search** *41* suchen
seat *11T* Platz, Sitz
second-hand *50* gebraucht
secretarial *43* Sekretariats-
secretary *28* Sekretär/in
section *47* Abschnitt
secure *42* sicher
to **secure** *68* sichern
security *64T* Sicherheit
to **seek** *59* suchen
to **seep in** *95* einsickern, eindringen
segment *74* Teil, Segment
to **select** *85* auswählen
self-employed *16* selbstständig
to **sell** *107* sich verkaufen
seller *21* Verkäufer
senior *11T* leitende/r
to **sense** *59* spüren, erspüren
sense, to **make ~** *36* sinnvoll sein
sentiment *35* Gefühl, Sentimentalität
to **separate** *51* trennen
separate(ly) *29* einzeln
series *34* Reihe, Serie
seriously *59* im Ernst
to **serve** *25* dienen
service *6* Dienstleistung
service provider *108* Dienstleister
session *9* Sitzung
set *72* Gruppe, Menge; *73* fest;
to **set sth up** *15* etw einrichten, aufbauen
to **set up a business** *16* ein Unternehmen gründen
set-back *92* Rückschlag
to **settle** *99* begleichen, bezahlen
to **shadow sb** *56* bei jdm hospitieren
share *10* Aktie, Anteil
to **share sth** *10* sich etw teilen
shareholder *10* Aktionär/in, Anteilseigner/in
sharp *95* scharf
sharply *54* drastisch, rapide
sheeting *65* Blech, Platte
to **ship** *19* verschicken, versenden, verschiffen
shipping *64T* Versand
shipping agent *64T* Spediteur
shop floor *63* Fertigungs-, Produktionsbereich
short circuit switch *81* Kurzschlussschalter, Kurzschließer
short-list *103* engere Auswahl
short-listed, to **be ~** *103* in die engere Auswahl kommen
short production run *61* Kleinserie
shoulder *36* Schulter
to **show sth off** *112* etw zur Geltung bringen
to **shut down** *67* schließen
sight *55T* Sehenswürdigkeit
sign *65* Schild, Verkehrszeichen
to **sign off** *51* einen Brief beenden, unterschreiben
to **sign up** *15* sich anmelden
signatory *83* Unterzeichner/in
signature *83* Unterschrift
significant(ly) *13* erheblich, bedeutend
silence *59* Schweigen
similar *28* ähnlich
since *74* da
sincere *35* aufrichtig
sincerity *35* Aufrichtigkeit
single room *42* Einzelzimmer
to **sit back** *79* sich zurücklehnen
to **sit in on sth** *19* bei etw dabei/ anwesend sein
site, on **~** *7T* vor Ort
skiing *107* Skifahren
skill *21* Fähigkeit, Fertigkeit
skilled *64T* geschult
slash, forward ~ *31* Schrägstrich
sleek *76T* elegant, schnittig
sleeve *76T* Hülle
slightly *54* geringfügig
slitter *7* Längsschneidemaschine, Streifenschneider
to **slouch** *59* sich lümmeln
to **slow down** *33* langsamer werden/sprechen
smart *76T* schick, elegant
to **smoke** *38* rauchen
smoker *38* Raucher/in
smoking area *43* Raucherbereich
smooth *21* glatt, problemlos, einwandfrei
snack *43T* Imbiss
sociology *59* Soziologie
to **soften** *32* abmildern
sole trader *10* Einzelunternehmer
solicitor *10* Anwalt/Anwältin (für Zivilrecht)
solid *65* solide, tüchtig, beachtlich
solution *36* Lösung
to **solve** *69* lösen
somehow *98* irgendwie
soon, as ~ as *19* sobald
sophisticated *112* fortschrittlich, raffiniert
to **sort sth out** *69* etw in Ordnung bringen, sich um etw kümmern; *71* klären, lösen
source *81* Quelle
sourcing *63* Beschaffung
spare part *17* Ersatzteil
to **speak up** *33* lauter sprechen
specialist magazine *77* Fachzeitschrift
to **specialize in sth** *61* sich auf etw spezialisieren
specialty *7T* Spezialität, Spezialgebiet
specific *71* bestimmt, speziell
specifically *76T* eigens, speziell
specification *63* Spezifikation, Vorgabe
to **specify** *34P* (genau) angeben, bestimmen
speed *7T* Geschwindigkeit
speed, to **get up to ~** *79* sich auf den neuesten Stand bringen
speedy *41* schnell
to **spell** *30* buchstabieren
spend *74* Ausgaben
spending *22* Ausgaben
splendid *42* prachtvoll, herrlich, großartig
to **split** *51* teilen, aufteilen
spoilt, to **be ~ for choice** *42* die Qual der Wahl haben
sporty *76T* sportlich
to **spot** *73* entdecken, erkennen
to **spread** *10* sich verbreiten
spring *88* Frühling, Frühjahr
stable *54* stabil
staff *21* Personal
stage *60* Phase, Abschnitt, Stadium
stairs *17* Treppe
stakes *24* Rangliste
stamping press *7* Stanzmaschine
to **stand out** *112* herausragen
standard, to **be up to ~** *68* den Vorgaben entsprechen
standardized *25* standardisiert
star *42* Stern
stare, blank ~ *59* starrer Gesichtsausdruck
to **start out** *10* (zunächst) beginnen
to **state** *76* sagen, erklären
state *35* Zustand
state-of-the-art *7T* auf dem neuesten Stand der Technik
statistical breakdown *74* statistische Aufschlüsselung

statistics *(pl)* 7T Statistik(en)
steel 24 Stahl
step 19 Schritt
to **step** 27 treten, gehen
sticker 79 Aufkleber
to **stink** 59 stinken
to **stipulate** 66 fordern, festlegen
to **stock sth** 27 etw (Ware) führen, ins Sortiment nehmen
stock, in ~ 64T auf Lager
stock level 25 Lagerbestand
to **store** 62 lagern
straight 30T sofort, gleich
straight ahead 17T geradeaus
straightforward 79 einfach, unkompliziert
strap 76T Gurt, Schlaufe
strategy 47 Strategie
to **streamline** 61 rationalisieren
strength 110 Stärke
stressed (out) 103 gestresst, fix und fertig
stressful 104 anstrengend, stressig
strict 90 streng
to **stir up** 78 aufwirbeln
to **stroll** 42 schlendern, gehen
to **structure** 9 strukturieren
to **study** 90 studieren, prüfen
to **stuff** 15 stopfen
to **sub-contract** 69 (als Zulieferer) unter Vertrag nehmen
sub-contractor 69 Zulieferer, Subunternehmer
sub-heading 66 Zwischenüberschrift
subject line 83 Betreffzeile
to **submit** 82 einreichen
subsidiary 7T Niederlassung
to **suggest** 50 vorschlagen
suggestion 49 Vorschlag
to **suit** 84 passen
suitability 109 Eignung
suitable 48 geeignet
suitcase 55T Koffer
suite 42 Suite
to **sum up** 57T zusammenfassen
to **summarize** 28 zusammenfassen
summary 22 Zusammenfassung
supplier 13 Lieferant/in, Zulieferer
supplies 64 Vorräte, Ware
supply 64T Lieferung, Versorgung
to **supply** 7 liefern; 81 zur Verfügung stellen
support 15 Unterstützung, Kundendienst
to **support** 51 unterstützen
to **suppose** 55T annehmen, glauben
suppose, I ~ so. 57T Mag sein. Kann schon sein.
sure, to **make ~** 9 sicherstellen, gewährleisten, sich vergewissern
surface 25 Oberfläche
surname 41 Nachname
surplus 63 überschüssig
survey 47 Umfrage, Studie
swing, to **get into full ~** 59 richtig ins Rollen kommen
to **switch to** 36 wechseln zu
switch, short circuit ~ 81 Kurzschlussschalter, Kurzschließer
switchgear 81 Schaltanlage

T

to **tailor sth to sth** 103 etw auf etw zuschneiden
tailor-made 82 maßgeschneidert
to **take over** 25 (die Führung) übernehmen
to **take place** 32 stattfinden
tank 44 Tank
to **target sb** 74 jdn (als Zielgruppe) ansprechen, jdn als Zielgruppe haben
to **target sth at sb/sth** 74 etw an jdn/etw richten
target group 71 Zielgruppe
tartan check 76T Schottenkaro
tax 85 Steuer
technical drawing 90 technische Zeichnung
technician 7T Techniker/in
technique 67 Methode, Technik
temporary 107 befristet
to **tend to do sth** 35 dazu neigen, etw zu tun
tender 80 Angebot, Ausschreibung
tense 59 angespannt
term, in the long ~ 16 langfristig
term, in the short ~ 16 kurzfristig
terminal 38 Anschluss, Anschlussleiste; 85 Entladestation, -stelle, Terminal
terms 13 Konditionen, Bedingungen
terms, preferential ~ 82 Sonderkonditionen
terms and conditions 41 Konditionen, (Allgemeine) Geschäftsbedingungen
theme 51 Motto, Thema
thickness 65 Dicke, Stärke
thin 49 dünn
third party 90 Dritte/r
thoroughly 25 gründlich; 53 völlig
thought 95 Gedanke, Meinung
threaded bolt 64T Gewindebolzen, Gewindestange
threaded bush 64T Gewindebuchse
three-part 7 dreiteilig
to **throw** 101 werfen; ~ sth up 112 etw zutage fördern
tied up, to **be ~** 84 beschäftigt sein, zu tun haben
tight 108 engere Auswahl
time, at a ~ 36 auf einmal, jeweils
time, for the ~ being 16 einstweilen, vorerst
time, on ~ 34 pünktlich
time difference 57T Zeitverschiebung
time frame 108 Zeitrahmen
time off 105 Freizeit
timetable 23 Zeitplan, Stundenplan
titanium 62 Titan
to **die for** 42 umwerfend
tone 32 Ton
tool 36 Werkeug
total, in ~ 15 insgesamt
total order value 90 Gesamtbestellwert, Gesamtauftragswert
tough 77 solide, widerstandsfähig
track, to **keep ~** 64 nachverfolgen
trade 85 Handel
trade fair 6 Handelsmesse, Fachmesse
traffic jam 34 Stau
to **train sb** 20 jdn ausbilden
to **train as …** 111 eine Ausbildung zum/zur … machen
trainee 7T Auszubildende/r
traineeship 16 Ausbildung, Lehre
training 19 Schulung, Ausbildung
training officer 55 Ausbildungsleiter/in
to **transfer** 30 weiterleiten, weitergeben; 65 übertragen; 98 überweisen
to **transform** 112 (grundlegend) verändern
transit 91 Transport
transit, in ~ 91 beim Transport
translator 11T Übersetzer/in
transparency 9 Overhead-Folie
travel expenses 47 Reisespesen
trouble, to **take the ~** 25 sich die Mühe machen
to **turn out** 7T produzieren
to **turn right/left** 17T rechts/links abbiegen
to **turn your back to sb** 9 jdm den Rücken zudrehen
turn-around time 63 Durchlaufzeit, Bearbeitungszeitraum
turnkey system 7T Komplettsystem
turnover 7 Umsatz
twin room 44 Zweibettzimmer
typical 76T typisch

U

ultimately *24* letzendlich, letztlich
unbeatable *77* unschlagbar
unclear(ly) *33* undeutlich, unklar
unconventional *79* unkonventionell
underscore *31* Unterstrich
understanding *21* Verständnis
unfortunately *31T* leider, unglücklicherweise
unique selling point *78* Alleinstellungsmerkmal
unit *10* Bau, Gebäude, Halle; *63* Einheit
unit, housing ~ *61* Gehäuse
unit price *88* Einzelpreis, Preis pro Stück
university *21* Universität
unlike *47* anders als
unlikely *76T* unwahrscheinlich
to **unload** *85* entladen
unpaid *98* unbezahlt
unperceived *24* nicht wahrgenommen
unproductive *78* unproduktiv
unspoken *24* unausgesprochen
unsure *71* unsicher
untypical *76T* untypisch
unusable *95* unbrauchbar
unusual *76T* ungewöhnlich
to **unwind** *42* sich entspannen, abschalten
up to, to **be ~ sth** *76T* etw vorhaben, etw anstellen
up to speed, to **get ~** *79* sich auf den neuesten Stand bringen
up to standard, to **be ~** *68* den Vorgaben entsprechen
upcoming *94* bevorstehend
to **update** *71* aktualisieren, auf den neusten Stand bringen
upset *95* verärgert
upstairs *11T* (nach) oben
uptake *71* Aufnahme
upward *52* nach oben
urgent *27* dringend
use, to **make ~ of sth** *42* etw nutzen, benutzen
user interface *65* Benutzeroberfläche

V

vacancy *108* offene Stelle, Stellenangebot, -ausschreibung
vacant *112* frei
to **vacate** *43T* räumen
vacation *108* Ferien
valid *82* gültig
valuable *73* wertvoll
value *79* Wert
value, total order ~ *90* Gesamtbestellwert, Gesamtauftragswert
variety *10* Sorte
various *60* verschieden
VAT (value added tax) *44* Mehrwertsteuer
vehicle *44* Fahrzeug
verbally *90* mündlich
versus *68* gegenüber
vibes *59* Schwingungen, Atmosphäre
view *42* Aussicht, Ausblick
virtual *112* virtuell
visual *25* visuell, Sicht-
visual aids/visuals *9* visuelle Hilfsmittel
vocational college *21* Berufsfachschule
volume *10* Umfang, Volumen
voucher *101* Gutschein

W

walker *74* Wanderer
walking distance, within ~ *43T* in Laufweite
wallet *91* Brieftasche, Portemonnaie (für Herren)
warehouse *64* Lager, Lagerhalle
waste *61* Verschwendung, Vergeudung
to **waste** *35* verschwenden, vergeuden
wasted *25* nicht genutzt, brachliegend
wasteful *47* verschwenderisch
water-resistant *76* wasserabweisend
waterproof *76T* wasserdicht
waterproofed *76T* wasserdicht imprägniert
watertight *77* wasserdicht
weakness *110* Schwäche
wear *27* Bekleidung, Kleidung
weekly *48* wöchentlich
to **weigh** *36* wiegen
weird *76T* seltsam, verrückt, bizarr
welding machine *7* Schweißmaschine
well received, to **be ~** *52* gut (beim Publikum etc.) ankommen
wet *77* nass
whilst *101* während
to **whip sth out** *59* etw zücken
wholesale *50* Großhandel
willing *85* bereit, willens
willingness *79* Bereitschaft
to **win** *68* gewinnen
wireless *42* drahtlos
wise *47* klug
word power *73* etwa: Wortschatz, Sprachkenntnis
word spider *72* Wortnetz
to **work sth out** *15* etw ausrechnen, etw herausfinden
to **work overtime** *93* Überstunden machen
work experience *71* Praktikum; 107 Berufserfahrung
workforce *7T* Belegschaft
working breakfast *84P* Arbeitsfrühstück
working day *99* Werktag
working environment *108* Arbeitsumfeld
working hours *105* Arbeitszeit(en)
workload *25* Arbeitspensum
workmate *56P* Arbeitskollege/-in
works council *17* Betriebsrat
worldwide *7* weltweit
worried *43T* besorgt
worth *40* wert; *64* Wert
to **wrap sth up** *53* etw abschließen
writing, in ~ *90* schriftlich, in Schriftform

Y

Yours sincerely *50* Hochachtungsvoll, Mit freundlichen Grüßen

Basic industry vocabulary (German–English)

Firmenorganisation – *Company organization*	
Aktiengesellschaft (AG)	Public Limited Company (plc) *BE;* open corporation *AE*
Aktie	share
Aktionär/in, Teilhaber/in	shareholder
Einzelunternehmen	sole proprietor
Gesellschaft mit beschränkter Haftung (GmbH)	Limited Company (Ltd) *BE;* closed corporation *AE*
Kommanditgesellschaft (KG)	limited partnership
Personengesellschaft, offene Handelsgesellschaft (OHG)	(general) partnership

Firmenabteilungen – *Company departments*	
Buchhaltung	accounts (department)
Einkauf(sabteilung)	purchasing (department)
Forschung(s-) und Entwicklung (sabteilung)	research and development (department, R&D)
Geschäftsführung, Vorstand	board (of directors)
Lager(halle)	warehouse
Marktforschung (sabteilung)	market research (department)
Personal(abteilung)	human resources (department, HR)
Rechnungswesen	finance (department)
Rechtswesen	legal department
Rezeption, Empfang	reception
Verkauf(sabteilung), Vertrieb	sales (department)
Vertrieb	distribution (department)
Verwaltung	administration
Zentrale	head office, headquarters

Mitarbeiter/innen – *Members of staff*	
Abteilungsleiter/in	head of department
Arbeitgeber/in, Unternehmer/in	employer
Arbeitnehmer/in, Beschäftigte/r	employee
Arbeitsplatz	workplace
Ausbildung	training
Buchhalter/in	accountant
Industriekaufmann/-frau	industrial management assistant
Empfangsmitarbeiter/in	receptionist
Gehalt	salary
Geschäftsführer/in	managing director (MD), chief executive officer (CEO)
Handelsvertreter/in	sales representative
Kollege, Kollegin	colleague
Lehre	apprenticeship
Manager/in	manager
Personal	staff
Persönliche/r Assistent/in	personal assistant (PA)
Qualifikation, Abschluss	qualification
Sekretär/in	secretary

Bürotätigkeiten – *Office activities*	
etw ausrichten	to take a message
Berichte schreiben	to write reports
Briefe beantworten	to reply to letters
etw faxen	to fax sth
Mitteilungen, Vermerke, Notizen schreiben	to write memos
ein Telefongespräch annehmen	to answer the telephone
Textverarbeitung	word processing
Überstunden machen	to work overtime
Unterlagen, Schriftstücke	paperwork
etw weiterleiten	to forward sth

Geschäftsbriefe – *Commercial correspondence*	
Absatz	paragraph
Absender	sender
Adresse	address
anhängen (E-Mail)	to attach sth
Anhang	attachment
Anlage(n)	enclosure (enc)
Anrede	salutation
Antwort	reply
beifügen (Brief)	to enclose
Betreff(zeile)	subject (line)
Briefkopf	letter head
Datum	date
Einschreiben	registered mail/post
Empfänger/in	addressee
Entschuldigungsschreiben	letter of apology
Mit den besten Wünschen	Best wishes
Mit freundlichen Grüßen (Hochachtungsvoll)	Yours faithfully
Mit freundlichen Grüßen	Yours sincerely
Mit freundlichen Grüßen, Viele Grüße	Best wishes, Regards
Mit herzlichen Grüßen	Best wishes, Cordially *AE*
Schlussformel	complimentary close
Unterschrift	signature
Zeichen	reference (ref)
zu Händen	attention (attn)

Basic industry vocabulary (German–English)

Besprechungen/Präsentationen – *Meetings/ presentations*	
Abwesenheit	absence
Bericht	report
Einladung	invitation
Liniendiagramm	line chart
Protokoll	minutes *pl*
Säulendiagramm	bar chart
die Sitzung leiten	to take the chair
stattfinden	take place
Tagesordnung(spunkt)	(item on the) agenda
teilnehmen	to participate
Teilnehmer/in	participant
Termin	date, appointment
Tortendiagramm	pie chart
Verschiedenes	any other business (AOB)
Vortrag	talk; lecture
vortragen	to report; to state

Dienstreisen – *Business trips*	
absagen, stornieren	to cancel
Anforderung	requirement
Ausstellung	exhibition
etw besuchen, an etw teilnehmen	to attend sth
Bitte, Anfrage	request
einfacher Flug	one-way flight
Hin- und Rückflug	return flight
Messe	(trade) fair
Passagier	passenger
Reservierung, Buchung	reservation
Unterkunft	accommodation
verschieben	to postpone

Geschäftspartner und Händler – *Business partners and traders*	
Einzelhändler/in	retailer
Exporteur	exporter
Großhändler	wholesaler
Importeur	importer
Käufer/in	buyer
Klient/in	client
Konkurrent/in	competitor
Konkurrenz	competition
Kunde, Kundin	customer, client
Lieferant	supplier
Spediteur	carrier; forwarding agent; freight forwarder
Verkäufer/in	seller

Geschäftsvorgänge – *Business transactions*	
Anfrage	enquiry
Angebot, Kostenvoranschlag	quotation
Auftrag, Bestellung	order
einen Auftrag erteilen	to place an order
einen Auftrag erledigen	to fill an order
Auftragsbestätigung	acknowledgement/ confirmation
einen Auftrag bestätigen	to acknowledge an order
Bestellformular	order form
Bestellnummer	order number
Erhalt, (Waren-)Eingang	receipt (of goods)
Lieferbedingungen	terms of delivery *pl*
liefern	to deliver
Lieferung	delivery
Muster	sample
Probeauftrag	trial order
Reklamation, Beschwerde	complaint
Sendung	consignment
Umsatz	turnover
Verkäufe, Umsatz	sales *pl*
Versandanzeige, Versandmitteilung	advice of dispatch
Versandpapiere	shipping documents *pl*
versenden	to ship, dispatch
Vertrag	contract
Ware(n), (Lager-)Bestand	stock
Zahlungsanzeige	advice of payment
Zahlungsbedingungen	terms of payment *pl*

Zahlung – *Payment*	
Dokumente gegen Akzept	documents against acceptance
Dokumente gegen Zahlung	documents against payment
Dokumentenakkreditiv	documentary letter of credit
fällig, ausstehend	overdue
Konto, Kreditkonto	account
letzte Mahnung	final demand
Mahnung	reminder
MwSt = Mehrwertsteuer	VAT = value added tax
Nicht(be)zahlung	non-payment
Rabatt, Nachlass	discount
Rate	instalment
Rechnung	bill, invoice
Skonto, Barzahlungsrabatt	cash discount
überweisen	to remit, to transfer
Überweisung, Zahlung	bank transfer, remittance
Vorauszahlung, Vorkasse	cash in advance
Wechsel	bill of exchange
zahlbar bei Lieferung, per Nachnahme	cash on delivery (COD)

Irregular verbs

be – was/were – been	*sein*
beat – beat – beaten	*schlagen, besiegen*
become – became – become	*werden*
begin – began – begun	*anfangen, beginnen*
bleed – bled – bled	*bluten*
break – broke – broken	*brechen*
bring – brought – brought	*bringen*
build – built – built	*bauen*
burn – burnt/burned – burnt/burned	*(ver)brennen*
buy – bought – bought	*kaufen*
catch – caught – caught	*fangen*
choose – chose – chosen	*wählen*
come – came – come	*kommen*
cost – cost – cost	*kosten*
cut – cut – cut	*schneiden*
do – did – done	*tun, machen*
draw – drew – drawn	*zeichnen*
dream – dreamt/dreamed – dreamt/dreamed	*träumen*
drink – drank – drunk	*trinken*
drive – drove – driven	*fahren*
eat – ate – eaten	*essen*
fall – fell – fallen	*fallen*
feed – fed – fed	*füttern, ernähren*
feel – felt – felt	*(sich) fühlen, empfinden*
fight – fought – fought	*kämpfen*
find – found – found	*finden*
fit – fit/fitted – fit/fitted	*passen*
fly – flew – flown	*fliegen*
forget – forgot – forgotten	*vergessen*
freeze – froze – frozen	*frieren*
get – got – got (*AE* gotten)	*bekommen*
give – gave – given	*geben*
go – went – gone	*gehen, fahren*
grow – grew – grown	*wachsen*
hang – hung – hung	*hängen*
have – had – had	*haben*
hear – heard – heard	*hören*
hide – hid – hidden	*(sich) verstecken*
hit – hit – hit	*schlagen*
hold – held – held	*halten, festhalten*
keep – kept – kept	*behalten*
know – knew – known	*kennen, wissen*
lay – laid – laid	*legen*
lean – leant/leaned – leant/leaned	*(sich) lehnen, neigen*
learn – learnt/learned – learnt/learned	*lernen*

leave – left – left	*abfahren, verlassen, weggehen*
let – let – let	*lassen*
lie – lay – lain	*liegen*
light – lit – lit	*anzünden, beleuchten, anmachen*
lose – lost – lost	*verlieren*
make – made – made	*machen*
mean – meant – meant	*meinen, bedeuten*
meet – met – met	*treffen*
pay – paid – paid	*bezahlen*
put – put – put	*setzen, stellen, legen*
quit – quit/quitted – quit/quitted	*verlassen, aufhören*
read – read – read	*lesen*
ride – rode – ridden	*reiten, fahren*
rise – rose – risen	*(an)steigen, aufgehen*
run – ran – run	*laufen, rennen*
say – said – said	*sagen*
see – saw – seen	*sehen*
sell – sold – sold	*verkaufen*
send – sent – sent	*senden, schicken*
set – set – set	*setzen, stellen*
show – showed – shown	*zeigen*
shut – shut – shut	*schließen*
sing – sang – sung	*singen*
sit – sat – sat	*sitzen*
sleep – slept – slept	*schlafen*
smell – smelt/smelled – smelt/smelled	*riechen*
speak – spoke – spoken	*sprechen*
spell – spelt/spelled – spelt/spelled	*buchstabieren*
spend – spent – spent	*ausgeben, verbringen*
stand – stood – stood	*stehen*
steal – stole – stolen	*stehlen*
swim – swam – swum	*schwimmen*
take – took – taken	*nehmen*
teach – taught – taught	*unterrichten, beibringen*
tear – tore – torn	*zerreißen*
tell – told – told	*sagen, erzählen*
think – thought – thought	*denken*
throw – threw – thrown	*werfen*
understand – understood – understood	*verstehen*
wake – woke – woken	*aufwachen/aufwecken*
wear – wore – worn	*tragen (Kleidung)*
win – won – won	*gewinnen*
write – wrote – written	*schreiben*

Quellen

Bildquellen

S. 6/a/shutterstock, S. 6/b/Fotofinder/Keystone/Volkmar Schulz, S. 6/c/Corbis/KIM KYUNG-HOON, S. 6/d/Fotofinder/Bildagentur-online/Tetra, S. 6/e/Picture-Alliance/YNA/Yonhap, S. 6/f/Fotolia/Africa Studio, S. 7/a-f/Cantec GmbH,/ S. 8/Cantec GmbH, S. 10/1/Shutterstock/auremar, S. 10/2/Shutterstock/wavebreakmedia ltd, S. 10/3/Corbis/moodboard, S. 11/Alamy/Asia Images Group Pte Ltd, S. 14/Fotofinder/Klaphake/teamwork, S. 15/Shutterstock/Monkey Business Images, S. 16/a/Shutterstock/Andresr, S. 16/b/Shutterstock/mango-stock, S. 16/c/Alamy/PhotoAlto, S. 16/d/Shutterstock/Elena Elisseeva, S. 16/e/Shutterstock/prism68, S. 16/f/Shutterstock/QQ7, S. 17/Cantec GmbH, S. 21/1/Shutterstock/Diego Cervo, S. 21/2/Shutterstock/Minerva Studio, S. 21/3/Shutterstock/Olga Sapegina, S. 21/4/Shutterstock/StockLite, S. 21/5/Shutterstock/ostill, S. 22/1/Shutterstock/StockLite, S. 22/2/shutterstock, S. 24/Soudronic, S. 25/Shutterstock/Dongliu, S. 27/Shutterstock/auremar, S. 28/Shutterstock/gnohz, S. 29/Shutterstock/Mihai Simonia, S. 30/Istockphoto/diego_cervo, S. 31/Shutterstock/Nikolay Mikhalchenko, S. 32/Shutterstock/Pablo Eder, S. 33/hinten/Shutterstock/iconspro, S. 34/Shutterstock, S. 36/1/Shutterstock/Anna Chelnokova, S. 36/2/Shutterstock/Oleksiy Mark, S. 37/1/Shutterstock/pjcross, S. 37/2/Shutterstock/Jaroslaw Kubak, S. 37/3/Shutterstock/Shots Studio, S. 37/4/Shutterstock/ARENA Creative, S. 38/Shutterstock/Geanina Bechea, S. 40/Alamy/luciopix, S. 42/1/Shutterstock/Sam Strickler, S. 42/2/Shutterstock/StockLite, S. 42/3/Shutterstock/Monkey Business Images, S. 42/4/Shutterstock/Gabi Moisa, S. 43/1/Shutterstock/justone, S. 43/2/Shutterstock/John Lock, S. 43/3/Shutterstock/John Lock, S. 43/4/Shutterstock/Miguel Angel Salinas Salinas, S. 43/5/Shutterstock/Dragana Gerasimoski, S. 43/6/Shutterstock/scherbet, S. 43/7/Shutterstock/patrimonio designs limited, S. 47/Shutterstock/Becky Stares, S. 48/a/Alamy/Image Source/IS457, S. 48/b/Shutterstock/Monkey Business Images, S. 48/c/Corbis/moodboard, S. 48/d/Alamy/F1online digitale Bildagentur GmbH, S. 49/Shutterstock/bluecrayola, S. 50/shutterstock, S. 51/shutterstock, S. 52/Alamy/OJO Images Ltd, S. 55/Picture Alliance/DeFodi, S. 59/Shutterstock/Pieter Beens, S. 60/a/Schaeffer AG, S. 60/b/Fotofinder/ecopix Fotoagentur, S. 61/Schaeffer AG, S. 62/Schaeffer AG, S. 64/Schaeffer AG, S. 68/Shutterstock/Guy Erwood, S. 70/a/Alamy/Pixsooz, S. 70/b/Shutterstock/pcruciatti, S. 70/c/Shutterstock/Helder Almeida, S. 70/d/Shutterstock/Sergej Khakimullin, S. 71/Andres Industries AG, S. 76/123RF/Yuri Arcurs (Hintergrund), S. 77/Andres Industries AG, S. 78/1/Shutterstock/Booka, S. 78/2/Shutterstock/kret87, S. 78/3/Shutterstock/tkemot, S. 78/4/Alamy/David Hoffman Photo Library, S. 79/1/Fotofinder/Keystone, S. 80/1/Shutterstock/lenetstan, S. 80/2/Shutterstock/Kati Molin, S. 80/1/shutterstock, S. 80/2/Shutterstock/Lisa S., S. 81/Ritter Starkstromtechnik, S. 82/1/2/Firma Ritter Starkstromtechnik, S. 83/Shutterstock/Madlen, S. 86/Alamy/Asia Images Group Pte Ltd, S. 87/Fotofinder/vario images, S. 89/Shutterstock/Olga Miltsova, S. 90/Firma Ritter, S. 92/Shutterstock/P72, S. 92/Shutterstock/Voronin76, S. 93/Shutterstock/StockLite, S. 96/Shutterstock/A1Stock, S. 99/Shutterstock/Monkey Business Images, S. 101/biteadvantage, S. 102/a/Fotofinder/VISUM/Marion Losse, S. 102/b/Picture-Alliance/Fotoreport monster.de, S. 102/c/Alamy/vario images GmbH & Co.KG/Christoph Papsch, S. 103/Picture-Alliance /Julian Stratenschulte, S. 110/Shutterstock/Ingrid W., S. 111/Shutterstock/ARENA Creative, S. 112/Alamy/i love images/teenagers, S. 127/Shutterstock/Edw, S. 128/1/Shutterstock/Alexander Kalina, S., S. 128/2/Shutterstock/AGITA LEIMANE, S. 128/3/Shutterstock/Jojje,

Cartoons/Illustrations: Oxford Designers Illustrators: S. 13, S. 18, S. 35, S. 45, S. 63, S. 91, S. 124
Gabriele Heinisch: S. 26, S. 33, S. 59

Textquellen

- Unit 1, page 15, The Website Setup Guide: http://websitesetupguide.com/
- Unit 2, page 24, Green's the word: http://www.soudronic.com/node/359
- Unit 3, page 35, Telephone greetings that customers – and employees – will love, adapted from: http://www.proedgeskills.com/Customer_Service_Articles/telephone_greetings_that_custome.htm
- Unit 4, page 47, How to put the brakes on rising travel costs, adapted from: http://www.microsoft.com/midsizebusiness/businessvalue/business-travel-expenses.mspx
- Unit 5, page 59, I hate meetings and they stink, abridged from: http://www.govloop.com/profiles/blogs/i-hate-meetings-and-they-stink
- Unit 10, page 112, Virtual job-hunting: Technology fills situations vacant, abridged from: www.bbc.co.uk/news/business-12194581

Danksagung

Wir bedanken uns bei folgenden Firmen, die uns freundlicherweise Material für dieses Lehrwerk zur Verfügung gestellt haben.

Andres Industries AG, Berlin
Cantec GmbH & Co. KG, Essen
Ritter Starkstromtechnik GmbH & Co. KG, Wilnsdorf
Schaeffer AG, Berlin
Schneider Electric GmbH, Ratingen